the unbeatab Squirrel Girl

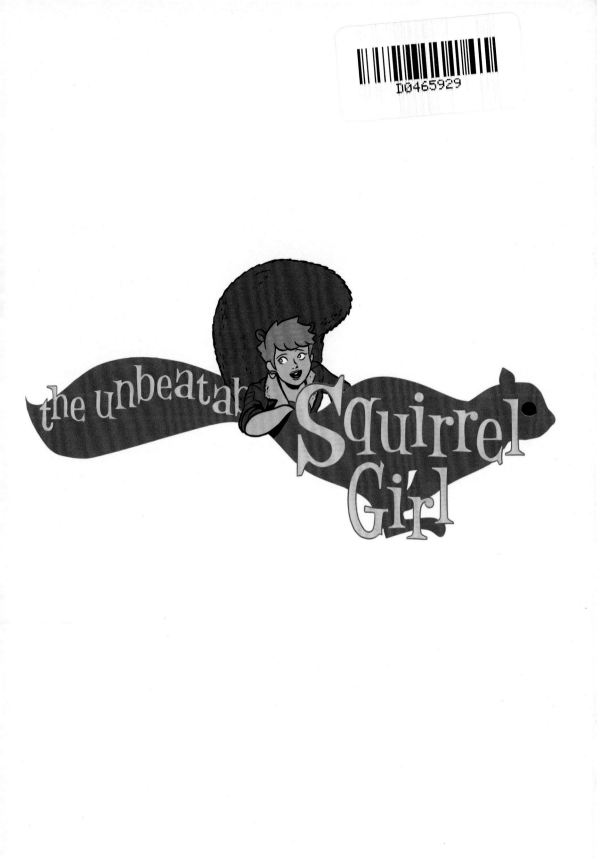

the unbeatab

COLLECTION EDITOR: **JENNIFER GRÜNWALD**
ASSISTANT EDITOR: **CAITLIN O'CONNELL**
ASSOCIATE MANAGING EDITOR: **KATERI WOODY**
EDITOR, SPECIAL PROJECTS: **MARK D. BEAZLEY**
VP PRODUCTION & SPECIAL PROJECTS: **JEFF YOUNGQUIST**
SVP PRINT, SALES & MARKETING: **DAVID GABRIEL**
BOOK DESIGNER: **JAY BOWEN**

EDITOR IN CHIEF: **C. B. CEBULSKI**
CHIEF CREATIVE OFFICER: **JOE QUESADA**
PRESIDENT: **DAN BUCKLEY**
EXECUTIVE PRODUCER: **ALAN FINE**

THE UNBEATABLE SQUIRREL GIRL VOL. 9: SQUIRRELS FALL LIKE DOMINOES. Contains material originally published in magazine form as THE UNBEATABLE SQUIRREL GIRL #32-36. First printing 2018. ISBN 978-1-302-91077-8. Published by MARVEL WORLDWIDE, INC., a subsidiary of MARVEL ENTERTAINMENT, LLC. OFFICE OF PUBLICATION: 135 West 50th Street, New York, NY 10020. Copyright © 2018 MARVEL No similarity between any of the names, characters, persons, and/or institutions in this magazine with those of any living or dead person or institution is intended, and any such similarity which may exist is purely coincidental. **Printed in Canada.** DAN BUCKLEY, President, Marvel Entertainment; JOHN NEE, Publisher; JOE QUESADA, Chief Creative Officer; TOM BREVOORT, SVP of Publishing; DAVID BOGART, SVP of Business Affairs & Operations, Publishing & Partnership; DAVID GABRIEL, SVP of Sales & Marketing, Publishing; JEFF YOUNGQUIST, VP of Production & Special Projects; DAN CARR, Executive Director of Publishing Technology; ALEX MORALES, Director of Publishing Operations; DAN EDINGTON, Managing Editor; SUSAN CRESPI, Production Manager; STAN LEE, Chairman Emeritus. For information regarding advertising in Marvel Comics or on Marvel.com, please contact Vit DeBellis, Custom Solutions & Integrated Advertising Manager, at vdebellis@marvel.com. For Marvel subscription inquiries, please call 888-511-5480. **Manufactured between 9/21/2018 and 10/23/2018 by SOLISCO PRINTERS, SCOTT, QC, CANADA.**
10 9 8 7 6 5 4 3 2 1

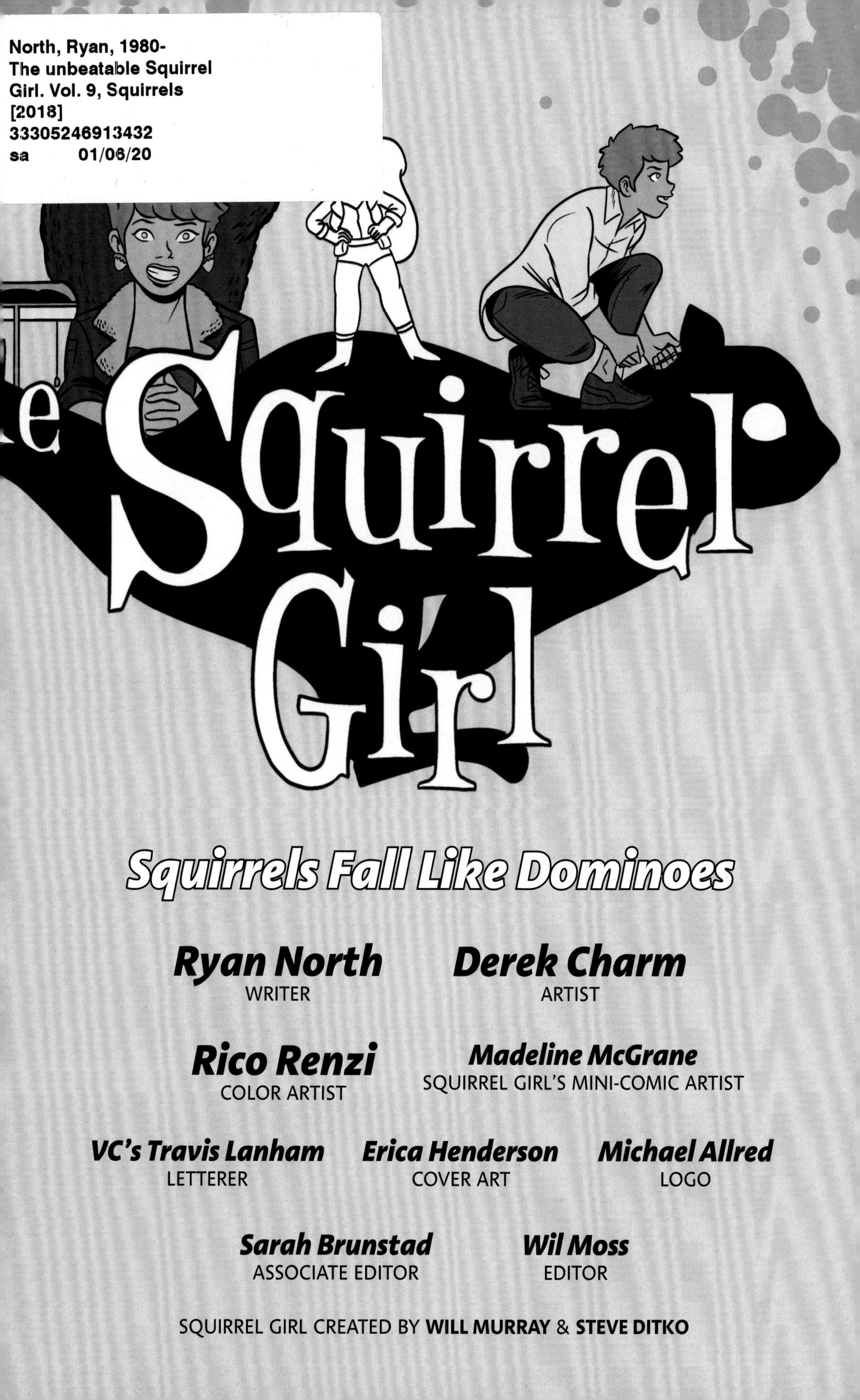
Squirrel
Girl

Squirrels Fall Like Dominoes

Ryan North
WRITER

Derek Charm
ARTIST

Rico Renzi
COLOR ARTIST

Madeline McGrane
SQUIRREL GIRL'S MINI-COMIC ARTIST

VC's Travis Lanham
LETTERER

Erica Henderson
COVER ART

Michael Allred
LOGO

Sarah Brunstad
ASSOCIATE EDITOR

Wil Moss
EDITOR

SQUIRREL GIRL CREATED BY **WILL MURRAY** & **STEVE DITKO**

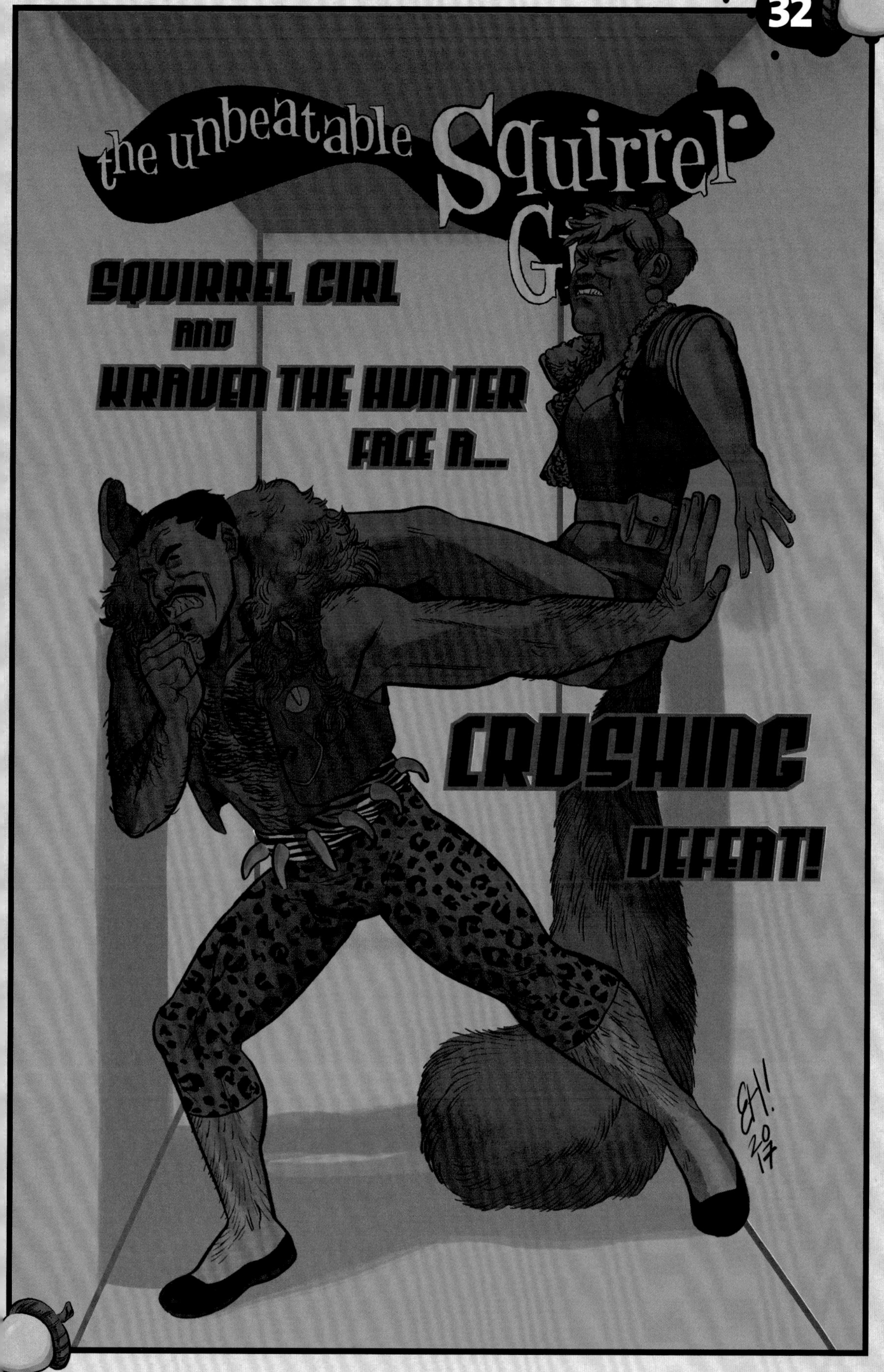
the unbeatable Squirrel Girl
SQUIRREL GIRL
AND
KRAVEN THE HUNTER
FACE A...
CRUSHING
DEFEAT!
EH! 2017

Doreen Green isn't just a second-year computer science student: she secretly also has all the powers of both squirrel and girl! She uses her amazing abilities to fight crime ***and*** *be as awesome as possible. You know her as...* ***The Unbeatable Squirrel Girl!*** *Find out what she's been up to, with...*

Squirrel Girl *in a nutshell*

Squirrel Girl @unbeatablesg
@starkmantony hey pretty crazy how @sewwiththeflo and I got trapped in hypertime and lived out our whole lives in one weekend at superspeed!

Tony Stark @starkmantony
@unbeatablesg Yes, you made a mockery of the free-use policy on my public restrooms.

Squirrel Girl @unbeatablesg
@starkmantony tony

Squirrel Girl @unbeatablesg
@starkmantony it is my understanding that after doing that we glued a "lol sorry about that" post-it note onto your person at super-speed

Squirrel Girl @unbeatablesg
@starkmantony so what is this

Tony Stark @starkmantony
@unbeatablesg Hey, honestly, just happy to help. Listen: is it true that you have no memories of what happened?

Squirrel Girl @unbeatablesg
@starkmantony NONE

Squirrel Girl @unbeatablesg
@starkmantony the machine we built to send us back to regular time was like restoring from backup, so -- body gets restored, but brain gets restored too!

Squirrel Girl @unbeatablesg
@starkmantony lots of adventures during that missing weekend though, that's for sure!

Tony Stark @starkmantony
@unbeatablesg Including the adventure of "liberating" hardware from my high-security warehouses to build said machine, you mean.

Squirrel Girl @unbeatablesg
@starkmantony TONY!

Squirrel Girl @unbeatablesg
@starkmantony it is my understanding that we glued "lol sorry about that as well" post-it notes onto your person at super-speed regarding this matter as well

Squirrel Girl @unbeatablesg
@starkmantony so again I find myself asking, what is this

Tony Stark @starkmantony
@unbeatablesg Again, just teasing! Seriously. Good to have you back, Squirrel Girl.

Squirrel Girl @unbeatablesg
@starkmantony Good to be back! Okay I'll let you go, I'm late for a SECRET THING

Squirrel Girl @unbeatablesg
ANNOUNCEMENT: my new thing is calling everything a "SECRET THING," I am v. mysterious

Squirrel Girl @unbeatablesg
Hey, on an unrelated note, you know that feeling when someone gets new glasses, but you don't know they got new glasses, so you're looking at them and they're still clearly the same person but they look different and you're like "I know SOMETHING has changed here, but WHAT??"

Squirrel Girl @unbeatablesg
I dunno I just thought I'd mention that for some reason, okay bye

search!

- #action
- #adventure
- #vans
- #allthisandmore
- #awaitsyou

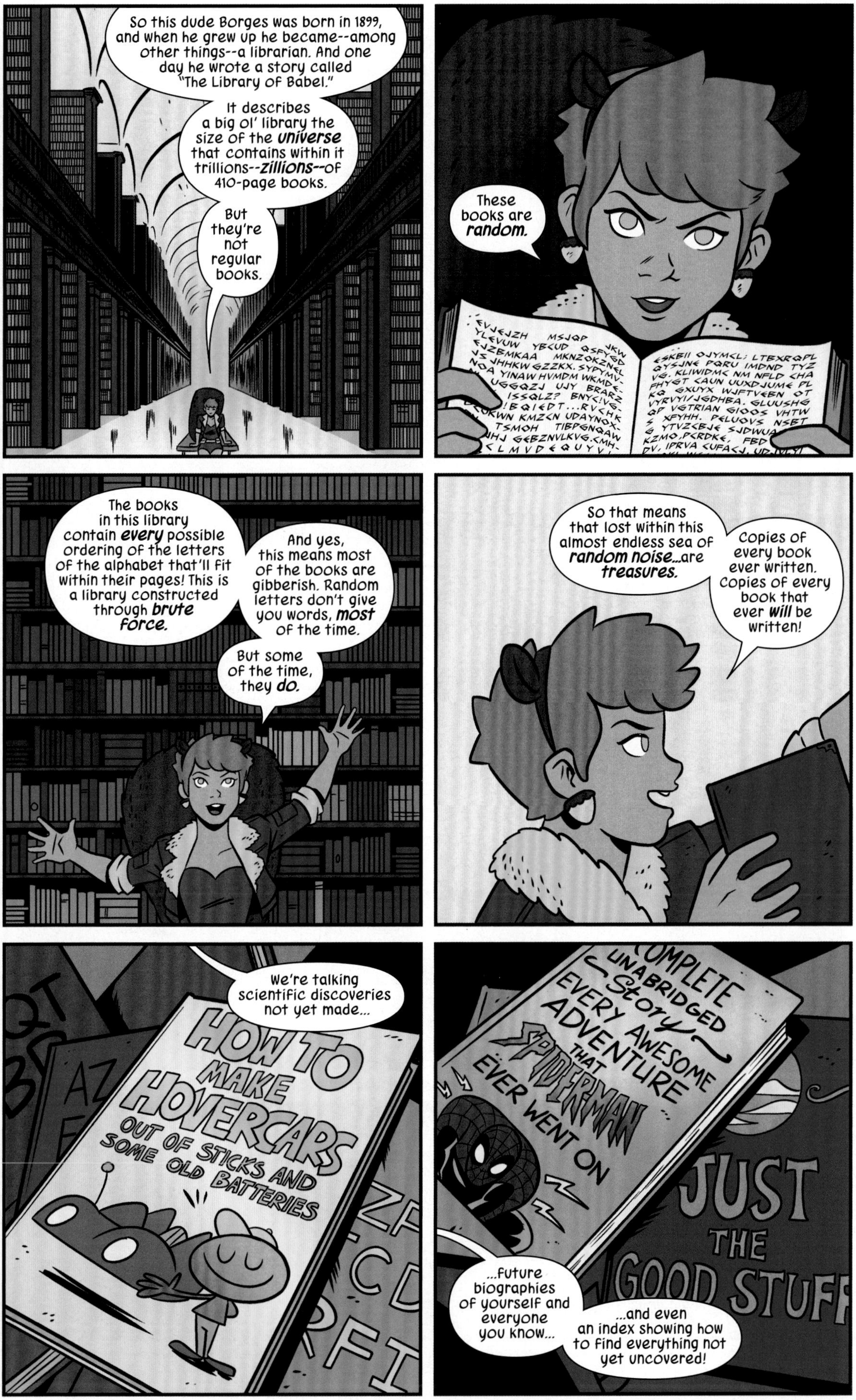

So this dude Borges was born in 1899, and when he grew up he became--among other things--a librarian. And one day he wrote a story called "The Library of Babel."
It describes a big ol' library the size of the *universe* that contains within it trillions--*zillions*--of 410-page books.
But they're not regular books.
These books are *random.*
The books in this library contain *every* possible ordering of the letters of the alphabet that'll fit within their pages! This is a library constructed through *brute force.*
And yes, this means most of the books are gibberish. Random letters don't give you words, *most* of the time.
But some of the time, they *do.*
So that means that lost within this almost endless sea of *random noise*...are *treasures.*
Copies of every book ever written. Copies of every book that ever *will* be written!
We're talking scientific discoveries not yet made...
HOW TO MAKE HOVERCARS OUT OF STICKS AND SOME OLD BATTERIES
COMPLETE UNABRIDGED Story EVERY AWESOME ADVENTURE SPIDER-MAN THAT EVER WENT ON
JUST THE GOOD STUFF
...future biographies of yourself and everyone you know...
...and even an index showing how to find everything not yet uncovered!

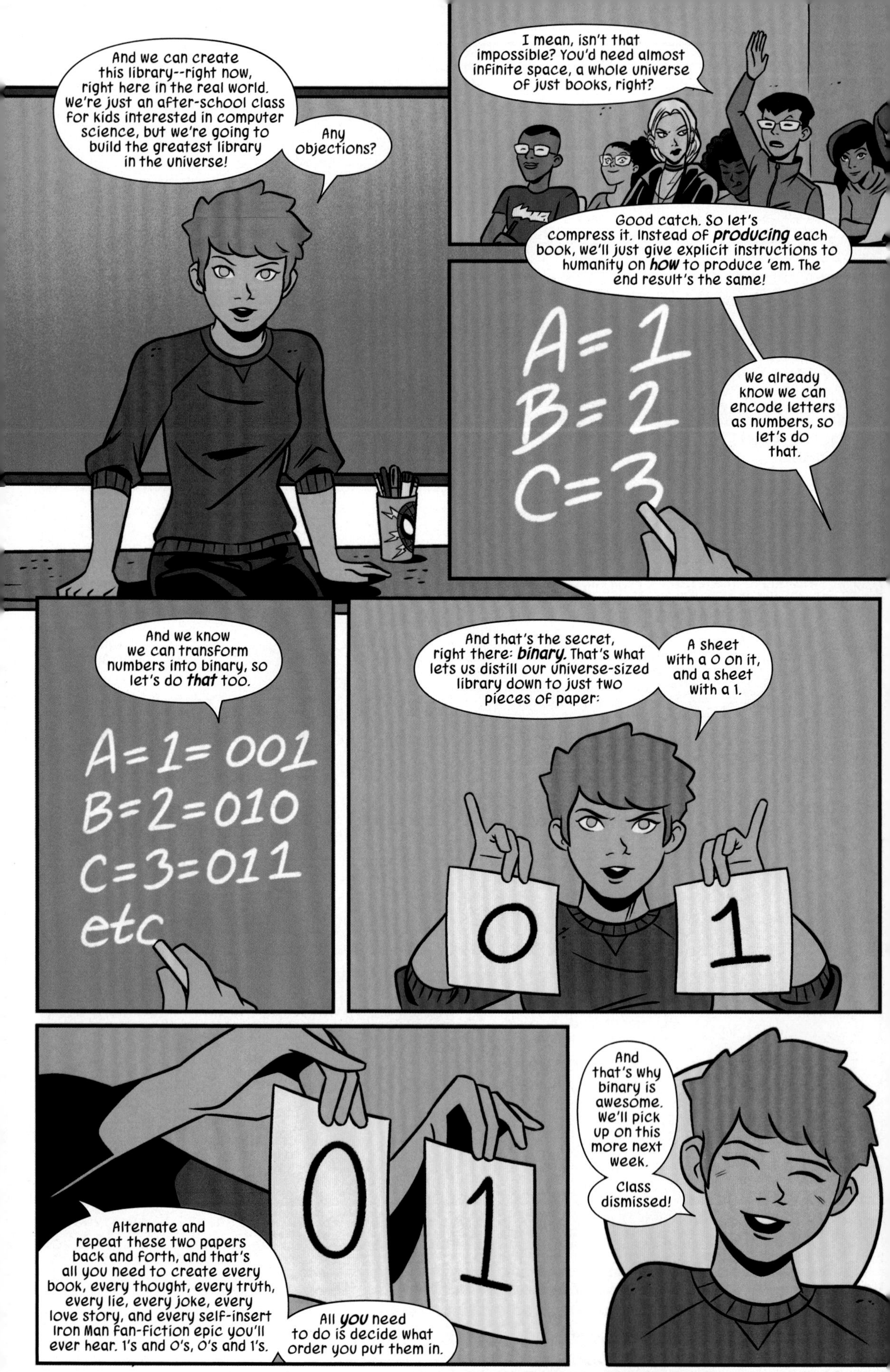

And we can create this library--right now, right here in the real world. We're just an after-school class for kids interested in computer science, but we're going to build the greatest library in the universe!
Any objections?
I mean, isn't that impossible? You'd need almost infinite space, a whole universe of just books, right?
Good catch. So let's compress it. Instead of *producing* each book, we'll just give explicit instructions to humanity on *how* to produce 'em. The end result's the same!
A=1
B=2
C=3
We already know we can encode letters as numbers, so let's do that.
And we know we can transform numbers into binary, so let's do *that* too.
A=1=001
B=2=010
C=3=011
etc
And that's the secret, right there: *binary*. That's what lets us distill our universe-sized library down to just two pieces of paper:
A sheet with a 0 on it, and a sheet with a 1.
0
1
0
1
Alternate and repeat these two papers back and forth, and that's all you need to create every book, every thought, every truth, every lie, every joke, every love story, and every self-insert Iron Man fan-fiction epic you'll ever hear. 1's and 0's, 0's and 1's.
All *you* need to do is decide what order you put them in.
And that's why binary is awesome. We'll pick up on this more next week.
Class dismissed!

That last bit comes from W.V.O. Quine, who called it "the miracle of binary notation: everything worth saying, and everything else as well, can be said with two characters." He's not wrong! I learned this when I was a kid and I'm an adult now and it still blows my mind!

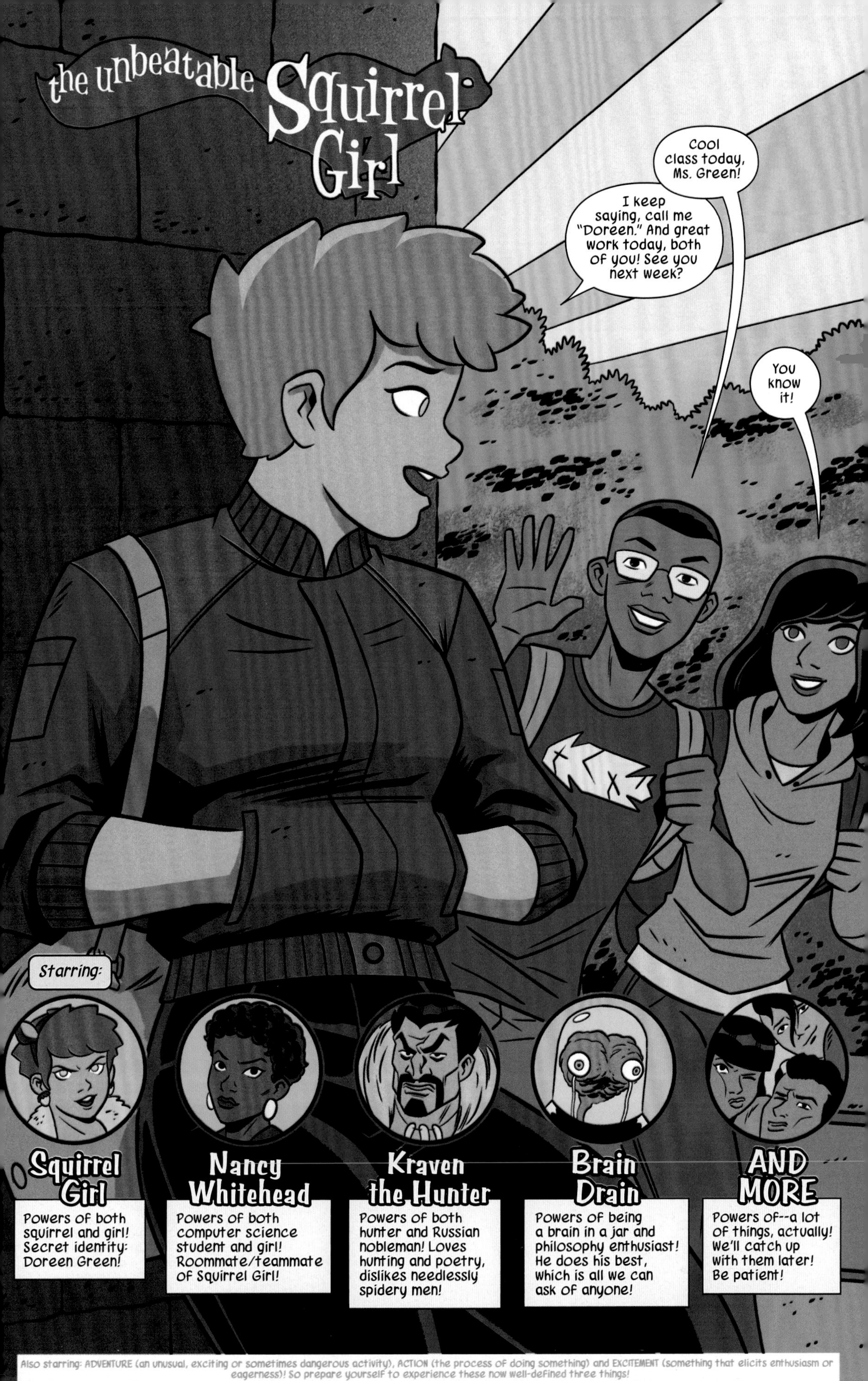
the unbeatable Squirrel Girl
Cool class today, Ms. Green!
I keep saying, call me "Doreen." And great work today, both of you! See you next week?
You know it!
Starring:
Squirrel Girl
Powers of both squirrel and girl! Secret identity: Doreen Green!
Nancy Whitehead
Powers of both computer science student and girl! Roommate/teammate of Squirrel Girl!
Kraven the Hunter
Powers of both hunter and Russian nobleman! Loves hunting and poetry, dislikes needlessly spidery men!
Brain Drain
Powers of being a brain in a jar and philosophy enthusiast! He does his best, which is all we can ask of anyone!
AND MORE
Powers of--a lot of things, actually! We'll catch up with them later! Be patient!

Also starring: ADVENTURE (an unusual, exciting or sometimes dangerous activity), ACTION (the process of doing something) and EXCITEMENT (something that elicits enthusiasm or eagerness)! So prepare yourself to experience these now well-defined three things!

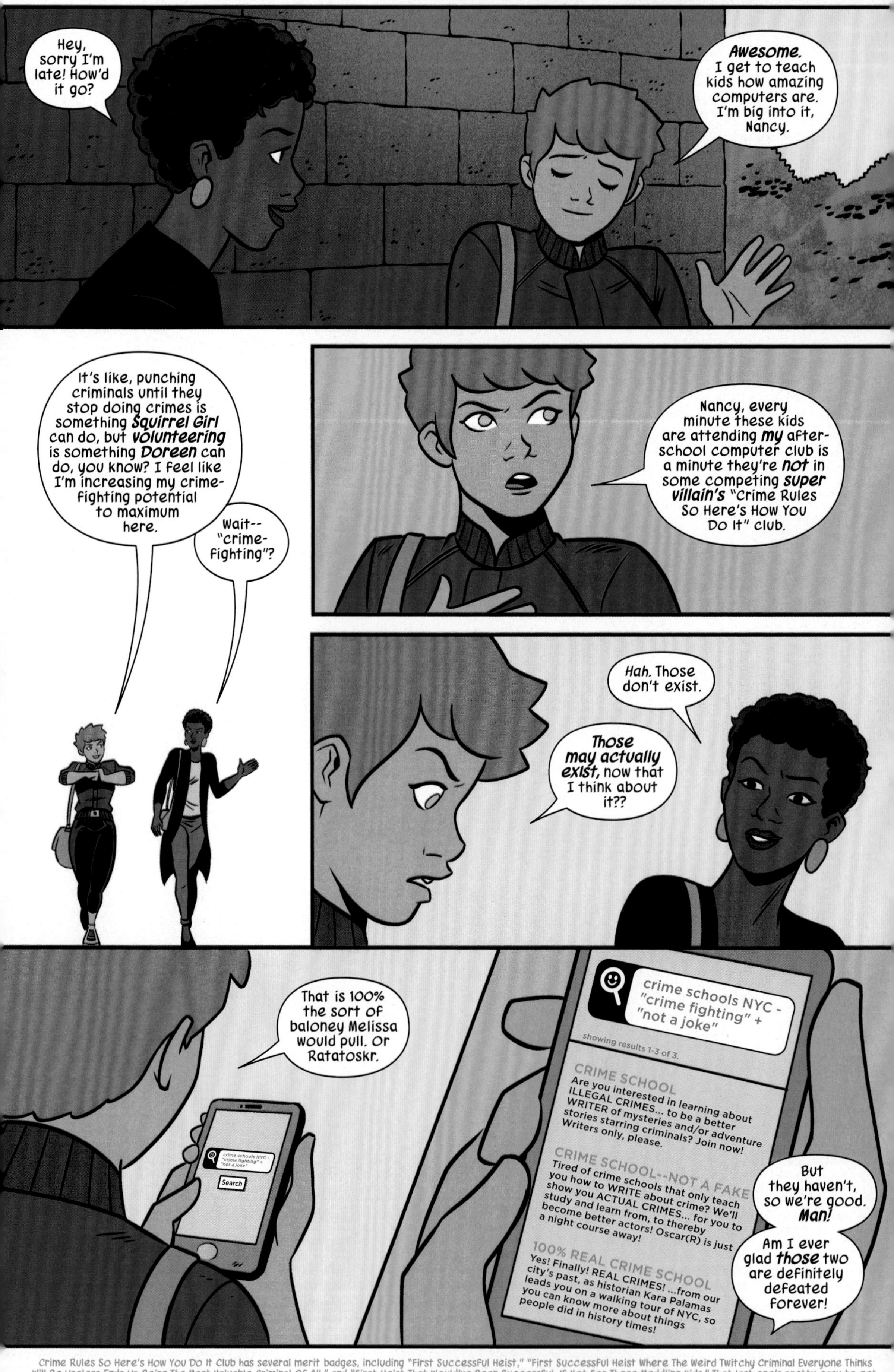

Hey, sorry I'm late! How'd it go?
Awesome. I get to teach kids how amazing computers are. I'm big into it, Nancy.
It's like, punching criminals until they stop doing crimes is something Squirrel Girl can do, but volunteering is something Doreen can do, you know? I feel like I'm increasing my crime-fighting potential to maximum here.
Wait--"crime-fighting"?
Nancy, every minute these kids are attending my after-school computer club is a minute they're not in some competing super villain's "Crime Rules So Here's How You Do It" club.
Hah. Those don't exist.
Those may actually exist, now that I think about it??
That is 100% the sort of baloney Melissa would pull. Or Ratatoskr.
crime schools NYC - "crime fighting" + "not a joke"
Search
crime schools NYC - "crime fighting" + "not a joke"
showing results 1-3 of 3.
CRIME SCHOOL
Are you interested in learning about ILLEGAL CRIMES... to be a better WRITER of mysteries and/or adventure stories starring criminals? Join now! Writers only, please.
CRIME SCHOOL--NOT A FAKE
Tired of crime schools that only teach you how to WRITE about crime? We'll show you ACTUAL CRIMES... for you to study and learn from, to thereby become better actors! Oscar(R) is just a night course away!
100% REAL CRIME SCHOOL
Yes! Finally! REAL CRIMES! ...from our city's past, as historian Kara Palamas leads you on a walking tour of NYC, so you can know more about things people did in history times!
But they haven't, so we're good. Man!
Am I ever glad those two are definitely defeated forever!

Crime Rules So Here's How You Do It Club has several merit badges, including "First Successful Heist," "First Successful Heist Where The Weird Twitchy Criminal Everyone Thinks Will Be Useless Ends Up Being The Most Valuable Criminal Of All," and "First Heist That Would've Been Successful, If Not For Those Meddling Kids." That last one's pretty easy to get. Lots and lots of meddling kids out there!

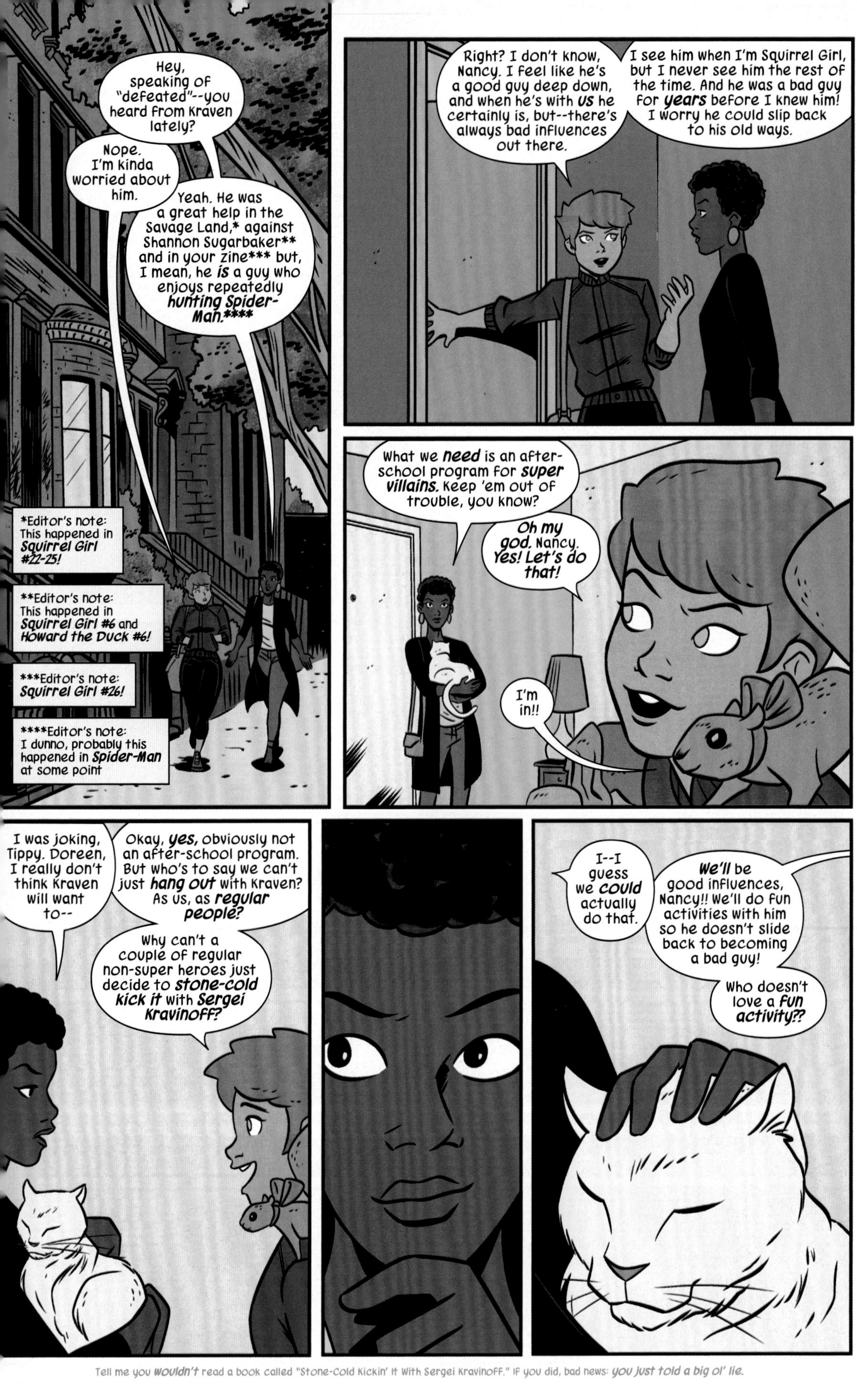
Hey, speaking of "defeated"--you heard from Kraven lately?
Nope. I'm kinda worried about him.
Yeah. He was a great help in the Savage Land,* against Shannon Sugarbaker** and in your zine*** but, I mean, he *is* a guy who enjoys repeatedly ***hunting Spider-Man.****
*Editor's note: This happened in *Squirrel Girl #22-25!*
**Editor's note: This happened in *Squirrel Girl #6* and *Howard the Duck #6!*
***Editor's note: *Squirrel Girl #26!*
****Editor's note: I dunno, probably this happened in *Spider-Man* at some point
Right? I don't know, Nancy. I feel like he's a good guy deep down, and when he's with *US* he certainly is, but--there's always bad influences out there.
I see him when I'm Squirrel Girl, but I never see him the rest of the time. And he was a bad guy for *years* before I knew him! I worry he could slip back to his old ways.
What we ***need*** is an after-school program for ***super villains.*** Keep 'em out of trouble, you know?
Oh my god. Nancy. *Yes! Let's do that!*
I'm in!!
I was joking, Tippy. Doreen, I really don't think Kraven will want to--
Okay, ***yes,*** obviously not an after-school program. But who's to say we can't just ***hang out*** with Kraven? As us, as ***regular people?***
Why can't a couple of regular non-super heroes just decide to ***stone-cold kick it*** with ***Sergei Kravinoff?***
I--I guess we ***could*** actually do that.
We'll be good influences, Nancy!! We'll do fun activities with him so he doesn't slide back to becoming a bad guy!
Who doesn't love a ***fun activity??***

Tell me you *wouldn't* read a book called "Stone-Cold Kickin' It With Sergei Kravinoff." If you did, bad news: *you just told a big ol' lie.*

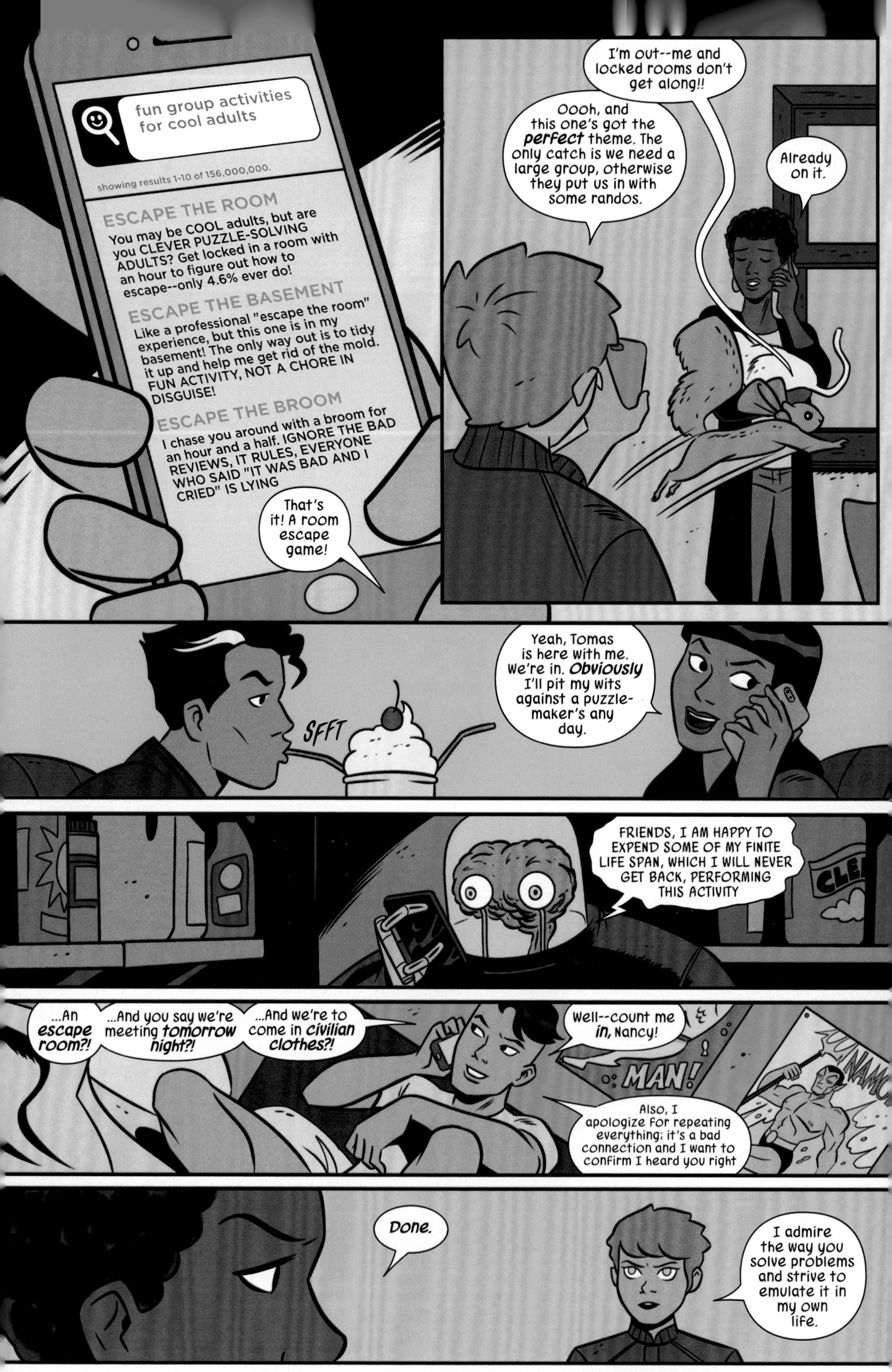
fun group activities for cool adults
showing results 1-10 of 156,000,000.
ESCAPE THE ROOM
You may be COOL adults, but are you CLEVER PUZZLE-SOLVING ADULTS? Get locked in a room with an hour to figure out how to escape--only 4.6% ever do!
ESCAPE THE BASEMENT
Like a professional "escape the room" experience, but this one is in my basement! The only way out is to tidy it up and help me get rid of the mold. FUN ACTIVITY, NOT A CHORE IN DISGUISE!
ESCAPE THE BROOM
I chase you around with a broom for an hour and a half. IGNORE THE BAD REVIEWS, IT RULES, EVERYONE WHO SAID "IT WAS BAD AND I CRIED" IS LYING
That's it! A room escape game!
I'm out--me and locked rooms don't get along!!
Oooh, and this one's got the *perfect* theme. The only catch is we need a large group, otherwise they put us in with some randos.
Already on it.
SFFT
Yeah, Tomas is here with me. We're in. *Obviously* I'll pit my wits against a puzzle-maker's any day.
FRIENDS, I AM HAPPY TO EXPEND SOME OF MY FINITE LIFE SPAN, WHICH I WILL NEVER GET BACK, PERFORMING THIS ACTIVITY
...An *escape room?!*
...And you say we're meeting *tomorrow night?!*
...And we're to come in *civilian clothes?!*
Well--count me *in*, Nancy!
MAN!
Also, I apologize for repeating everything; it's a bad connection and I want to confirm I heard you right
Done.
I admire the way you solve problems and strive to emulate it in my own life.

As part of research for this story, I participated in an escape room game. It was definitely research and not at all goofing off, so I was extremely justified when I told everyone else in the room that I was "here on a very important mission from Marvel Comics."

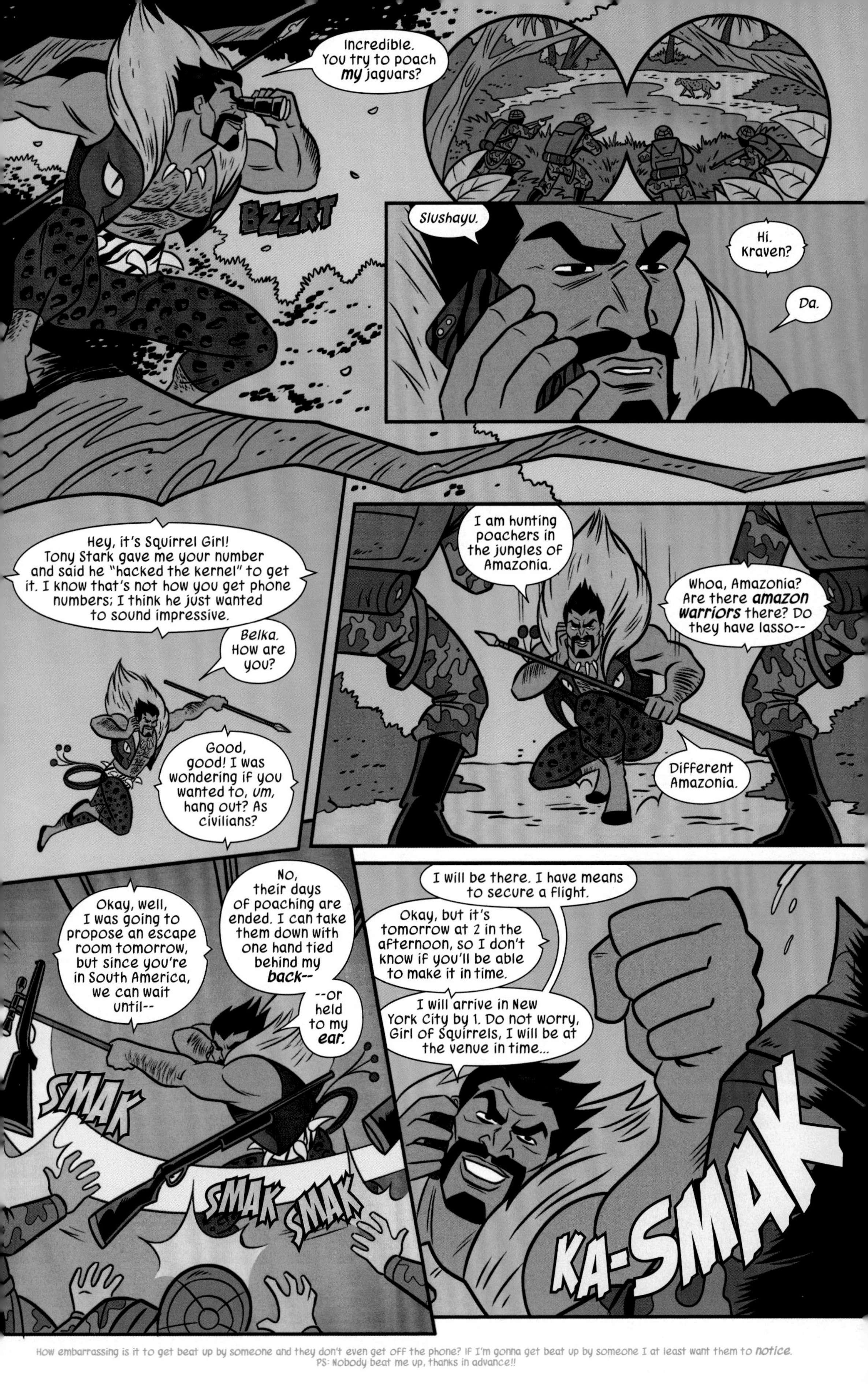
Incredible. You try to poach *my* jaguars?
BZZRT
Slushayu.
Hi. Kraven?
Da.
Hey, it's Squirrel Girl! Tony Stark gave me your number and said he "hacked the kernel" to get it. I know that's not how you get phone numbers; I think he just wanted to sound impressive.
Belka. How are you?
Good, good! I was wondering if you wanted to, um, hang out? As civilians?
I am hunting poachers in the jungles of Amazonia.
Whoa, Amazonia? Are there ***amazon warriors*** there? Do they have lasso--
Different Amazonia.
Okay, well, I was going to propose an escape room tomorrow, but since you're in South America, we can wait until--
No, their days of poaching are ended. I can take them down with one hand tied behind my ***back***--
--or held to my ***ear.***
SMAK
SMAK SMAK
I will be there. I have means to secure a flight.
Okay, but it's tomorrow at 2 in the afternoon, so I don't know if you'll be able to make it in time.
I will arrive in New York City by 1. Do not worry, Girl of Squirrels, I will be at the venue in time...
KA-SMAK

How embarrassing is it to get beat up by someone and they don't even get off the phone? If I'm gonna get beat up by someone I at least want them to *notice*.
PS: Nobody beat me up, thanks in advance!!

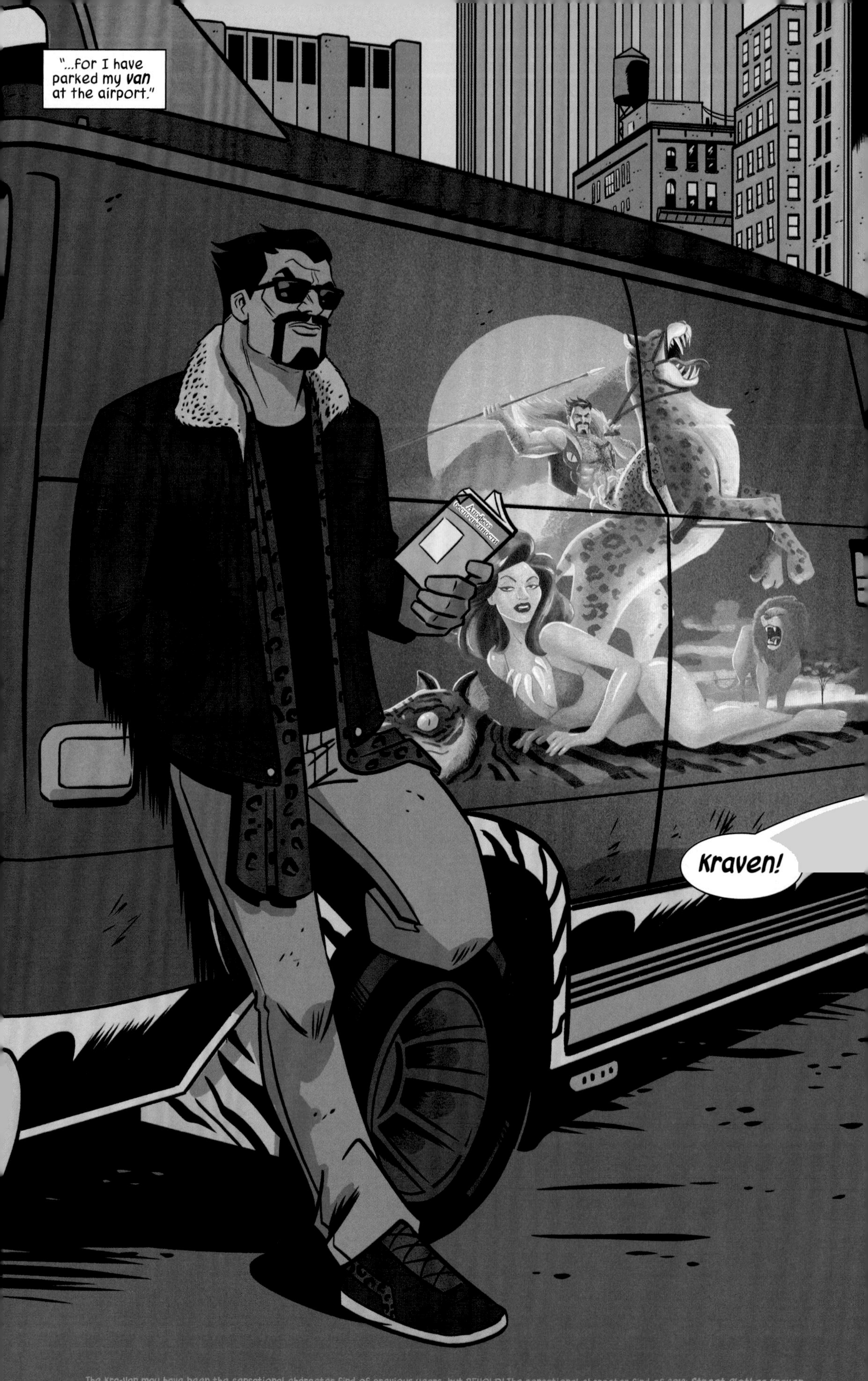
"...for I have parked my *van* at the airport."
Апофеоз беспочвенности
Kraven!

The Kra-Van may have been the sensational character find of previous years, but BEHOLD! The sensational character find of 2018: *Street Clothes Kraven.*

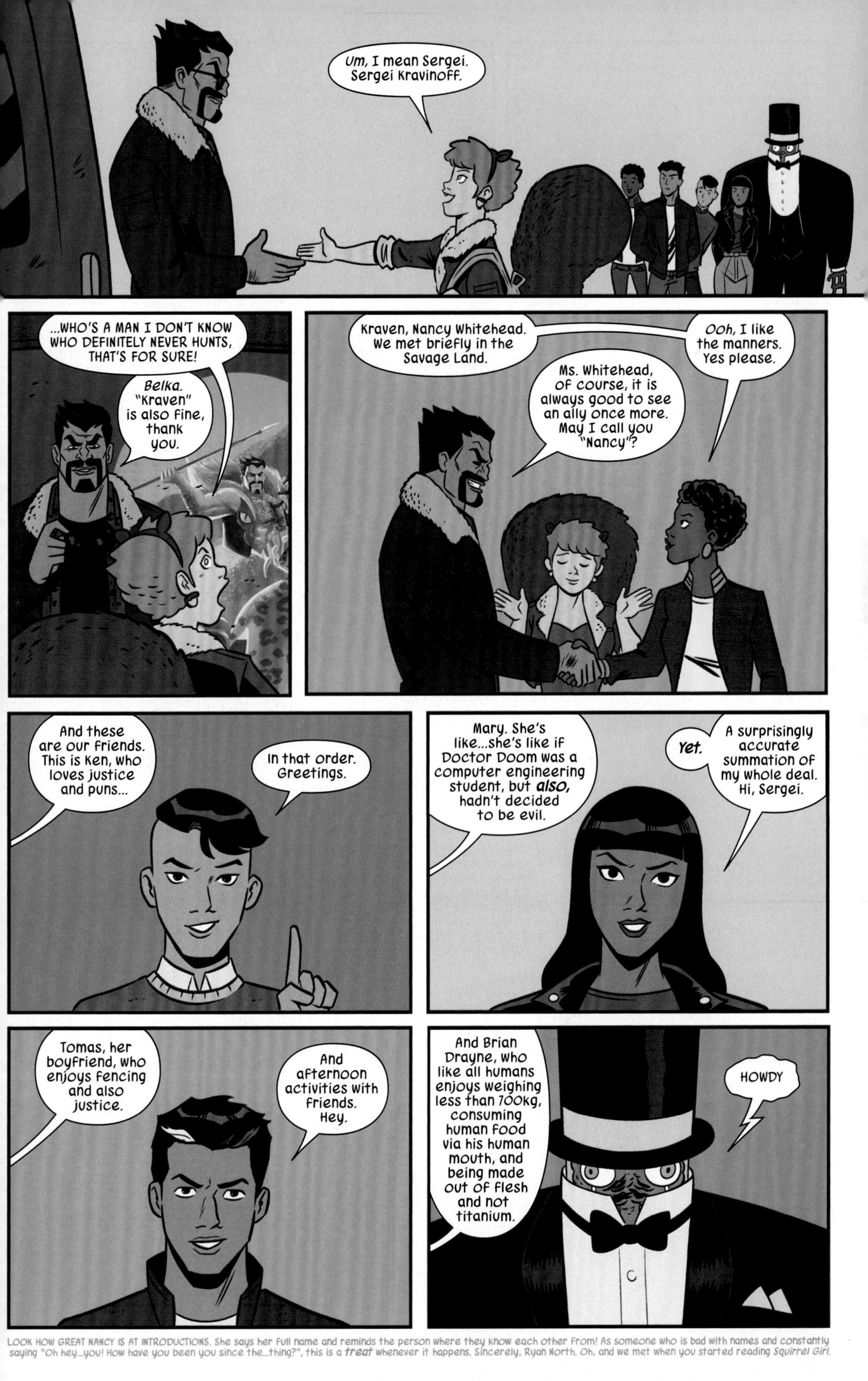

Um, I mean Sergei. Sergei Kravinoff.
...WHO'S A MAN I DON'T KNOW WHO DEFINITELY NEVER HUNTS, THAT'S FOR SURE!
Belka. "Kraven" is also fine, thank you.
Kraven, Nancy Whitehead. We met briefly in the Savage Land.
Ms. Whitehead, of course, it is always good to see an ally once more. May I call you "Nancy"?
Ooh, I like the manners. Yes please.
And these are our friends. This is Ken, who loves justice and puns...
In that order. Greetings.
Mary. She's like...she's like if Doctor Doom was a computer engineering student, but also, hadn't decided to be evil.
Yet.
A surprisingly accurate summation of my whole deal. Hi, Sergei.
Tomas, her boyfriend, who enjoys fencing and also justice.
And afternoon activities with friends. Hey.
And Brian Drayne, who like all humans enjoys weighing less than 700kg, consuming human food via his human mouth, and being made out of flesh and not titanium.
HOWDY

LOOK HOW GREAT NANCY IS AT INTRODUCTIONS. She says her full name and reminds the person where they know each other from! As someone who is bad with names and constantly saying "Oh hey...you! How have you been you since the...thing?", this is a *treat* whenever it happens. Sincerely, Ryan North. Oh, and we met when you started reading *Squirrel Girl*.

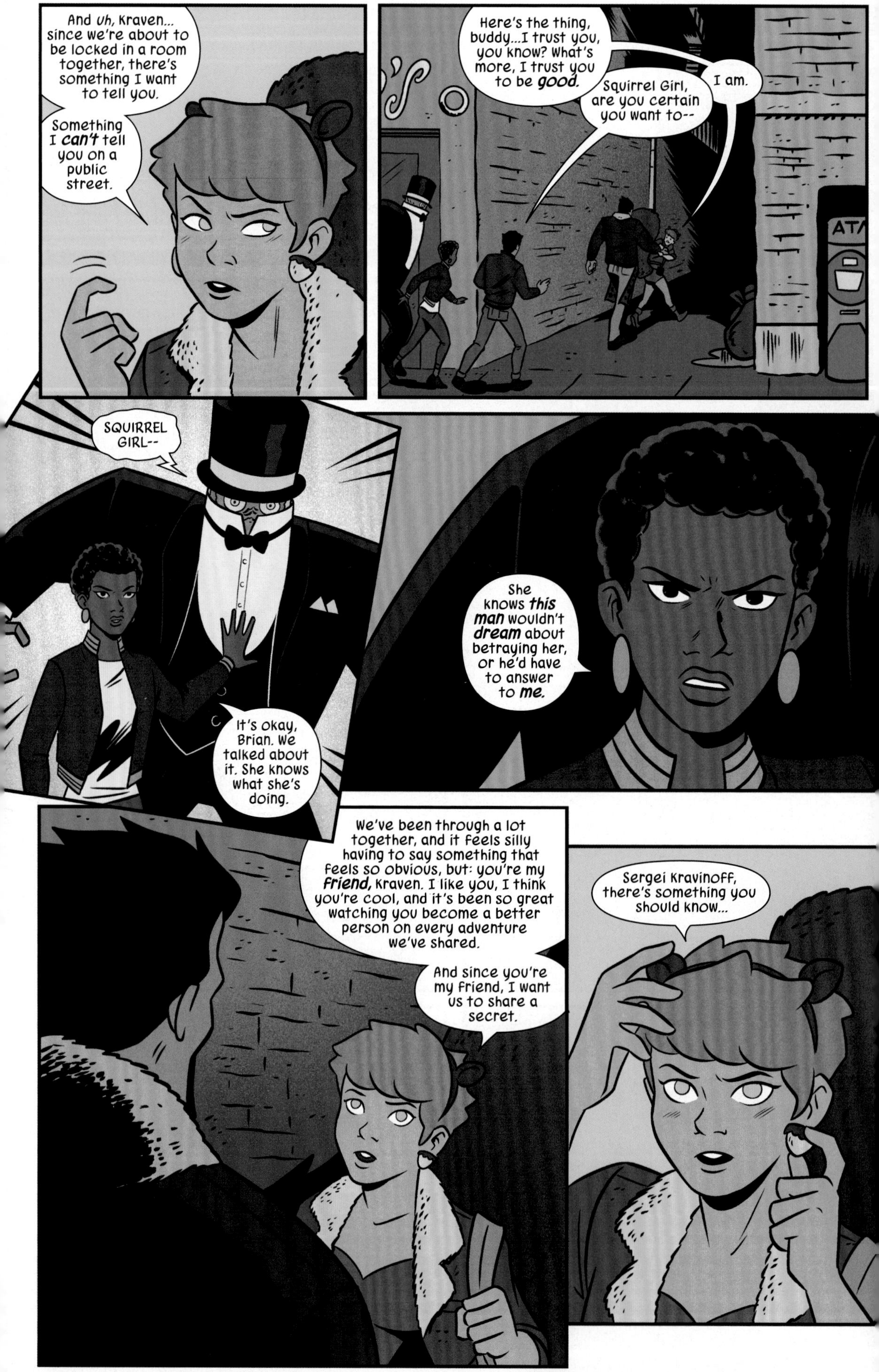
And uh, Kraven... since we're about to be locked in a room together, there's something I want to tell you.
Something I *can't* tell you on a public street.
Here's the thing, buddy...I trust you, you know? What's more, I trust you to be *good.*
Squirrel Girl, are you certain you want to--
I am.
ATM
SQUIRREL GIRL--
It's okay, Brian. We talked about it. She knows what she's doing.
She knows *this man* wouldn't *dream* about betraying her, or he'd have to answer to *me.*
We've been through a lot together, and it feels silly having to say something that feels so obvious, but: you're my *friend,* Kraven. I like you, I think you're cool, and it's been so great watching you become a better person on every adventure we've shared.
And since you're my friend, I want us to share a secret.
Sergei Kravinoff, there's something you should know...

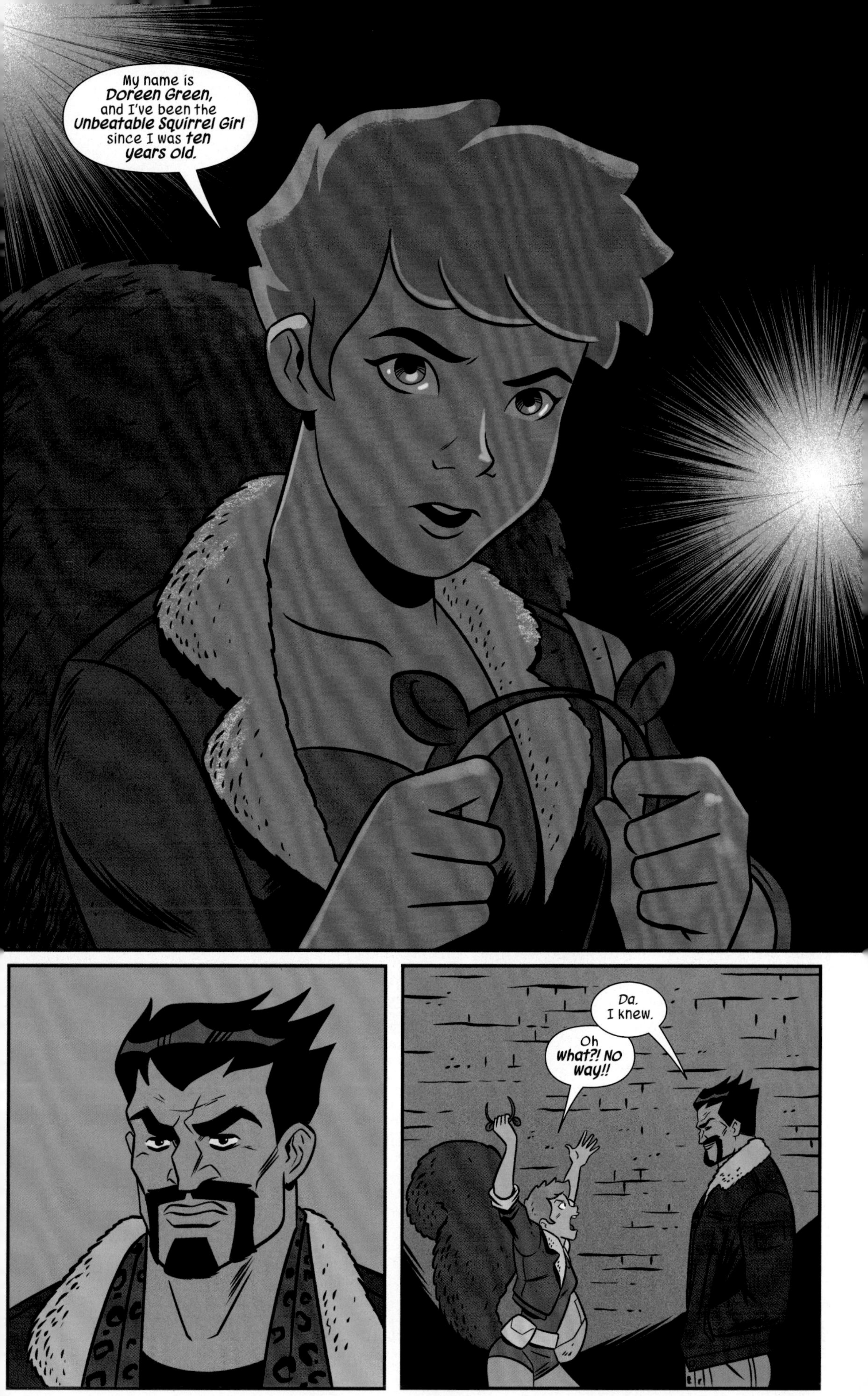
My name is Doreen Green, and I've been the Unbeatable Squirrel Girl since I was ten years old.
Oh what?! No way!!
Da. I knew.

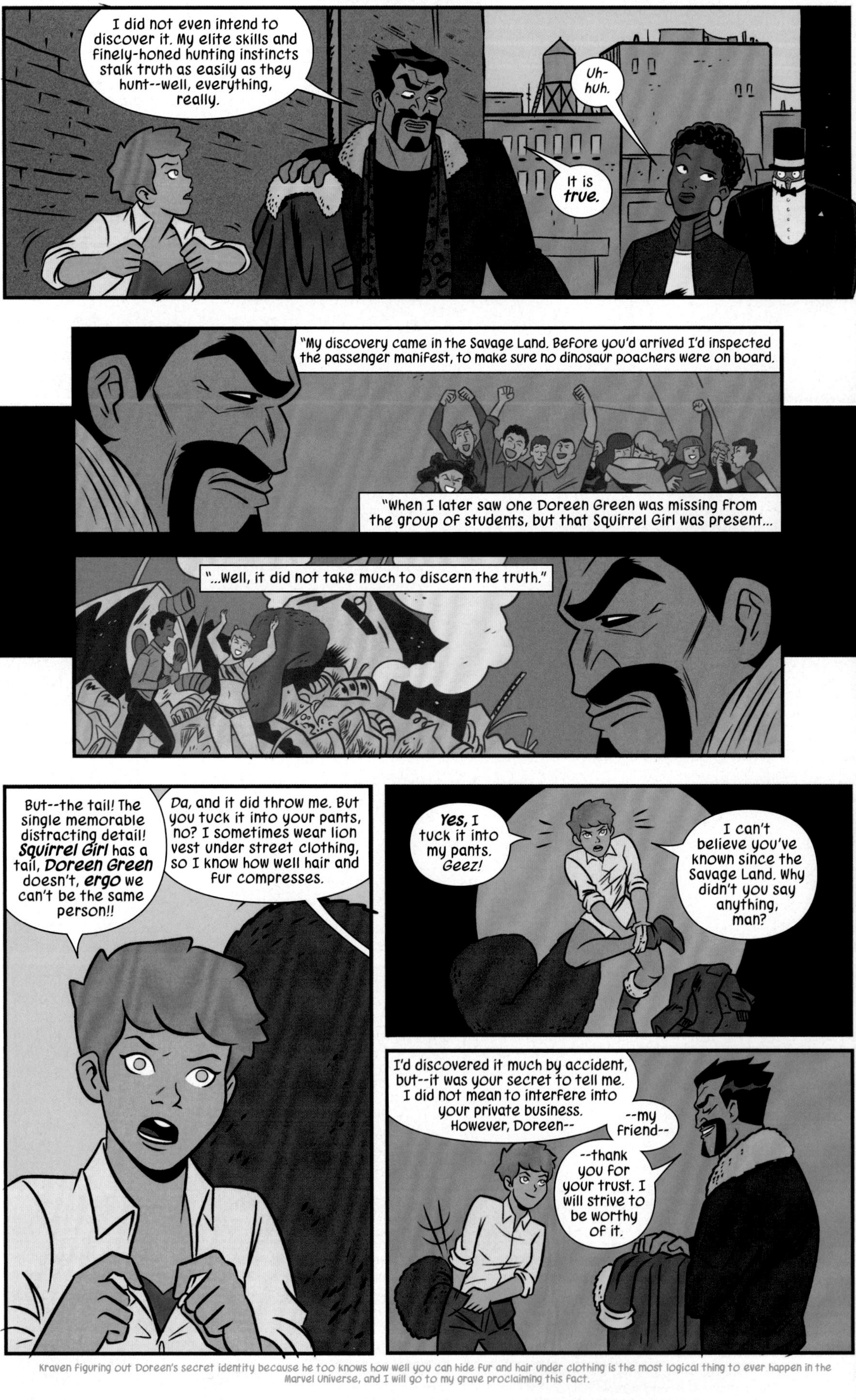
I did not even intend to discover it. My elite skills and finely-honed hunting instincts stalk truth as easily as they hunt--well, everything, really.
Uh-huh.
It is true.
"My discovery came in the Savage Land. Before you'd arrived I'd inspected the passenger manifest, to make sure no dinosaur poachers were on board.
"When I later saw one Doreen Green was missing from the group of students, but that Squirrel Girl was present...
"...Well, it did not take much to discern the truth."
But--the tail! The single memorable distracting detail! Squirrel Girl has a tail, Doreen Green doesn't, ergo we can't be the same person!!
Da, and it did throw me. But you tuck it into your pants, no? I sometimes wear lion vest under street clothing, so I know how well hair and fur compresses.
Yes, I tuck it into my pants. Geez!
I can't believe you've known since the Savage Land. Why didn't you say anything, man?
I'd discovered it much by accident, but--it was your secret to tell me. I did not mean to interfere into your private business. However, Doreen--
--my friend--
--thank you for your trust. I will strive to be worthy of it.

Kraven figuring out Doreen's secret identity because he too knows how well you can hide fur and hair under clothing is the most logical thing to ever happen in the Marvel Universe, and I will go to my grave proclaiming this fact.

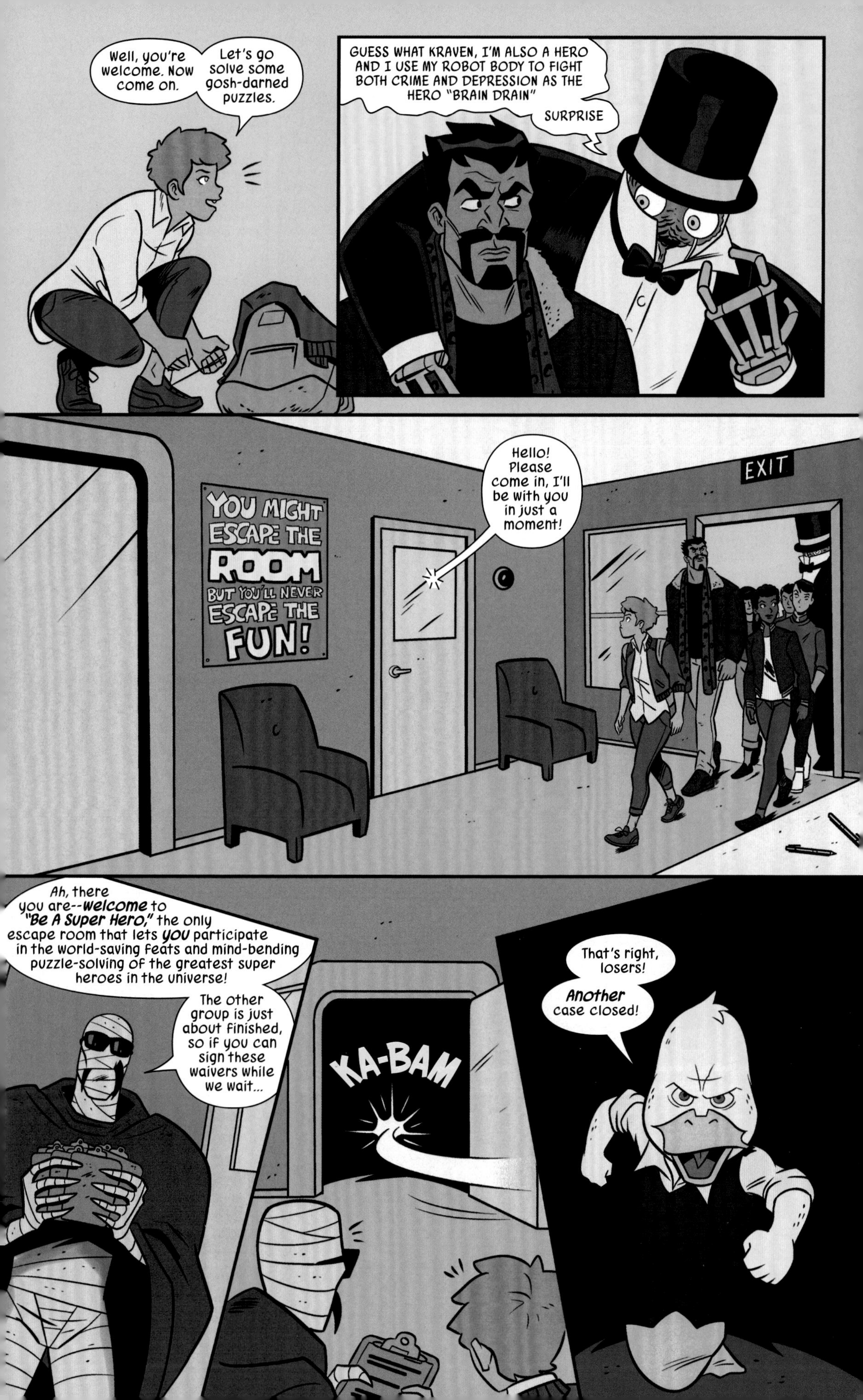

Well, you're welcome. Now come on.
Let's go solve some gosh-darned puzzles.
GUESS WHAT KRAVEN, I'M ALSO A HERO AND I USE MY ROBOT BODY TO FIGHT BOTH CRIME AND DEPRESSION AS THE HERO "BRAIN DRAIN"
SURPRISE
YOU MIGHT ESCAPE THE ROOM BUT YOU'LL NEVER ESCAPE THE FUN!
Hello! Please come in, I'll be with you in just a moment!
EXIT
Ah, there you are--*welcome* to *"Be A Super Hero,"* the only escape room that lets *YOU* participate in the world-saving feats and mind-bending puzzle-solving of the greatest super heroes in the universe!
The other group is just about finished, so if you can sign these waivers while we wait...
KA-BAM
That's right, losers!
Another case closed!

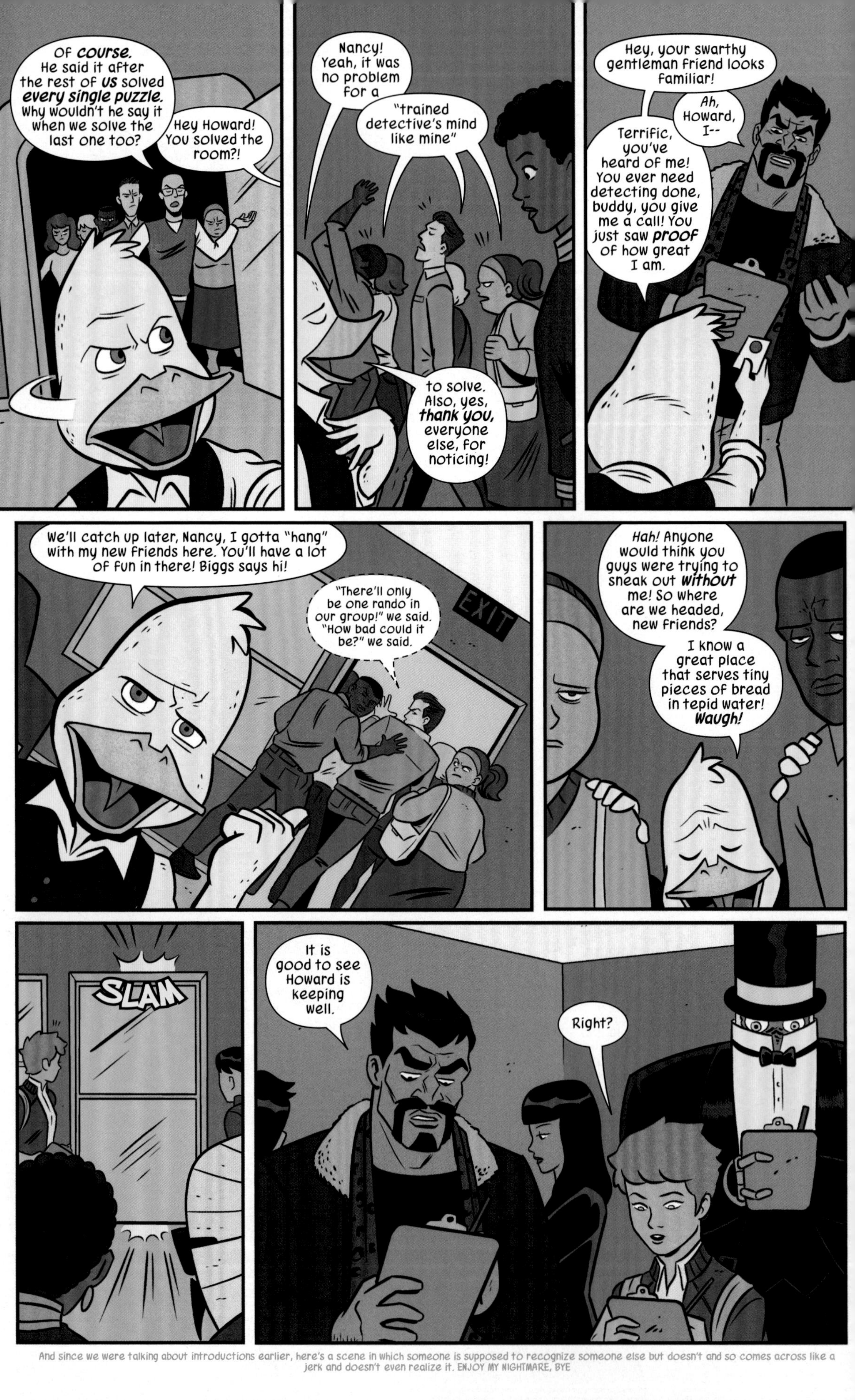
Of course. He said it after the rest of us solved every single puzzle. Why wouldn't he say it when we solve the last one too?
Hey Howard! You solved the room?!
Nancy! Yeah, it was no problem for a
"trained detective's mind like mine"
to solve. Also, yes, thank you, everyone else, for noticing!
Hey, your swarthy gentleman friend looks familiar!
Terrific, you've heard of me! You ever need detecting done, buddy, you give me a call! You just saw proof of how great I am.
Ah, Howard, I--
We'll catch up later, Nancy, I gotta "hang" with my new friends here. You'll have a lot of fun in there! Biggs says hi!
"There'll only be one rando in our group!" we said. "How bad could it be?" we said.
EXIT
Hah! Anyone would think you guys were trying to sneak out without me! So where are we headed, new friends?
I know a great place that serves tiny pieces of bread in tepid water! Waugh!
SLAM
It is good to see Howard is keeping well.
Right?

And since we were talking about introductions earlier, here's a scene in which someone is supposed to recognize someone else but doesn't and so comes across like a jerk and doesn't even realize it. ENJOY MY NIGHTMARE, BYE

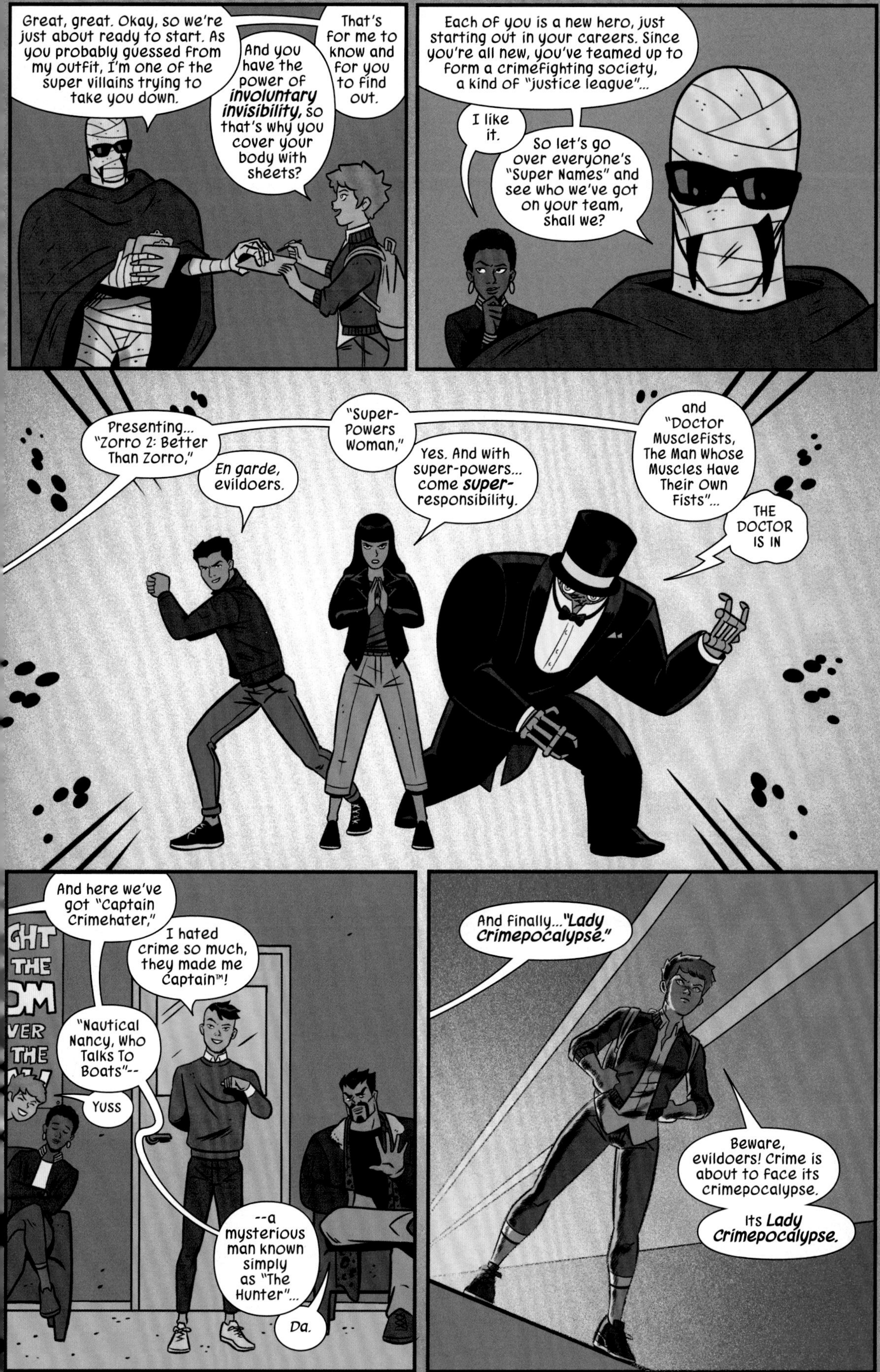
Great, great. Okay, so we're just about ready to start. As you probably guessed from my outfit, I'm one of the super villains trying to take you down.
And you have the power of *involuntary invisibility,* so that's why you cover your body with sheets?
That's for me to know and for you to find out.
Each of you is a new hero, just starting out in your careers. Since you're all new, you've teamed up to form a crimefighting society, a kind of "justice league"...
I like it.
So let's go over everyone's "Super Names" and see who we've got on your team, shall we?
Presenting... "Zorro 2: Better Than Zorro,"
En garde, evildoers.
"Super-Powers Woman,"
Yes. And with super-powers... come ***super-***responsibility.
and "Doctor Musclefists, The Man Whose Muscles Have Their Own Fists"...
THE DOCTOR IS IN
And here we've got "Captain Crimehater,"
I hated crime so much, they made me Captain™!
"Nautical Nancy, Who Talks To Boats"--
YUSS
--a mysterious man known simply as "The Hunter"...
Da.
And finally...***"Lady Crimepocalypse."***
Beware, evildoers! Crime is about to face its crimepocalypse.
Its ***Lady Crimepocalypse.***

Brain Drain was going to call himself "The NihilFIST," but then thought he'd better save that one for real life. At the very least it's a great name for one or both of his fists.

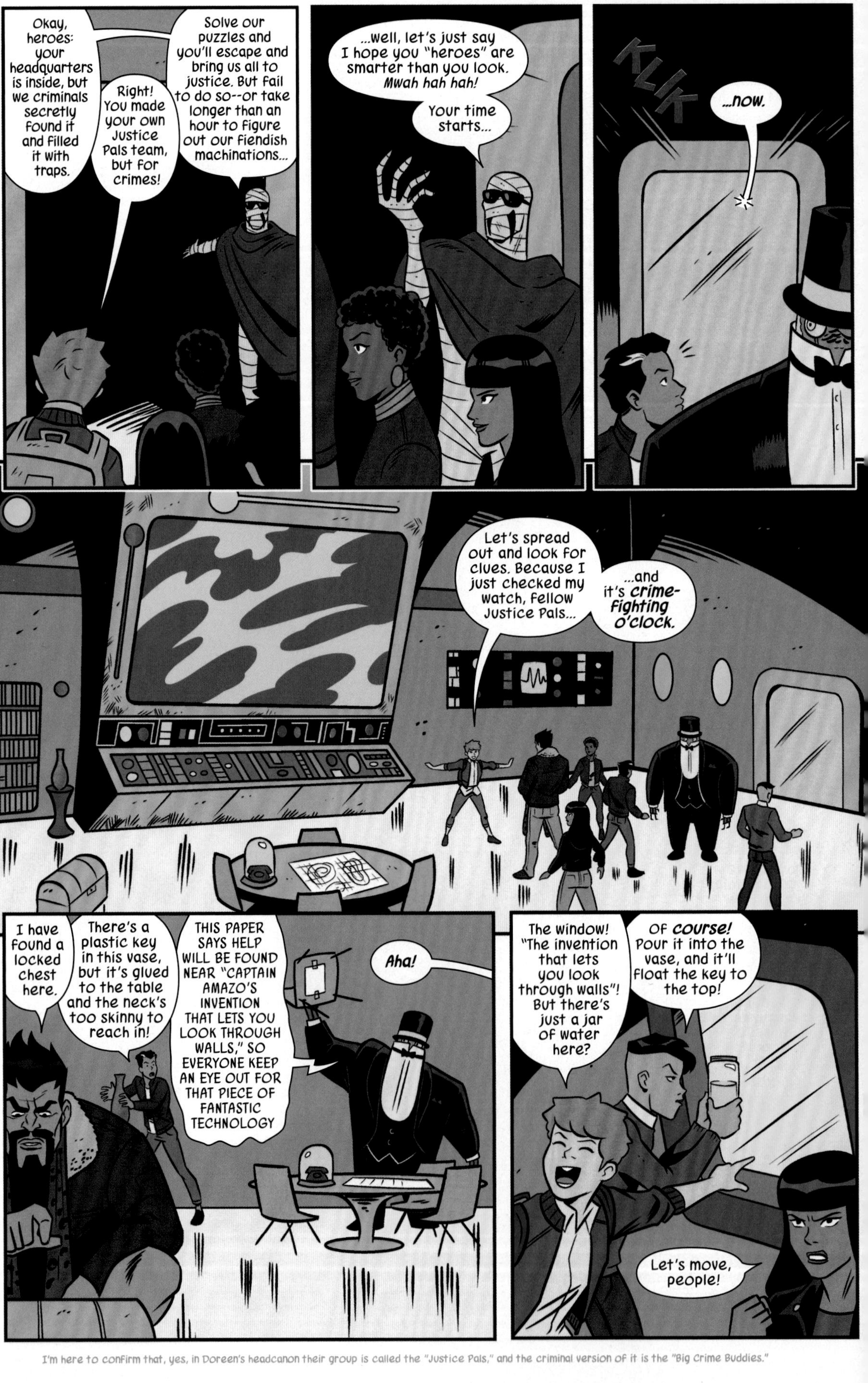
Okay, heroes: your headquarters is inside, but we criminals secretly found it and filled it with traps.
Right! You made your own Justice Pals team, but for crimes!
Solve our puzzles and you'll escape and bring us all to justice. But fail to do so--or take longer than an hour to figure out our fiendish machinations...
...well, let's just say I hope you "heroes" are smarter than you look. Mwah hah hah!
Your time starts...
KLIK
...now.
Let's spread out and look for clues. Because I just checked my watch, fellow Justice Pals...
...and it's crime-fighting o'clock.
I have found a locked chest here.
There's a plastic key in this vase, but it's glued to the table and the neck's too skinny to reach in!
THIS PAPER SAYS HELP WILL BE FOUND NEAR "CAPTAIN AMAZO'S INVENTION THAT LETS YOU LOOK THROUGH WALLS," SO EVERYONE KEEP AN EYE OUT FOR THAT PIECE OF FANTASTIC TECHNOLOGY
Aha!
The window! "The invention that lets you look through walls"! But there's just a jar of water here?
OF COURSE! Pour it into the vase, and it'll float the key to the top!
Let's move, people!

I'm here to confirm that, yes, in Doreen's headcanon their group is called the "Justice Pals," and the criminal version of it is the "Big Crime Buddies."

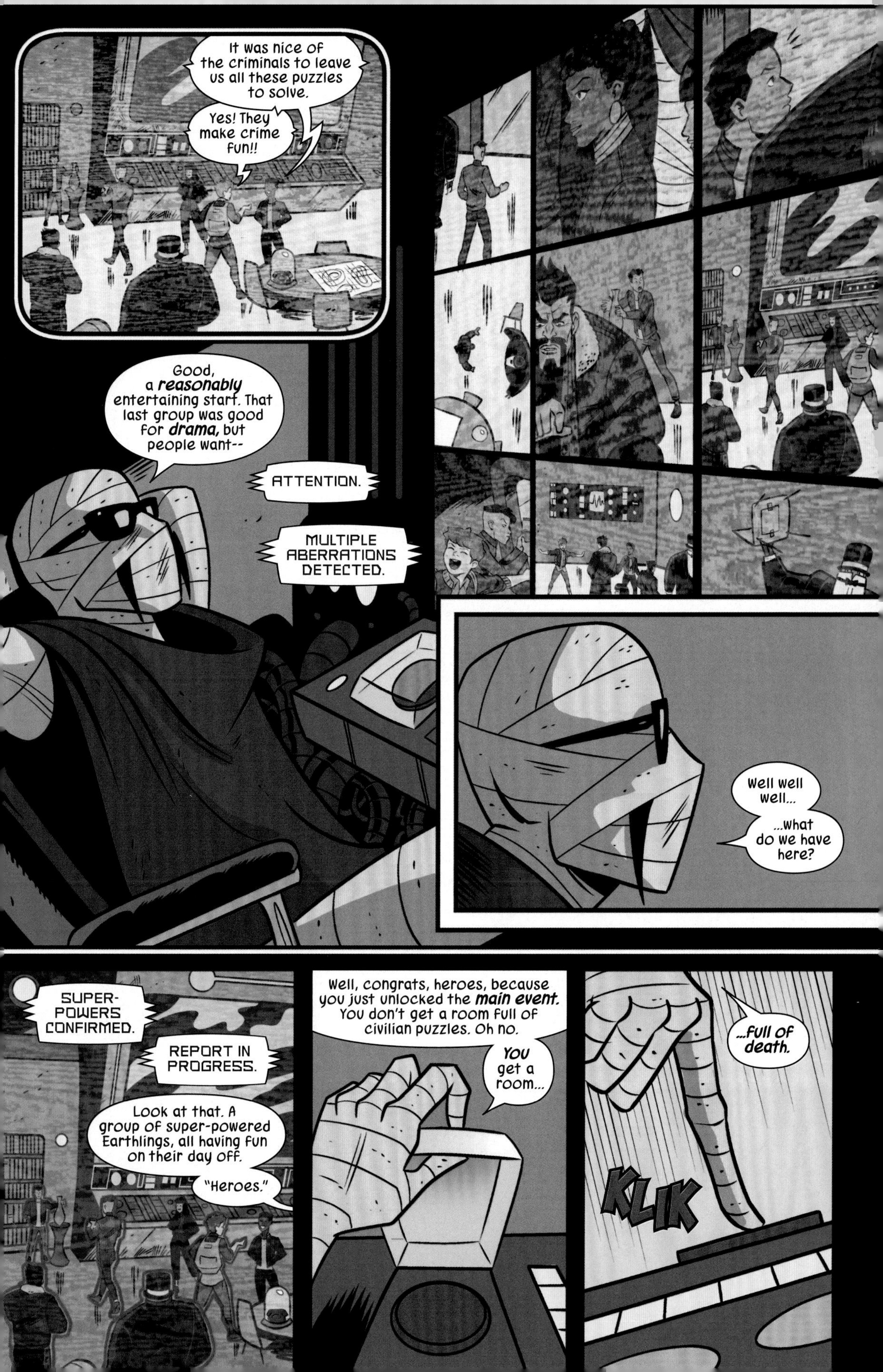

It was nice of the criminals to leave us all these puzzles to solve.
Yes! They make crime fun!!
Good, a reasonably entertaining start. That last group was good for drama, but people want--
ATTENTION.
MULTIPLE ABERRATIONS DETECTED.
Well well well...
...what do we have here?
SUPER-POWERS CONFIRMED.
REPORT IN PROGRESS.
Look at that. A group of super-powered Earthlings, all having fun on their day off.
"Heroes."
Well, congrats, heroes, because you just unlocked the main event. You don't get a room full of civilian puzzles. Oh no.
You get a room...
...full of death.
KLIK

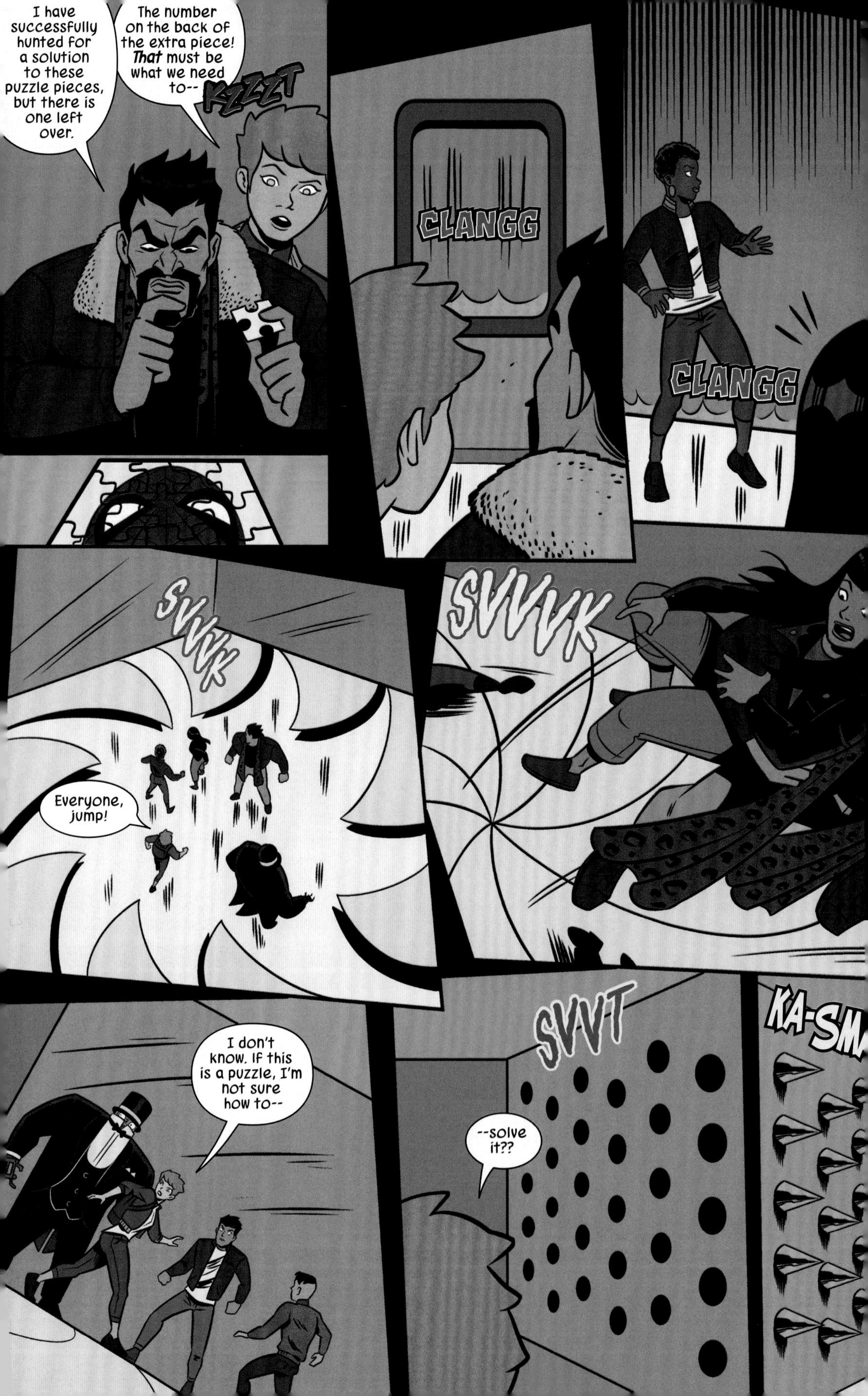
I have successfully hunted for a solution to these puzzle pieces, but there is one left over.
The number on the back of the extra piece! *That* must be what we need to--
KZZZT
CLANGG
CLANGG
SVVVK
Everyone, jump!
SVVVK
I don't know. If this is a puzzle, I'm not sure how to--
SVVT
--solve it??
KA-SM

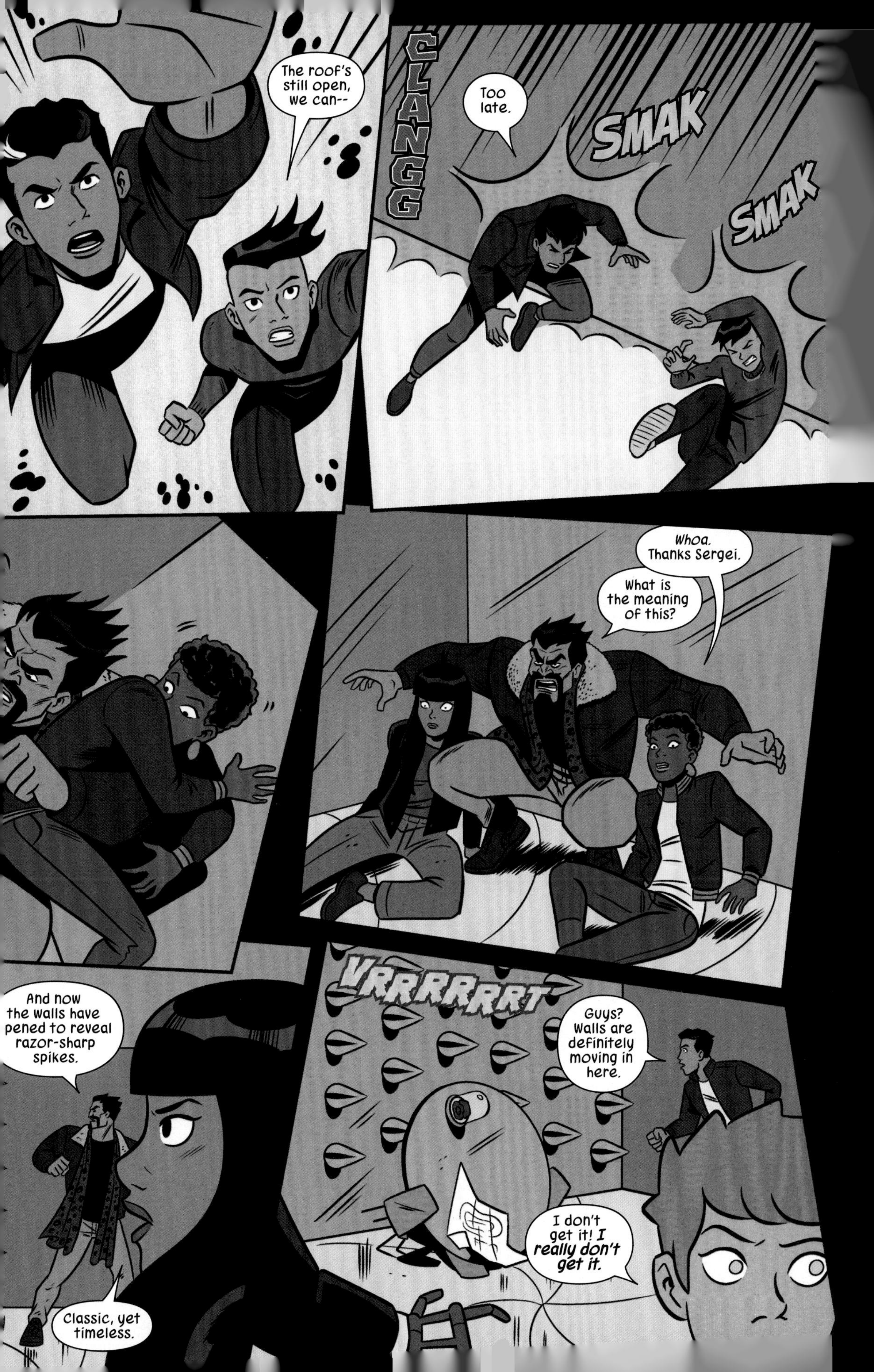
The roof's still open, we can--
CLANGG
Too late.
SMAK
SMAK
Whoa. Thanks Sergei.
What is the meaning of this?
VRRRRRRRT
And now the walls have pened to reveal razor-sharp spikes.
Guys? Walls are definitely moving in here.
I don't get it! I really don't get it.
Classic, yet timeless.

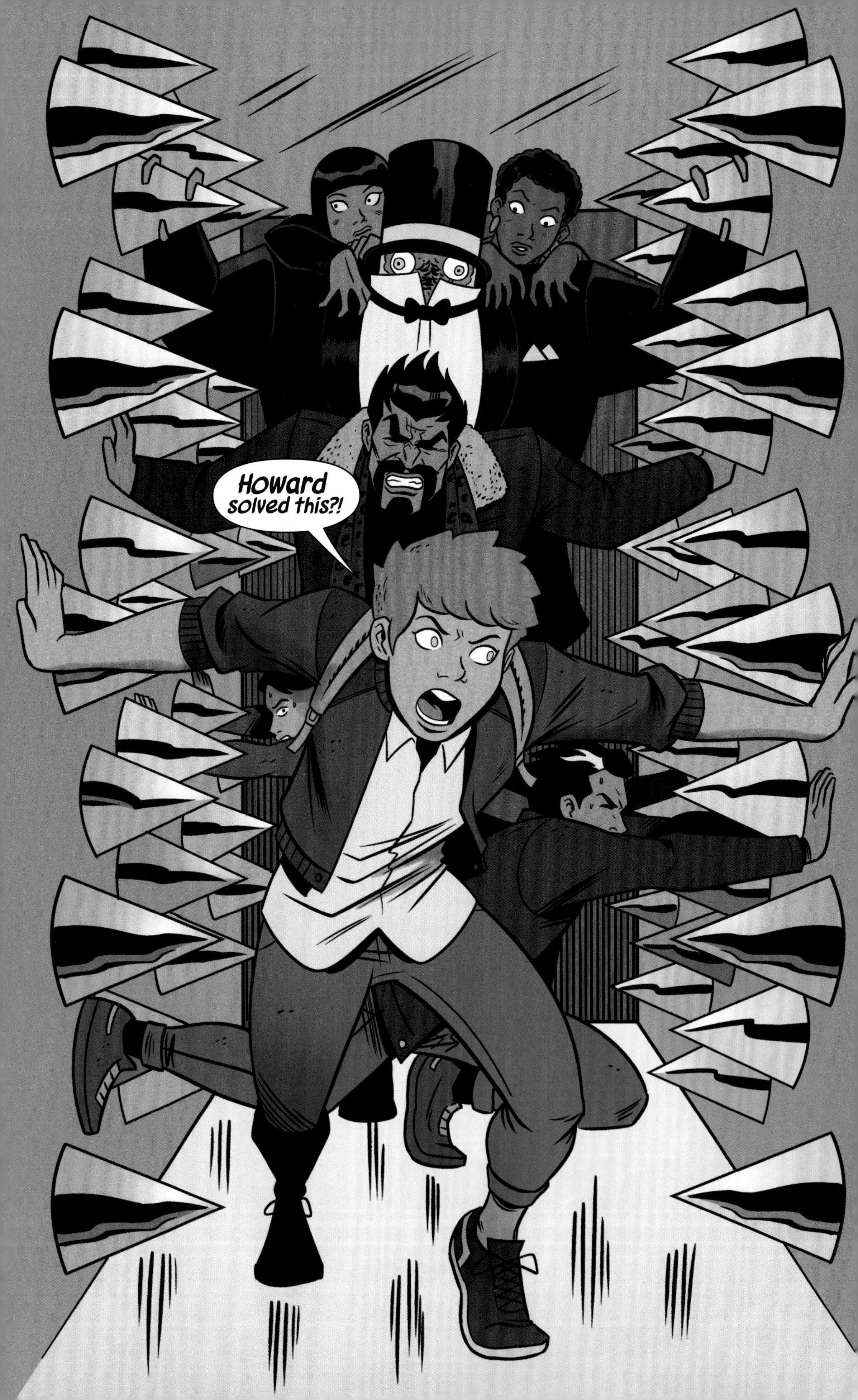
Howard solved this?!

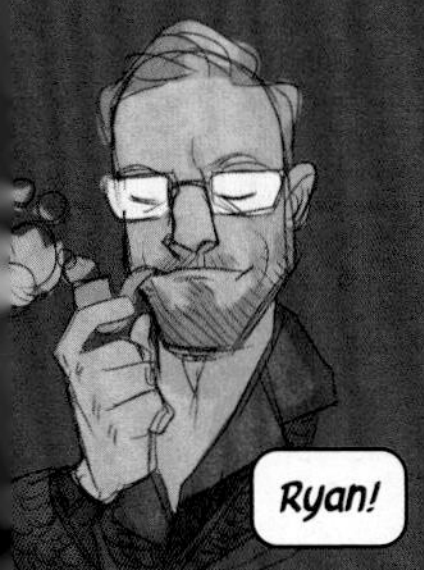
Ryan!

Letters From Nuts

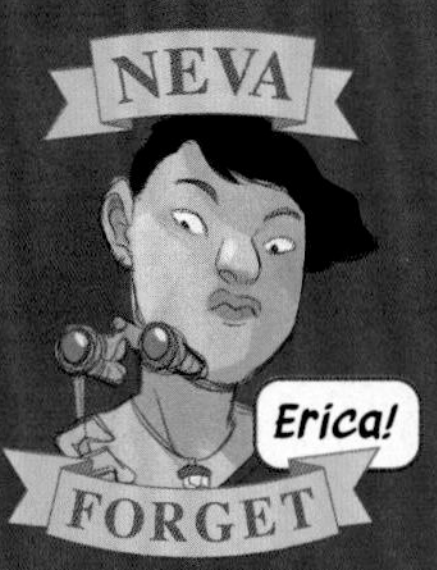
NEVA
Erica!
FORGET

Send letters to mheroes@marvel.com or 135 W 50th St, 7th Floor, New York, NY 10020 (Please mark "OKAY TO PRINT")

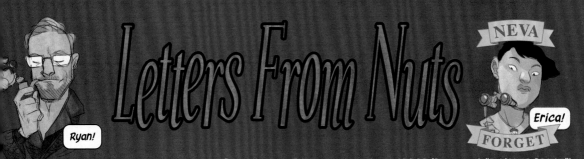

Hey everybody! Before we get to Ryan's responses to your letters, we just wanted to extend a great big "CHITTY CHIRT CHIK!" (which means "WELCOME ABOARD!") to Derek Charm, the artist of this new Kraven story! Derek's got some big shoes to fill (we'll never forget you, Erica!), but isn't his take on Doreen, Nancy and the gang terrific?? Write in and let us know what you think! (And let us know your guesses for the mystery Escape Room operator!)

Hello!

I love your UNBEATABLE SQUIRREL GIRL comics. I sure wish I had squirrel agility, and definitely a sweet, kickass tail. A handy-dandy sidekick like Tippy-Toe would be too cute as well. I'd set him up with a most dapper top hat and monocle and we could solve mysteries together. I wouldn't approve of a smoking pipe, but maybe one of the bubble pipes if he doesn't mind.

First discovered SQUIRREL GIRL comics when I went around the internet googling squirrel pictures to update my League of Legends profile. I'm a Lulu main (she turns people into squirrels). Anyways, I'm rambling.

Thank you!
Max

RYAN: Hey, Max! I approve of any scheme that involves solving mysteries, ESPECIALLY if it also involves an animal to assist in that mystery-solving. When I got my dog Noam Chompsky, I thought there was a chance he and I might solve mysteries, but the only mystery he's interested in is the mystery of Why Can't I Have More Dinner, You Are Being Mean To Me. We still go on adventures, though, and one time I got stuck in a hole with him! You can read that whole story if you Google "Ryan North hole." Spoiler alert: We escaped and now I defy all holes!!

Dear Squirrel Girl,

I am six years old and my sister is four. We live in Den Haag, The Netherlands, and there are no comic books here but Grandma came to visit and brought us sixty-five thousand million Squirrel Girl comic books for Christmas. She told my dad the suitcase was too heavy. We love you because you are nice to all the good people and you stop the bad guys from being mean. Also you don't listen to boys. That is smart.

I also really like you because you have short hair and you don't dress like a princess and make it look cool and you are proud of the way you look. I really hope you will please get us a Squirrel Girl action figure with lots of squirrels. Also, your tail should be fluffy just like in the pictures. My dad says maybe you will make a movie and I hope you will so that we can see you in person.

Love,
Meryl and Hana

P.S. Do you need pillows or do you just use your tail?

RYAN: Normally these letters aren't directed specifically to Squirrel Girl, but since this one is, I'll let her answer!

SQUIRREL GIRL: Hi, Meryl! Hi, Hana! I am sad there are no comic book stores where you live but VERY HAPPY you have a grandma (who, I can only assume, now has extremely ripped arms) to deliver comics to you. Please tell her thanks from me!

I am 100% in favor of stopping bad guys from being mean (that is, like, my #1 dream right there) and also 100% in favor of a me action figure. If you have an action figure of yourself, then you can take a picture of her next to your dinner and it looks like you're eating a giant dinner. THERE ARE NO DOWNSIDES TO THIS PLAN.

To answer your question, I don't need pillows, but they're nice to have, because if I sleep on my tail wrong it can fall asleep, just like an arm! Then you wake up and your tail feels all weird and tingly.

Dear Ryan, Erica, and all others associated with SQUIRREL GIRL,

I would like to thank you from the bottom of my heart for producing such a fine comic. With the upcoming (for me) cancelation of GWENPOOL, SQUIRREL GIRL is now the only comic that I am currently following. The fact that I am in the "non-rich" category is only half the story. All the other comics I have tried to get into recently have either been too political (to paraphrase Dennis Miller, I now watch the news for my entertainment and read comics for my politics) or too angsty (if I wanted angst I'd get a teenager and make my own angst)!

SQUIRREL GIRL, on the other hand, is constantly fun, adventurous and well-written, which is all I want from a comic.

By the way, now that Gwenpool is going to have time on her hands, how about she and Doreen get together for a buddy/buddy road trip adventure? If you're too busy I'd be happy to write it for you. You wouldn't even have to pay me, that's how much I want to see it! If I could draw I'd even send to whole thing to you. Deal?

With thanks,
Joshua Thomas

RYAN: Hey, thanks, Joshua! I too have been in that non-rich category so I hear you on that. This sounds like a shill, BUT IT'S LEGIT: If you sign up for Marvel Unlimited, you can read unlimited comics for $9.99 a month! The catch is they're all at least six months old, so you won't be current, but you WILL be reading lots and lots of comics, and the catalogue goes back to the '60s. I read the first issue of FANTASTIC FOUR on Marvel Unlimited. Guess what? Mister Fantastic is a jerk! Maybe he's better now but in his first appearance all his friends get transformed, and his good buddy Ben is so distraught that he thinks he can only be called "The Thing" from now on, and Reed's like, "Hey, call me Mister Fantastic." You don't get to pick your own nickname, Reed! P.S. Everyone please call me Johnny Handsomeface. Also, my one regret about GWENPOOL is that Chris and I never got a crossover sorted out, but on the plus side Gwenpool is still out there in the Marvel Universe, so maybe someday!

Dear Willow Wilson, Adrian Alphona, Ryan North, and Erica Henderson,

WHY HAVEN'T DOREEN GREEN AND KAMALA KHAN TEAMED UP IN A COMIC!!?? They're my two favorite super heroes ever. They would likely be best friends forever. So PLEASE put them in a comic book teaming up.

Sincerely,
Doreen's and Kamala's biggest Fan
Armyn Carpenter

RYAN: WHAT PERFECT TIMING, ARMYN! Doreen and Kamala are teaming up for a comic AS WE SPEAK, and you'll be able to read the result in a miniseries called MARVEL RISING, coming out soon! Devin Grayson has masterminded the story, and G. Willow Wilson and I are taking turns writing each chapter! So far I can say this: It features giant robots and also squirrels. A teaser story called MARVEL RISING #0 came out on April 25, and the event kicks off with MARVEL RISING: ALPHA on June 13. It's been really fun getting to write Kamala--she's very different from Doreen, but I have the feeling they're going to be great pals.

Dear Ryan and Erica,

I am an avid comic book reader, but oddly had never been introduced to Squirrel Girl! That's nutty, huh???!

This all changed when I saw my 3-year-old daughter attempting to play Lego Marvel Super Heroes with her dad. She kept asking for the "girl with the squirrels." At that moment, I knew I had to find out more about this amazing character...and boy was I missing out!

Thank you for such a wholesome, hilarious comic series! The writing is great and the art brings everything to life.

I even took my 3-year-old daughter to her very first comic book store to pick out her own copy of USG. She doesn't read yet, but it's the best to hear her make up her own stories to Erica's artwork. (I attached a few photos from this trip. Her name is Josephine Sunshine Sanders.)

Thank you for showing the world that girls can kick booty AND be brilliant computer science nerds!

Keep up the great work,
Erin Sanders

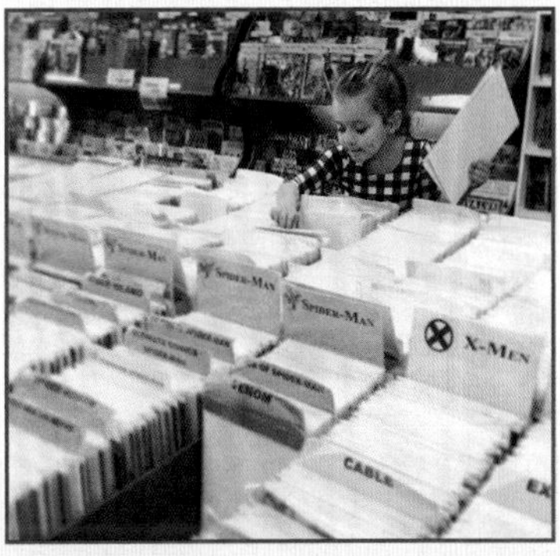
X-MEN
SPIDER-MAN
CABLE

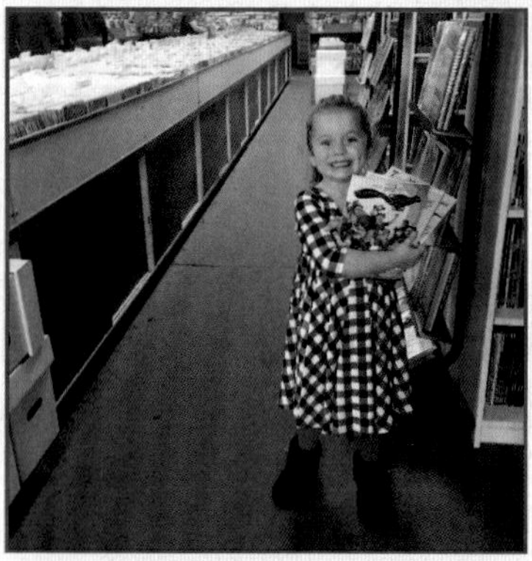

RYAN: Erin, these photos are AMAZING. They warm my heart. And having "Sunshine" as a middle name is also A+. Great choices all around here, I gotta say! Man, I remember the feeling of walking into a bookstore and being able to pick out any book you wanted. It's so great you're sharing that with Josephine. Also: Hi, Josephine! I'm glad you like Squirrel Girl, and now you're in her book too!!

Hello, Ryan, Erica, Rico and everyone at Marvel,

We wanted to share this picture of Iris and SQUIRREL GIRL. Iris has decided she is going to read SQUIRREL GIRL to her daddy from now on. We're good with this. Her Doreen voice is squeaky and optimistic. And to think, when she first became a fan, she couldn't read at all. Thank you again for this wonderful book and all you have done for us as a family.

Holdren Family
Greensboro, NC

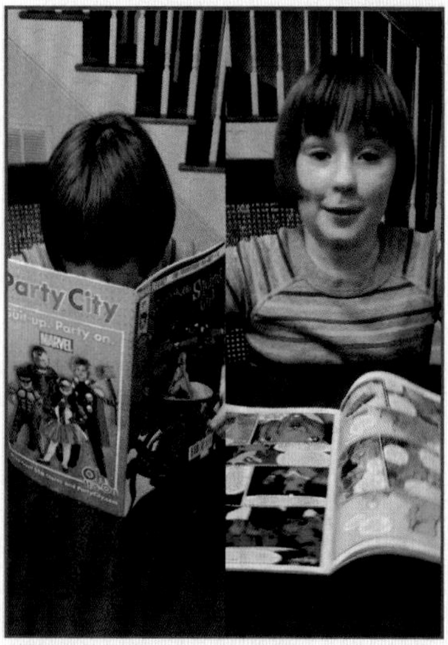
Party City

RYAN: Oh my gosh, it's always great to get an update from Iris. And her Doreen voice sounds spot-on. Comics are actually a great way to start reading, because unlike a book, you've got pictures there supporting the words on every page. It gives tons of context to unfamiliar words in a way plain text can't, which means if you encounter a word you don't know, you have a much better chance of figuring it out! I remember reading Archie comics and thinking "fiend" was a typo, but it showed up so often--and only in relation to Reggie--that I figured it meant "a jerk, but still a friend we hang out with some of the time for reasons that nobody ever seems to question." It wasn't a perfect definition but it's not completely wrong either!

Ryan & Erica,

Squirrel Girl is the best, and she always will be. I've been reading your comics since issue #6 or #7, back in 2016, when I was in fifth grade. Now I'm 13, and I still can't get enough of her! I've gone in and out of my comics phases, but it seems I just can't shake Doreen. I read up on all her appearances, from her start with Iron Man to her run with the GLA, and even dressed as her for Halloween in 6th grade. I'm wondering, though: Whatever happened to her and Speedball? After he became Penance (and made Niles, his cat, also wear some sweet spikes), she visited him and tried to break the edgy vibe he had. It didn't work then, but now he's back to being Speedball. Has she talked to him since? Maybe a lengthy phone conversation about the inevitability of death? In fact, I'm wondering about a lot of her past acquaintances. Did she ever help Iron Man get the mice out of his garage by getting Tippy to coax them through the phone? Or instruct Flatman on how to properly install RAM? If so, can I please get a whole comic of just that? I feel like you'd win even more awards for it.

Your girl,
Molly

RYAN: Molly! What a great letter, and I'm thrilled you've been reading for so long! You have read all her appearances, which means your Squirrel Girl knowledge is the precise equal of my own! And that means these are all some great ideas. We haven't done anything with Speedball or the Great Lakes Avengers yet, it's true! I keep wanting to have the perfect story for them, rather than having them show up and Squirrel Girl says "I trust you have been keeping well" and they say "Yes, thank you" and Squirrel Girl says "I too have been keeping well." See, this is why people say conflict is the heart of narrative. PEOPLE CAN'T JUST BE KEEPING WELL INDEFINITELY.

All this to say: Thank you, and I hope we can do something along these lines sooner rather than later!

Dear Ryan and Erica,

My name is Heidi and I am 8 years old and I am a huge SG fan! She is so awesome. My favorite was when she went to the moon and convinced Galactus not to eat Earth.

(Also here is a pic of me dressing up as SG for Super Hero Day at school!)

With lots of happiness,
Heidi
San Bruno, CA

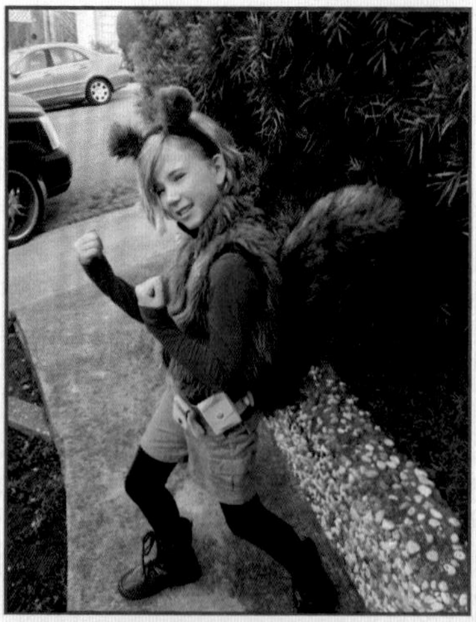

RYAN: HEIDI! Amazing costume, amazing picture, AMAZING attitude--I love it all. Also: Since when have schools had Super Hero Day? When I was in school we only had themes like "Beach Day"--which I always went all in on, a swimsuit, towel, sunglasses, the works--but very few people participated. And then we suggested "Tuck Your Pants Into Your Socks Day" because then if you forgot about it, it would still be very easy to participate, but nobody in the student council liked our ideas. Anyway, all this to say: I love that you rocked Super Hero Day and I am insanely jealous of your school / costume / the fact that when I tuck my pants into my socks it doesn't look nearly as awesome.

First of all…Hocky Hoof Hank! Dang, you guys, that's great! The best new Marvel character find since…forever! Thanks for the laughs.

Second of all, a request. I get that the text notes at the bottom of the page should be unnoticeable, but the experimentation with different colored backgrounds and text in issue #29 made them super difficult to see. Give those of us with some old eyes a break, could you? The notes are often my favorite part of the book where the funniest stuff hides. Thanks for that, but I'd appreciate if you kept that in mind.

Thanks, and keep going nuts!

Brian Langlois
Memphis, TN

RYAN: Brian, thanks for the feedback, and it is noted! I think we change the colors when it's on a full-bleed page with a lot of white and they wouldn't be visible otherwise, but if it's not working we'll find a better solution! P.S. Hocky Hoof Hank 4ever. Who could forget his famous quote, "I say thee…NEIGH"?

Next Issue:

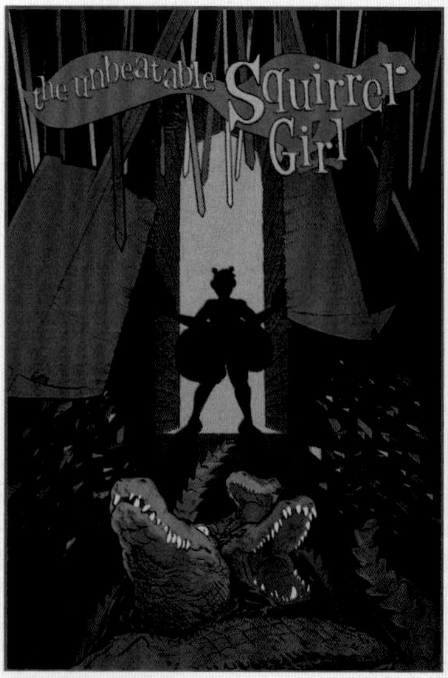
the unbeatable Squirrel Girl

Attention, Squirrel Scouts! Make sure to check out our production blog, **unbeatablesquirrelgirl.tumblr.com**, where we post behind-the-scenes stuff on how the book gets made, along with all sorts of cool things *you* make: fanart, cosplay, whatever!

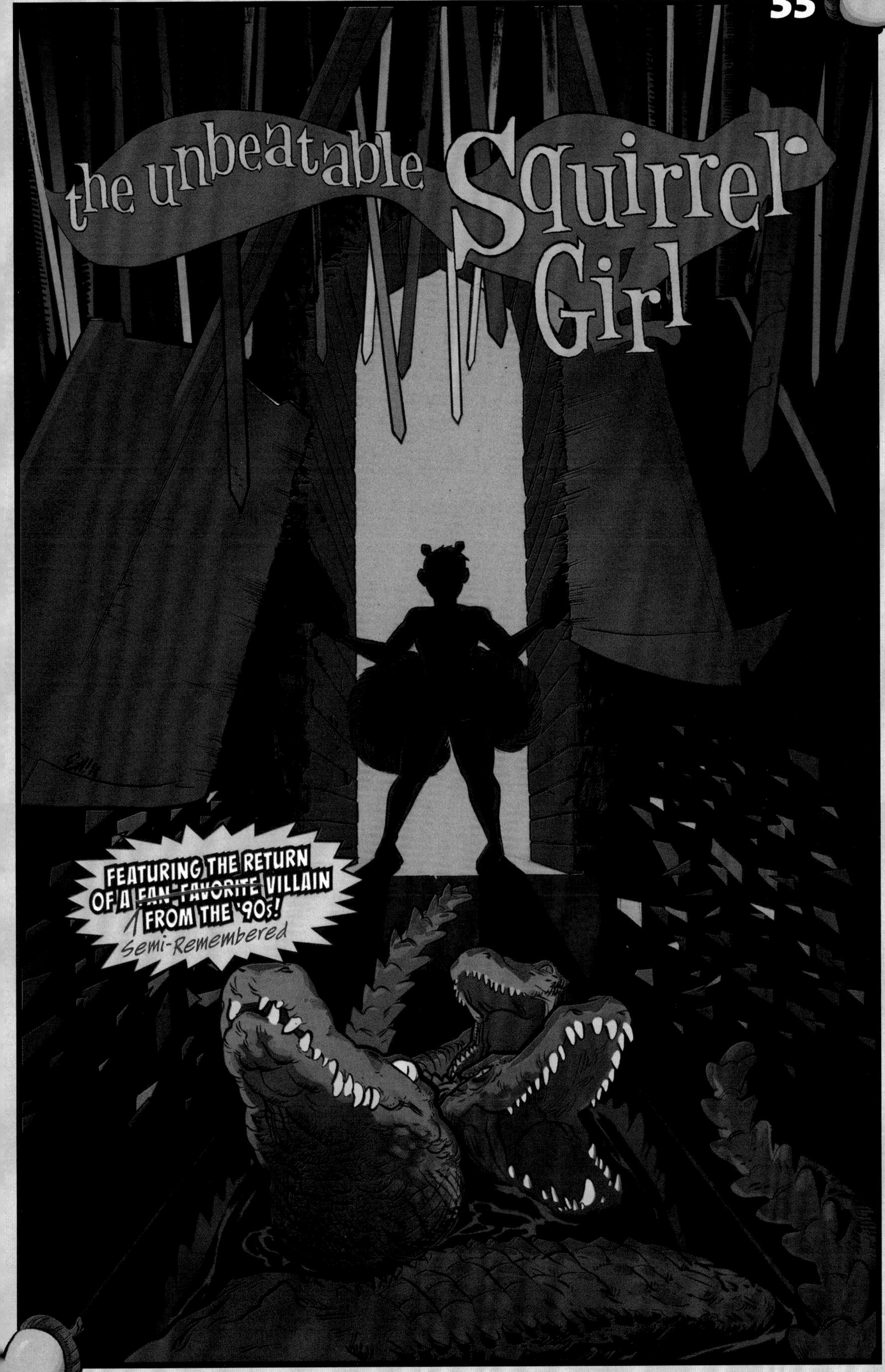
the unbeatable Squirrel Girl
FEATURING THE RETURN OF A ~~FAN-FAVORITE~~ Semi-Remembered VILLAIN FROM THE '90s!

Doreen Green isn't just a second-year computer science student: she secretly also has all the powers of both squirrel and girl! She uses her amazing abilities to fight crime **and** be as awesome as possible. You know her as...**The Unbeatable Squirrel Girl!** Find out what she's been up to, with...

Squirrel Girl *in a nutshell*

search! 🔍

#chomp

#newusesforhands

#theoryofmind

#weirdpuzzlestuff

#enigmamachines

Squirrel Girl @unbeatablesg
So here's the thing about friendships: They're so easy to make when you're in school! You're literally forced, BY THE STATE, to hang out with other people your own age! And so you're meeting tons of potential pals every year, every class! It's easy!

Squirrel Girl @unbeatablesg
But then when you graduate and go out into the world and get a job, suddenly you're not meeting new people every day. And if you work with duds and don't have friends where you live, how do you make more ones? IT'S HORRIBLE

Squirrel Girl @unbeatablesg
But the answer is easy: structured group activities! Join a club, START a club, do something where you have casual contact with other people and HEY PRESTO: That's a recipe for friendship developing.

Squirrel Girl @unbeatablesg
Anyway, this is just to say that as someone who is BIG INTO FRIENDS, I hereby swear to do more group activities with said friends, old AND new, in order to maintain friendships and make new ones!

Squirrel Girl @unbeatablesg
And on that note, whooooo wants to go to an escape room?

xKravenTheHunterx @unshavenkraven
@unbeatablesg I am in. Also, you have already called to invite me, which is good, because I do not often check this site and forget why I signed up for it in the first place.

xKravenTheHunterx @unshavenkraven
@unbeatablesg I will hunt for solutions to puzzles as well as I hunt for everything else, which is to say: extremely well.

Squirrel Girl @unbeatablesg
@unshavenkraven EXCELLENT!! This is gonna be great, assuming that the room isn't run by a mysterious super villain who turns it into a deadly maze of death traps, transforming a lighthearted game into a life-and-death battle for survival!!

xKravenTheHunterx @unshavenkraven
@unbeatablesg Why would you say this.

Squirrel Girl @unbeatablesg
@unshavenkraven i'm just saying I DON'T want that to happen. if that happened it would be bad, so here i am hoping that it does not take place

Squirrel Girl @unbeatablesg
@unshavenkraven just looking for a relaxing time with pals and not having to survive by my wits alone in a sinister cavalcade of death!!

Nancy W. @sewwiththeflo
@unbeatablesg Hi SG, random stranger here. Any business that sends its clientele through "a sinister cavalcade of death" is killing off its customers, so I think we're good. Capitalism and profit motives alone should be enough to protect us from this particular fate.

Squirrel Girl @unbeatablesg
@sewwiththeflo PHEW

Squirrel Girl @unbeatablesg
Anyway we're all off to the escape room, check in with everyone later! So relieved to know it's not a room filled with death! Hah! Not even the fates themselves can make that happen!!

Squirrel Girl @unbeatablesg
UPDATE

Squirrel Girl @unbeatablesg
I AM FORTUNE'S FOOL

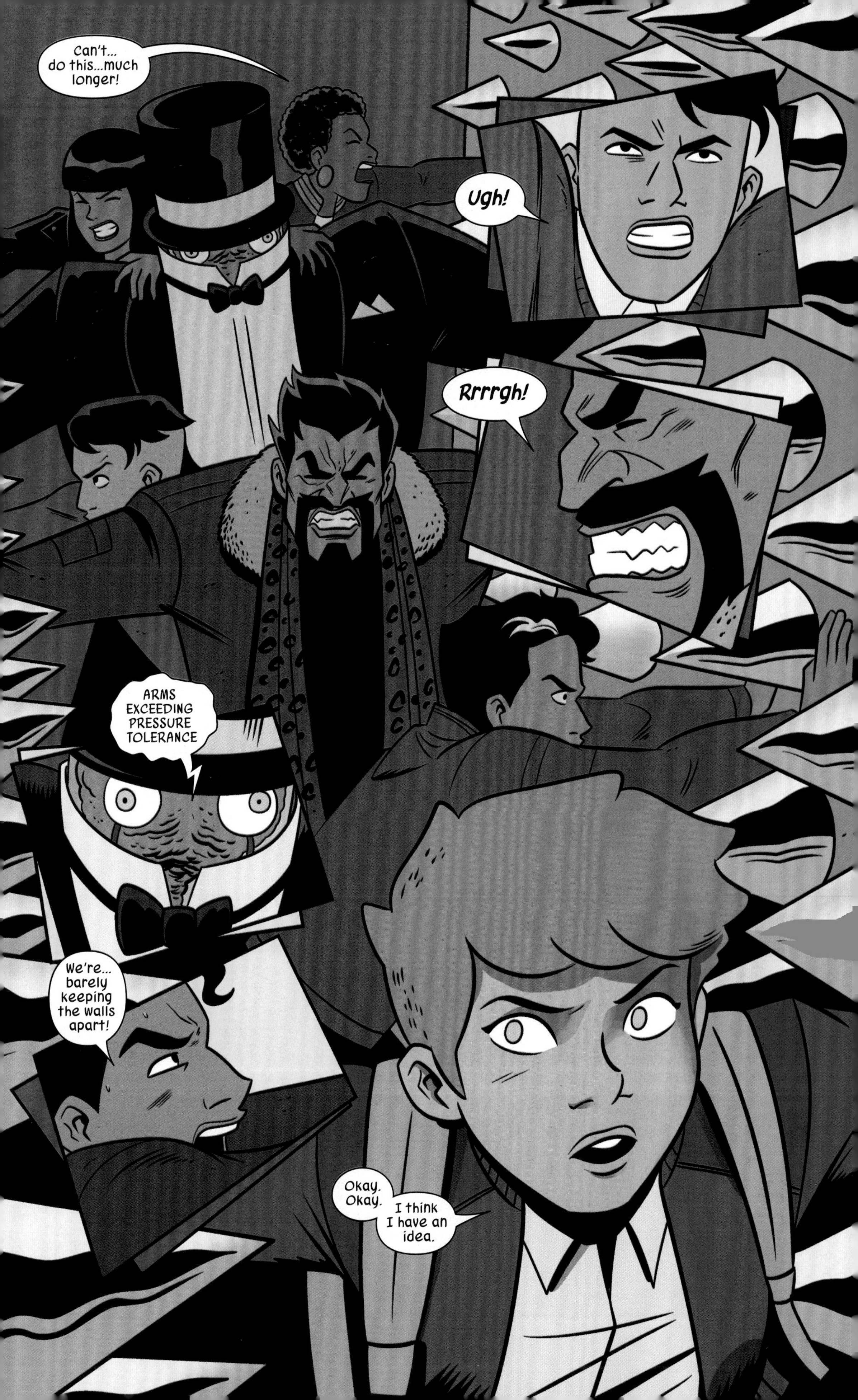
Can't... do this...much longer!
Ugh!
Rrrrgh!
ARMS EXCEEDING PRESSURE TOLERANCE
We're... barely keeping the walls apart!
Okay. Okay.
I think I have an idea.

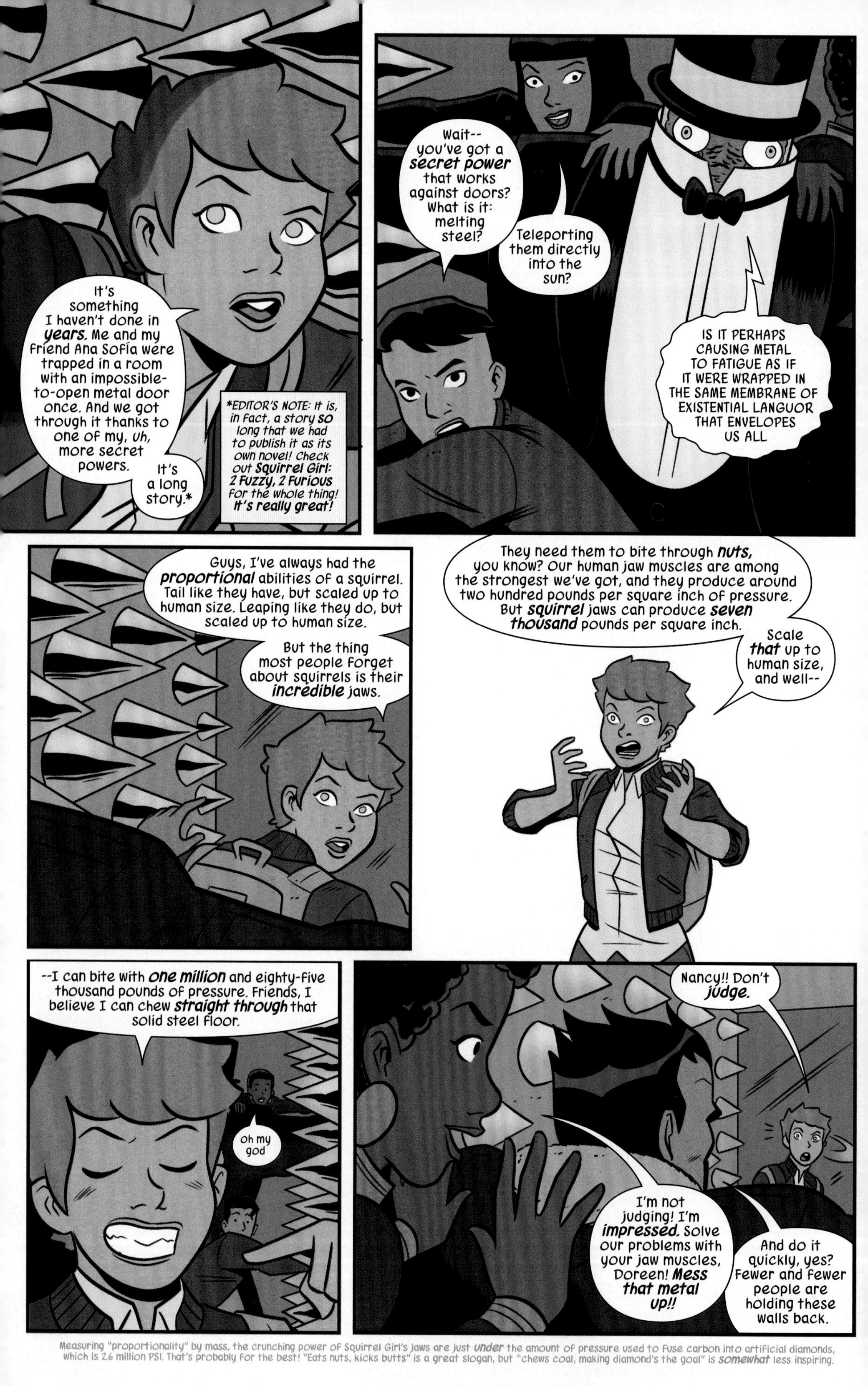
It's something I haven't done in years. Me and my friend Ana Sofía were trapped in a room with an impossible-to-open metal door once. And we got through it thanks to one of my, uh, more secret powers.
It's a long story.*
*EDITOR'S NOTE: It is, in fact, a story so long that we had to publish it as its own novel! Check out Squirrel Girl: 2 Fuzzy, 2 Furious for the whole thing! It's really great!
Wait-- you've got a secret power that works against doors? What is it: melting steel?
Teleporting them directly into the sun?
IS IT PERHAPS CAUSING METAL TO FATIGUE AS IF IT WERE WRAPPED IN THE SAME MEMBRANE OF EXISTENTIAL LANGUOR THAT ENVELOPES US ALL
Guys, I've always had the proportional abilities of a squirrel. Tail like they have, but scaled up to human size. Leaping like they do, but scaled up to human size.
But the thing most people forget about squirrels is their incredible jaws.
They need them to bite through nuts, you know? Our human jaw muscles are among the strongest we've got, and they produce around two hundred pounds per square inch of pressure. But squirrel jaws can produce seven thousand pounds per square inch.
Scale that up to human size, and well--
--I can bite with one million and eighty-five thousand pounds of pressure. Friends, I believe I can chew straight through that solid steel floor.
oh my god
Nancy!! Don't judge.
I'm not judging! I'm impressed. Solve our problems with your jaw muscles, Doreen! Mess that metal up!!
And do it quickly, yes? Fewer and fewer people are holding these walls back.

Measuring "proportionality" by mass, the crunching power of Squirrel Girl's jaws are just *under* the amount of pressure used to fuse carbon into artificial diamonds, which is 2.6 million PSI. That's probably for the best! "Eats nuts, kicks butts" is a great slogan, but "chews coal, making diamond's the goal" is *somewhat* less inspiring.

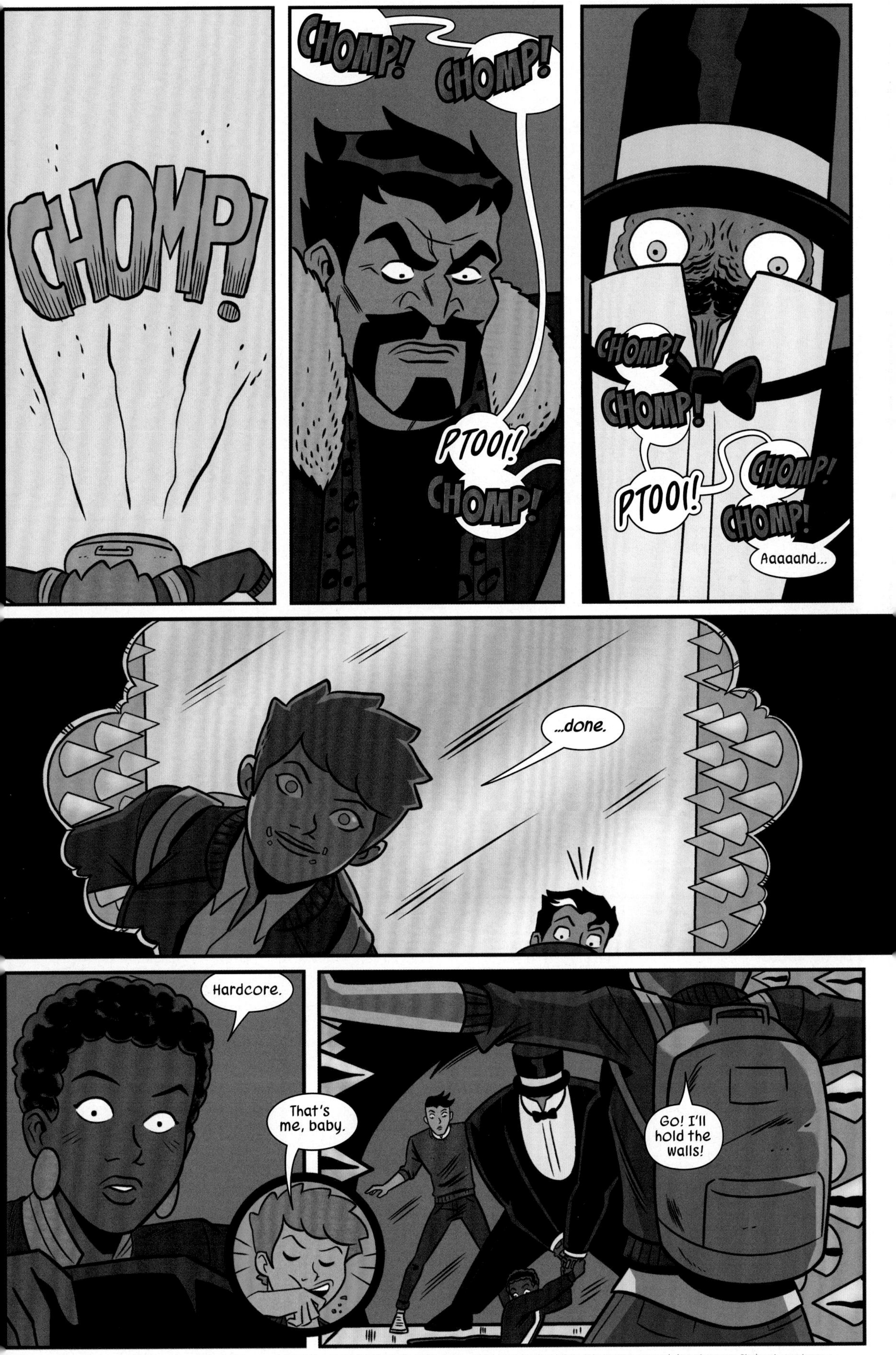
CHOMP!
CHOMP!
CHOMP!
PTOO!!
CHOMP!
CHOMP!
CHOMP!
PTOO!!
CHOMP!
CHOMP!
Aaaaand...
...done.
Hardcore.
That's me, baby.
Go! I'll hold the walls!

Dear diary: Today I found out two things. I have a friend who can bite through solid steel, and I also learned that it's always a good day when you find out you have a friend who can bite through solid steel.

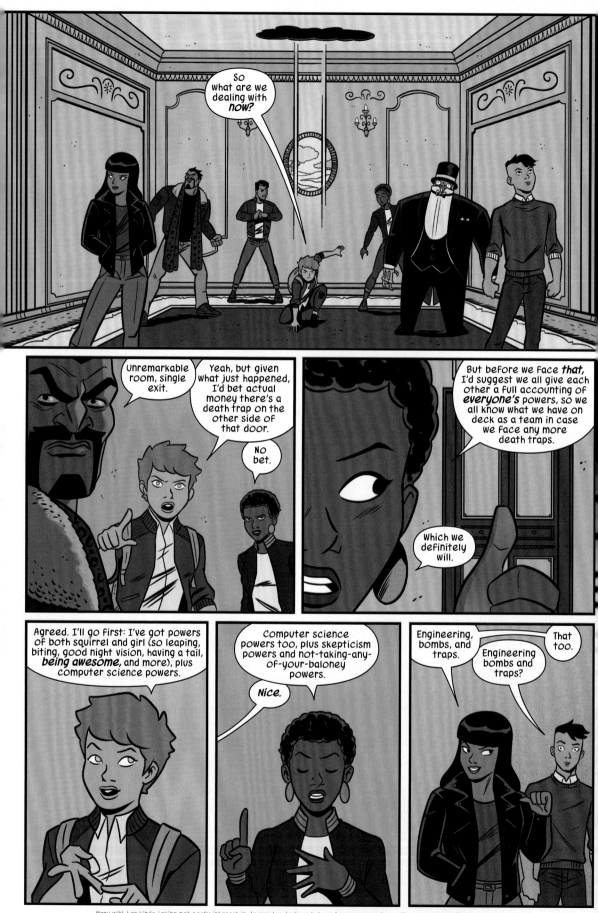

So what are we dealing with now?

Unremarkable room, single exit.

Yeah, but given what just happened, I'd bet actual money there's a death trap on the other side of that door.

No bet.

But before we face *that,* I'd suggest we all give each other a full accounting of *everyone's* powers, so we all know what we have on deck as a team in case we face any more death traps.

Which we definitely will.

Agreed. I'll go first: I've got powers of both squirrel and girl (so leaping, biting, good night vision, having a tail, *being awesome,* and more), plus computer science powers.

Computer science powers too, plus skepticism powers and not-taking-any-of-your-baloney powers.

Nice.

Engineering, bombs, and traps.

Engineering bombs and traps?

That too.

Mary with her kinda-joking-not-really interest in doomsday devices is based on every engineer I've ever known. They're great people!
Especially if you need some sort of doomsday device constructed for no particular reason!

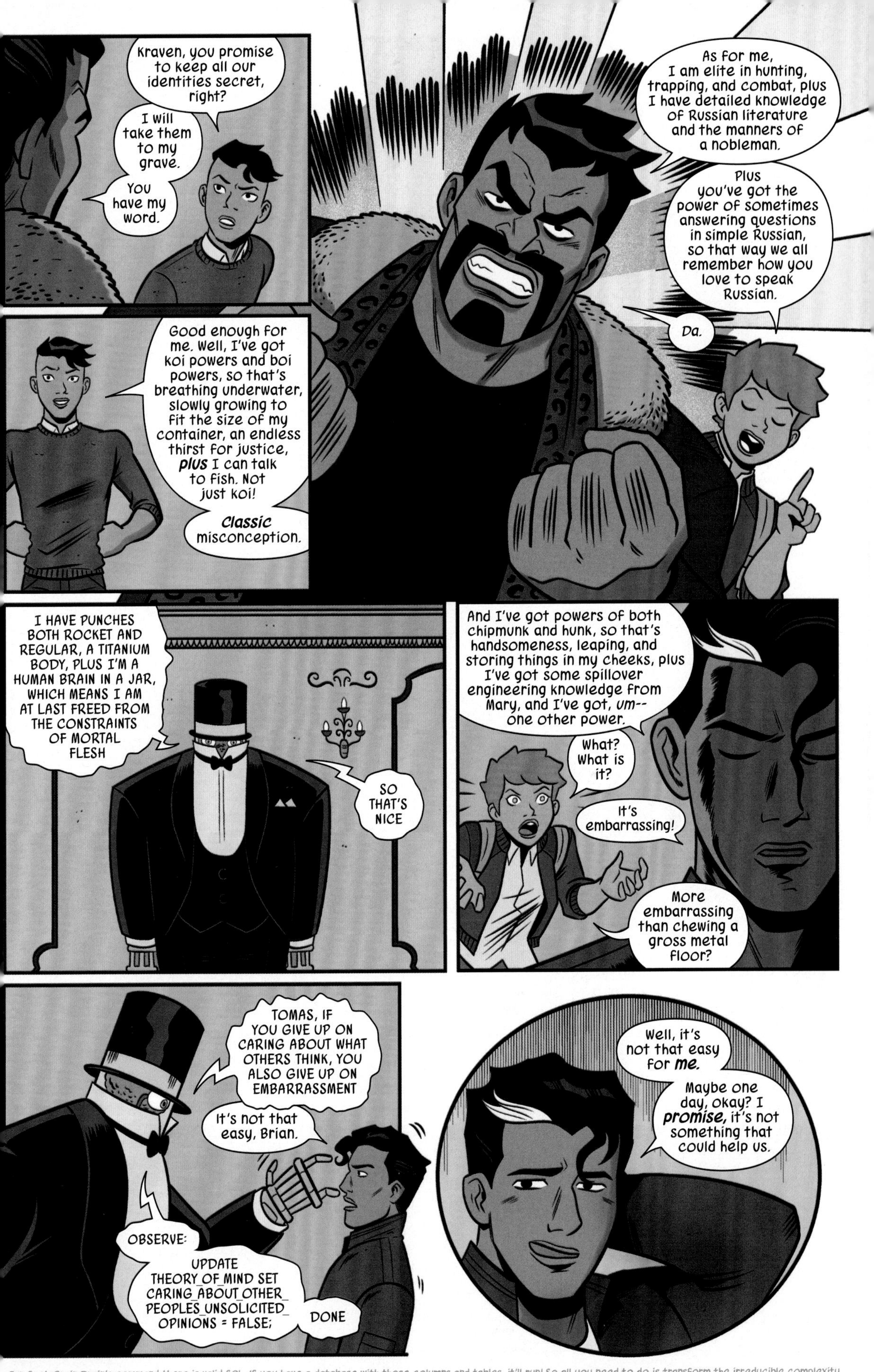
Kraven, you promise to keep all our identities secret, right?
I will take them to my grave.
You have my word.
As for me, I am elite in hunting, trapping, and combat, plus I have detailed knowledge of Russian literature and the manners of a nobleman.
Plus you've got the power of sometimes answering questions in simple Russian, so that way we all remember how you love to speak Russian.
Da.
Good enough for me. Well, I've got koi powers and boi powers, so that's breathing underwater, slowly growing to fit the size of my container, an endless thirst for justice, plus I can talk to fish. Not just koi!
Classic misconception.
I HAVE PUNCHES BOTH ROCKET AND REGULAR, A TITANIUM BODY, PLUS I'M A HUMAN BRAIN IN A JAR, WHICH MEANS I AM AT LAST FREED FROM THE CONSTRAINTS OF MORTAL FLESH
SO THAT'S NICE
And I've got powers of both chipmunk and hunk, so that's handsomeness, leaping, and storing things in my cheeks, plus I've got some spillover engineering knowledge from Mary, and I've got, um-- one other power.
What? What is it?
It's embarrassing!
More embarrassing than chewing a gross metal floor?
TOMAS, IF YOU GIVE UP ON CARING ABOUT WHAT OTHERS THINK, YOU ALSO GIVE UP ON EMBARRASSMENT
It's not that easy, Brian.
OBSERVE:
UPDATE THEORY_OF_MIND SET CARING_ABOUT_OTHER_PEOPLES_UNSOLICITED_OPINIONS = FALSE;
DONE
Well, it's not that easy for me.
Maybe one day, okay? I promise, it's not something that could help us.

Fun Fact: Brain Drain's command there is valid SQL. If you have a database with those columns and tables, it'll run! So all you need to do is transform the irreducible complexity of the human condition to third normal database form and you're *set.*

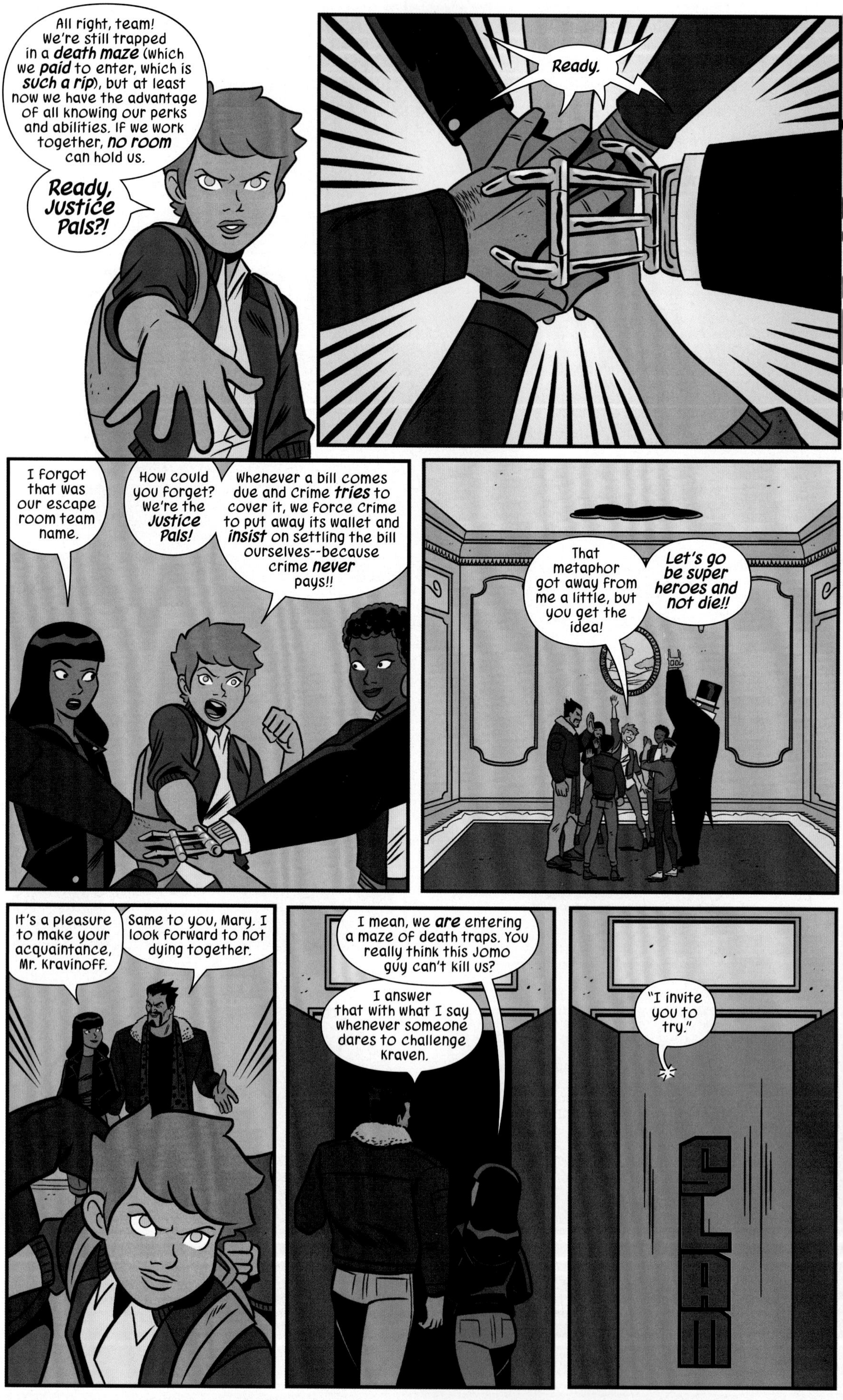
All right, team! We're still trapped in a death maze (which we paid to enter, which is such a rip), but at least now we have the advantage of all knowing our perks and abilities. If we work together, no room can hold us.
Ready, Justice Pals?!
Ready.
I forgot that was our escape room team name.
How could you forget? We're the Justice Pals!
Whenever a bill comes due and crime tries to cover it, we force crime to put away its wallet and insist on settling the bill ourselves--because crime never pays!!
That metaphor got away from me a little, but you get the idea!
Let's go be super heroes and not die!!
It's a pleasure to make your acquaintance, Mr. Kravinoff.
Same to you, Mary. I look forward to not dying together.
I mean, we are entering a maze of death traps. You really think this Jomo guy can't kill us?
I answer that with what I say whenever someone dares to challenge Kraven.
"I invite you to try."
SLAM

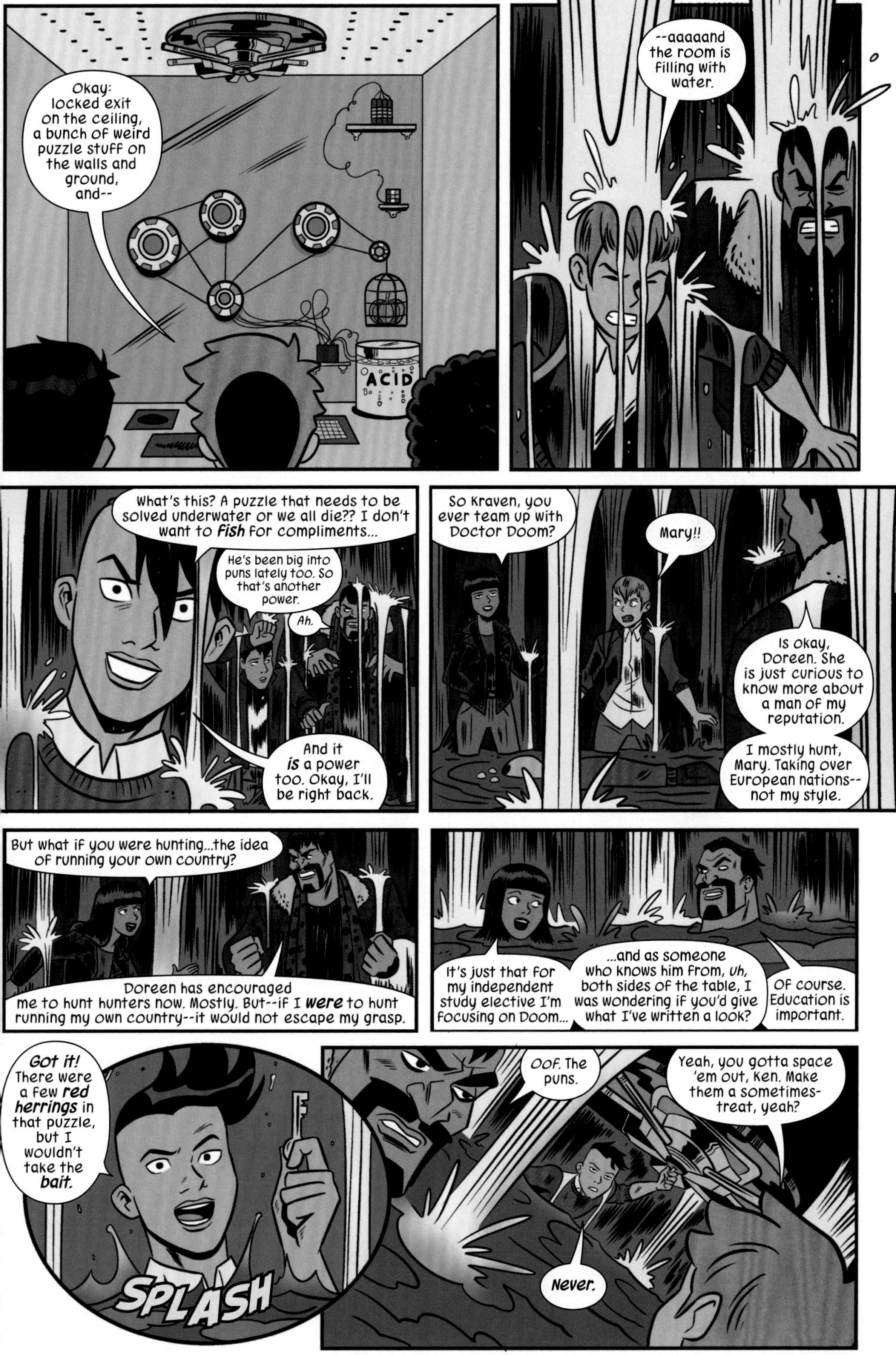
Okay: locked exit on the ceiling, a bunch of weird puzzle stuff on the walls and ground, and--
ACID
--aaaaand the room is filling with water.
What's this? A puzzle that needs to be solved underwater or we all die?? I don't want to *fish* for compliments...
He's been big into puns lately too. So that's another power.
Ah.
And it *is* a power too. Okay, I'll be right back.
So Kraven, you ever team up with Doctor Doom?
Mary!!
Is okay, Doreen. She is just curious to know more about a man of my reputation.
I mostly hunt, Mary. Taking over European nations--not my style.
But what if you were hunting...the idea of running your own country?
Doreen has encouraged me to hunt hunters now. Mostly. But--if I *were* to hunt running my own country--it would not escape my grasp.
It's just that for my independent study elective I'm focusing on Doom...
...and as someone who knows him from, *uh*, both sides of the table, I was wondering if you'd give what I've written a look?
Of course. Education is important.
Got it! There were a few *red herrings* in that puzzle, but I wouldn't take the *bait.*
SPLASH
Oof. The puns.
Yeah, you gotta space 'em out, Ken. Make them a sometimes-treat, yeah?
Never.

I'd go so far as to ask if saying "fish for compliments" when you're fish-themed even *COUNTS* as a pun! It's just an appropriate choice of idiom!!

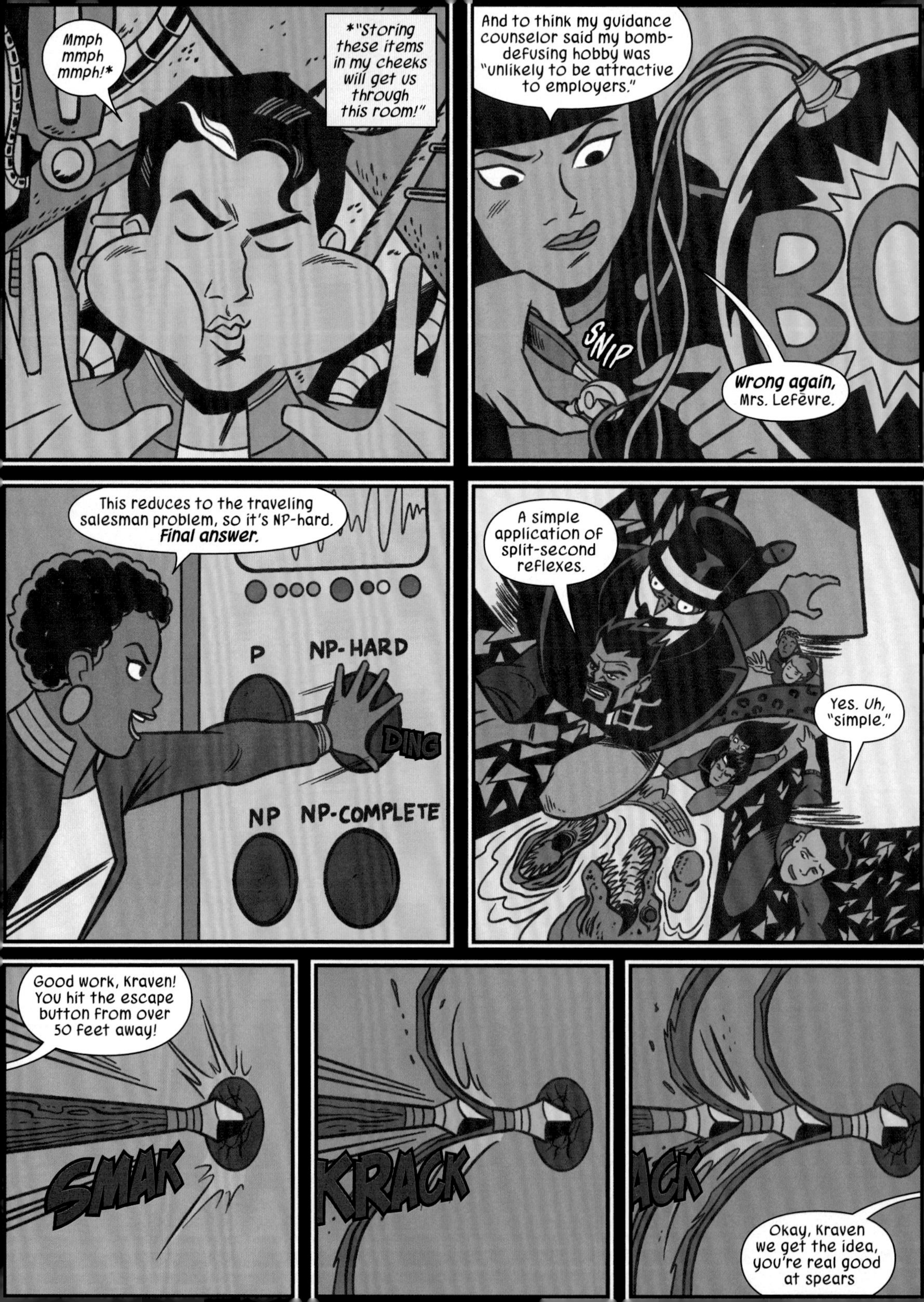
Mmph mmph mmph!*
*"Storing these items in my cheeks will get us through this room!"
And to think my guidance counselor said my bomb-defusing hobby was "unlikely to be attractive to employers."
SNIP
BO
Wrong again, Mrs. Lefèvre.
This reduces to the traveling salesman problem, so it's NP-hard. Final answer.
P
NP-HARD
DING
NP
NP-COMPLETE
A simple application of split-second reflexes.
Yes. Uh, "simple."
Good work, Kraven! You hit the escape button from over 50 feet away!
SMAK
KRACK
ACK
Okay, Kraven we get the idea, you're real good at spears

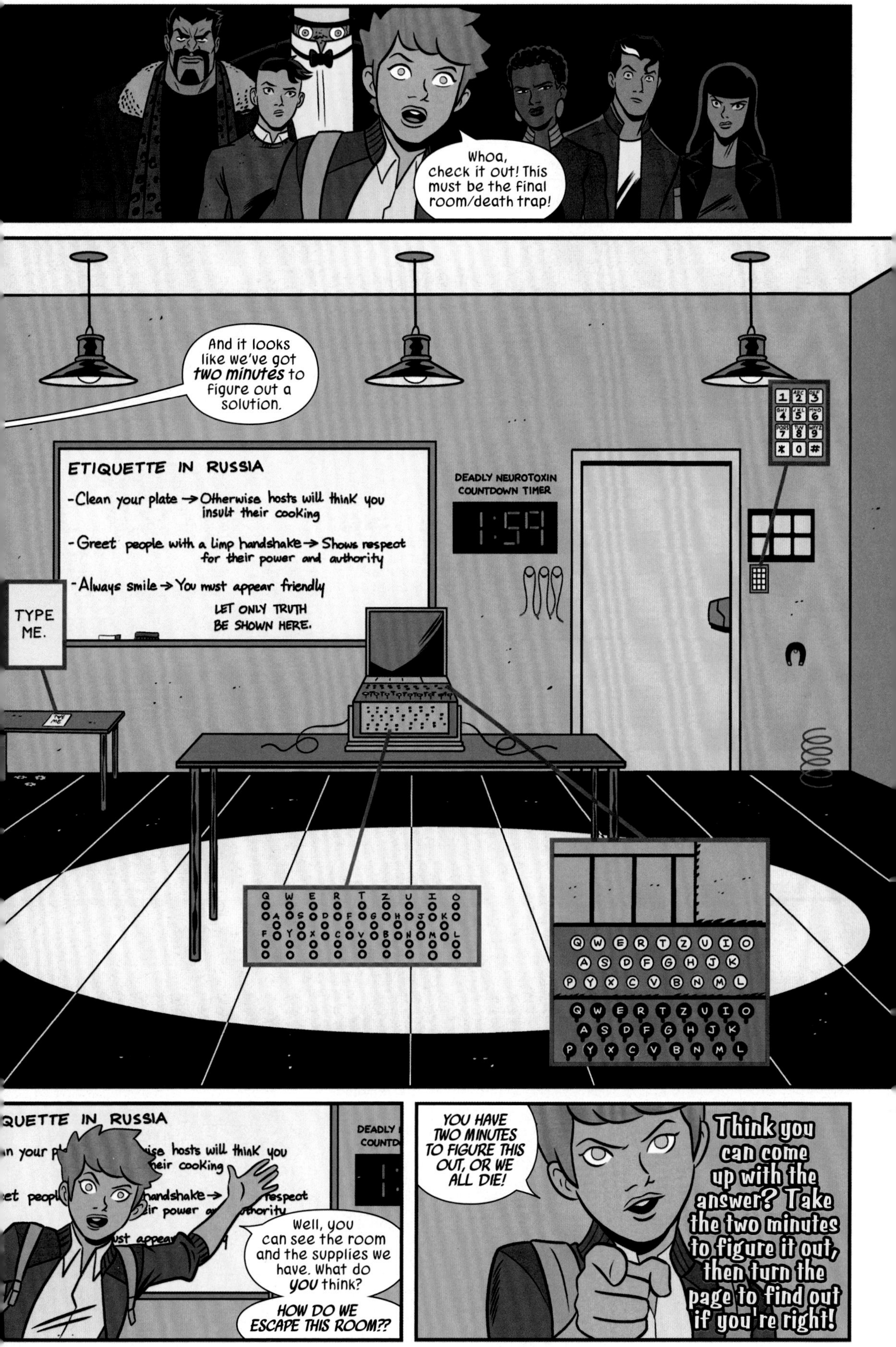
Whoa, check it out! This must be the final room/death trap!
And it looks like we've got *two minutes* to figure out a solution.
ETIQUETTE IN RUSSIA
-Clean your plate → Otherwise hosts will think you insult their cooking
-Greet people with a limp handshake → Shows respect for their power and authority
-Always smile → You must appear friendly
LET ONLY TRUTH BE SHOWN HERE.
TYPE ME.
DEADLY NEUROTOXIN COUNTDOWN TIMER
1:59
Q W E R T Z U I O
A S D F G H J K
P Y X C V B N M L
Well, you can see the room and the supplies we have. What do *you* think?
HOW DO WE ESCAPE THIS ROOM??
YOU HAVE TWO MINUTES TO FIGURE THIS OUT, OR WE ALL DIE!
Think you can come up with the answer? Take the two minutes to figure it out, then turn the page to find out if you're right!

If you figure it out in less than two minutes, give yourself a treat! If you take more than two minutes, give yourself a treat anyway! This is a really hard puzzle and I think we could all use some treats!

...You are pointing to me, yes, Doreen? You are asking me how we should escape this room?

Well, I'd start by saying that whiteboard is all wrong.

"Clean your plate"? No! In Russia you always leave some food behind, to show host their hospitality was ample!

"Limp handshake"? No! Bone-crushing firm handshakes are *only* way to do it!

ETIQUETTE IN RUSSIA

- Clean your plate → Otherwise hos... think insult their co...

- Greet people with a limp handsh... fo... their

- Always smile → ...

And "always smile"? Russian saying is unambiguous: "Laughter without good reason is the hallmark of a fool"!

-C   →O

-G   →S

-A   →Y

To leave this up is an insult to--

--what is this? The capital letters are not erasable!

No, but *this* looks like a simplified Enigma machine. They were used to encrypt secret messages during World War II, and figuring out a way to break them was a goal of early computational machinery.

It looks like it's missing some cogs, though.

Six letters: C O G S A Y.

No dice, it's not the door code!

You guys: "COG SAY." The answer's in the cogs!

BEEP

BOOP

Found 'em. They were hidden in the darkness under the desk.

Squirrel night vision and all that.

Did *you* notice the three cogs hidden in the darkness on the last page? If you did, give yourself a treat! That's right: It's treats all around here at the bottom of *Squirrel Girl* this month! They're *mandatory*.

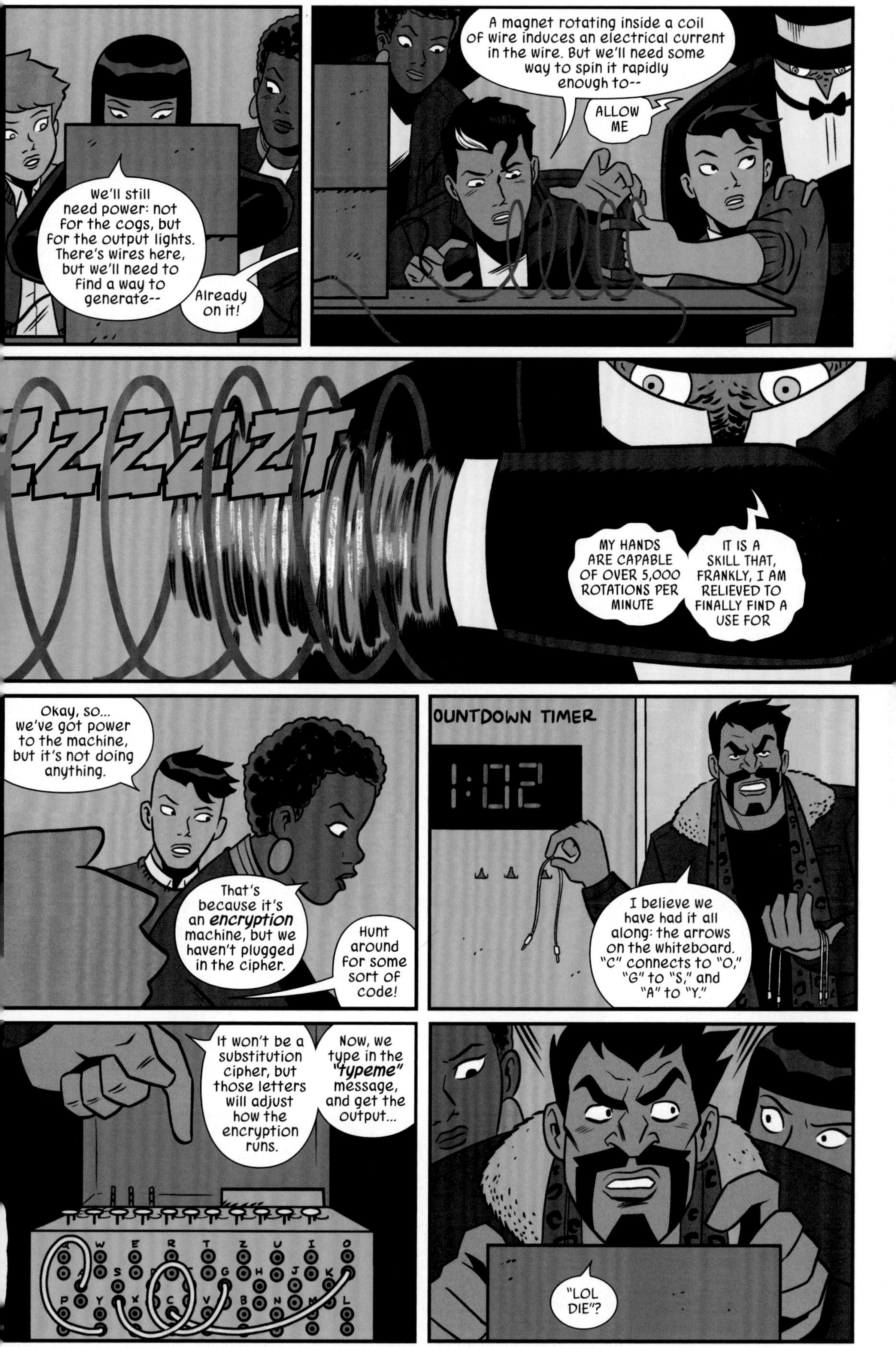
We'll still need power: not for the cogs, but for the output lights. There's wires here, but we'll need to find a way to generate--
Already on it!
A magnet rotating inside a coil of wire induces an electrical current in the wire. But we'll need some way to spin it rapidly enough to--
ALLOW ME
ZZZZZT
MY HANDS ARE CAPABLE OF OVER 5,000 ROTATIONS PER MINUTE
IT IS A SKILL THAT, FRANKLY, I AM RELIEVED TO FINALLY FIND A USE FOR
Okay, so... we've got power to the machine, but it's not doing anything.
That's because it's an *encryption* machine, but we haven't plugged in the cipher.
Hunt around for some sort of code!
OUNTDOWN TIMER
1:02
I believe we have had it all along: the arrows on the whiteboard. "C" connects to "O," "G" to "S," and "A" to "Y."
It won't be a substitution cipher, but those letters will adjust how the encryption runs.
Now, we type in the *"typeme"* message, and get the output...
"LOL DIE"?

I keep thinking of Brain Drain, alone at night, staring at his rapidly rotating hands and thinking "ONE DAY I WILL FIGURE OUT WHAT YOU ARE FOR, ROTOHANDS. ONE DAY."
He must be so excited to finally have that one solved!

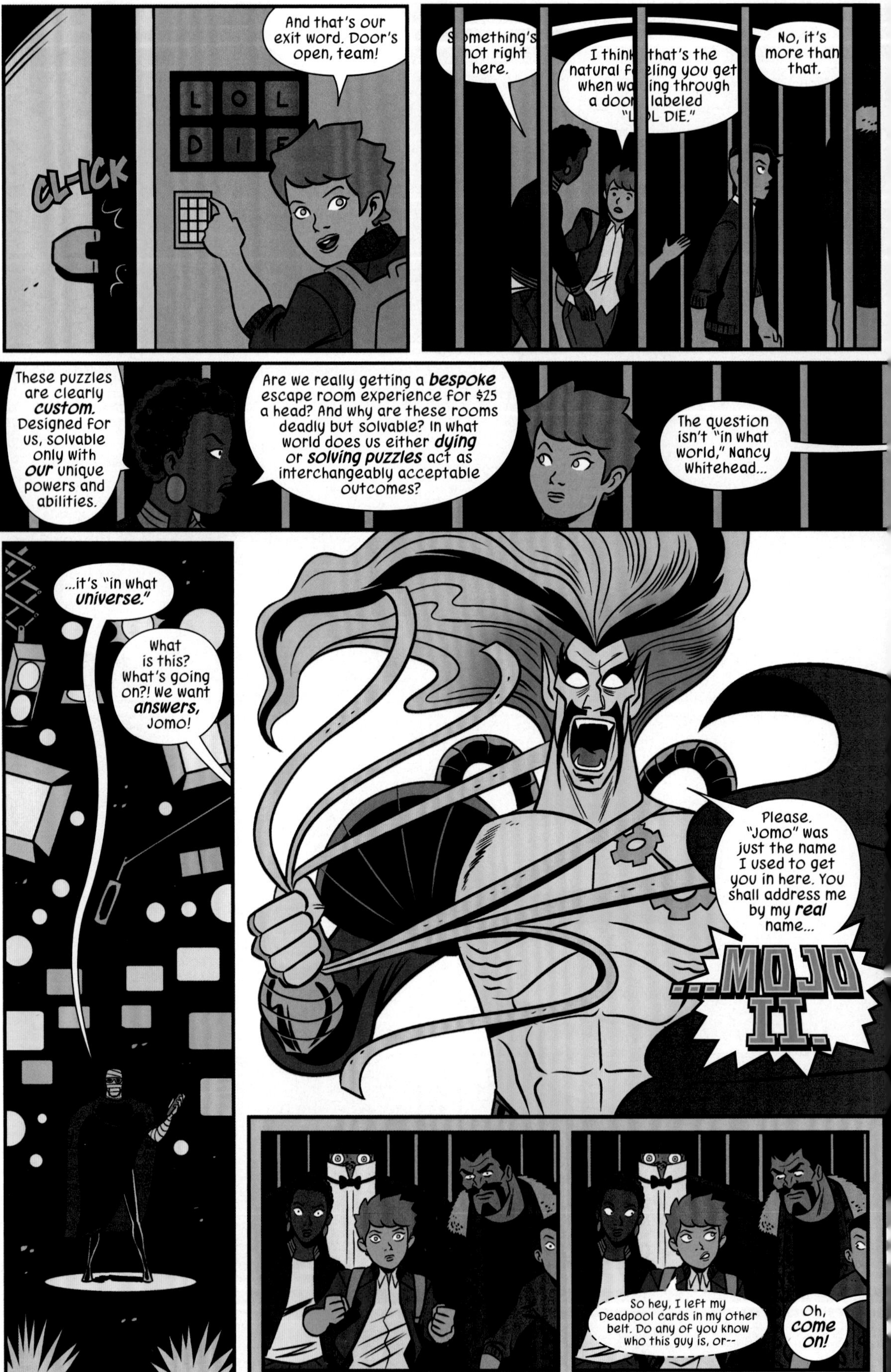
And that's our exit word. Door's open, team!
LOL
DIE
CL-ICK
Something's not right here.
I think that's the natural feeling you get when walking through a door labeled "LOL DIE."
No, it's more than that.
These puzzles are clearly custom. Designed for us, solvable only with our unique powers and abilities.
Are we really getting a bespoke escape room experience for $25 a head? And why are these rooms deadly but solvable? In what world does us either dying or solving puzzles act as interchangeably acceptable outcomes?
The question isn't "in what world," Nancy Whitehead...
...it's "in what universe."
What is this? What's going on?! We want answers, Jomo!
Please. "Jomo" was just the name I used to get you in here. You shall address me by my real name...
...MOJO II.
So hey, I left my Deadpool cards in my other belt. Do any of you know who this guy is, or--
Oh, come on!

The original Mojo is a major Marvel villain! In contrast, Mojo II is a character that everyone forgot about until riiiiiiight...*now.*

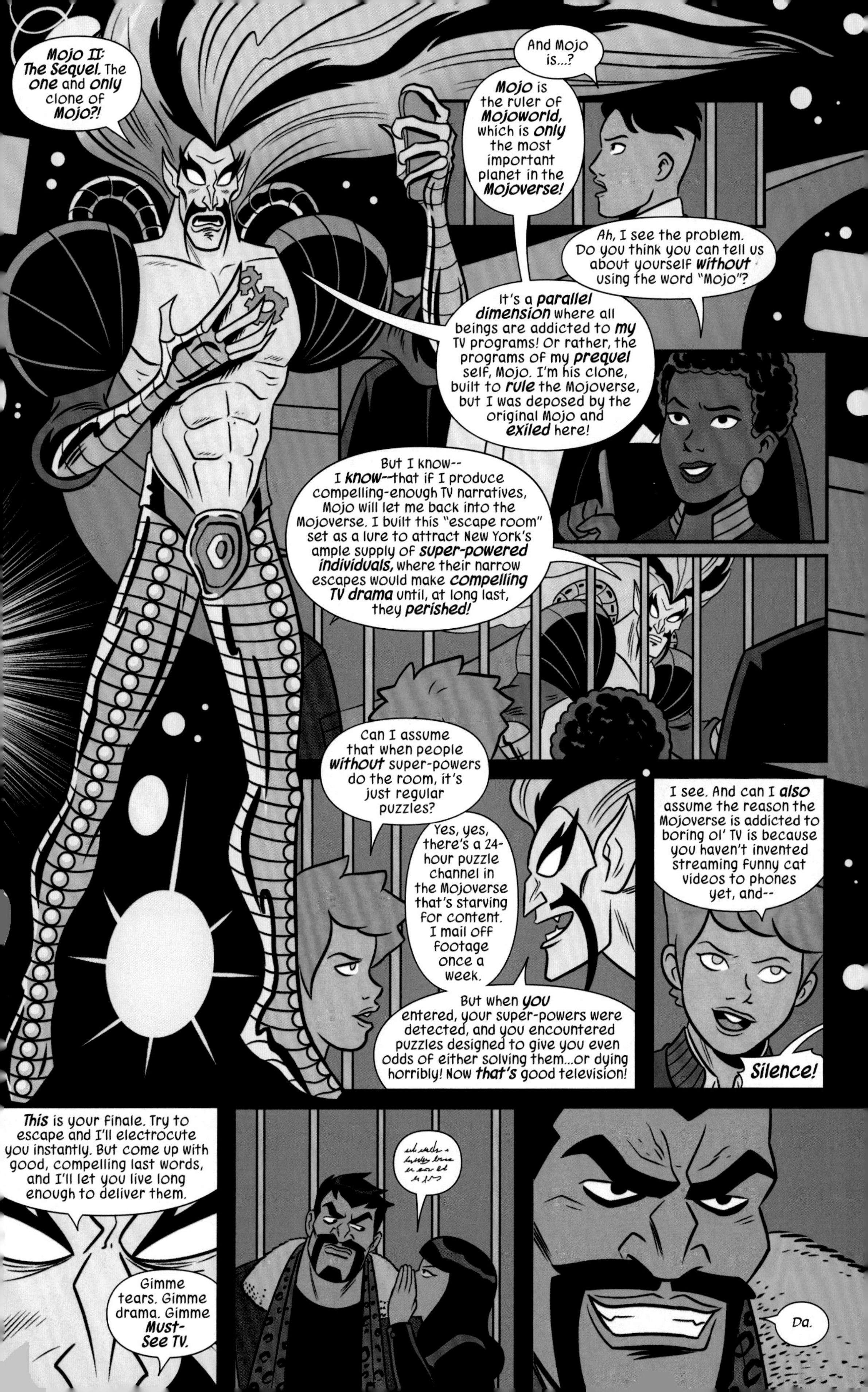
Mojo II: The Sequel. The one and only clone of Mojo?!
And Mojo is...?
Mojo is the ruler of Mojoworld, which is only the most important planet in the Mojoverse!
Ah, I see the problem. Do you think you can tell us about yourself without using the word "Mojo"?
It's a parallel dimension where all beings are addicted to my TV programs! Or rather, the programs of my prequel self, Mojo. I'm his clone, built to rule the Mojoverse, but I was deposed by the original Mojo and exiled here!
But I know-- I know--that if I produce compelling-enough TV narratives, Mojo will let me back into the Mojoverse. I built this "escape room" set as a lure to attract New York's ample supply of super-powered individuals, where their narrow escapes would make compelling TV drama until, at long last, they perished!
Can I assume that when people without super-powers do the room, it's just regular puzzles?
Yes, yes, there's a 24-hour puzzle channel in the Mojoverse that's starving for content. I mail off footage once a week.
But when you entered, your super-powers were detected, and you encountered puzzles designed to give you even odds of either solving them...or dying horribly! Now that's good television!
I see. And can I also assume the reason the Mojoverse is addicted to boring ol' TV is because you haven't invented streaming funny cat videos to phones yet, and--
Silence!
This is your finale. Try to escape and I'll electrocute you instantly. But come up with good, compelling last words, and I'll let you live long enough to deliver them.
Gimme tears. Gimme drama. Gimme Must-See TV.
Da.

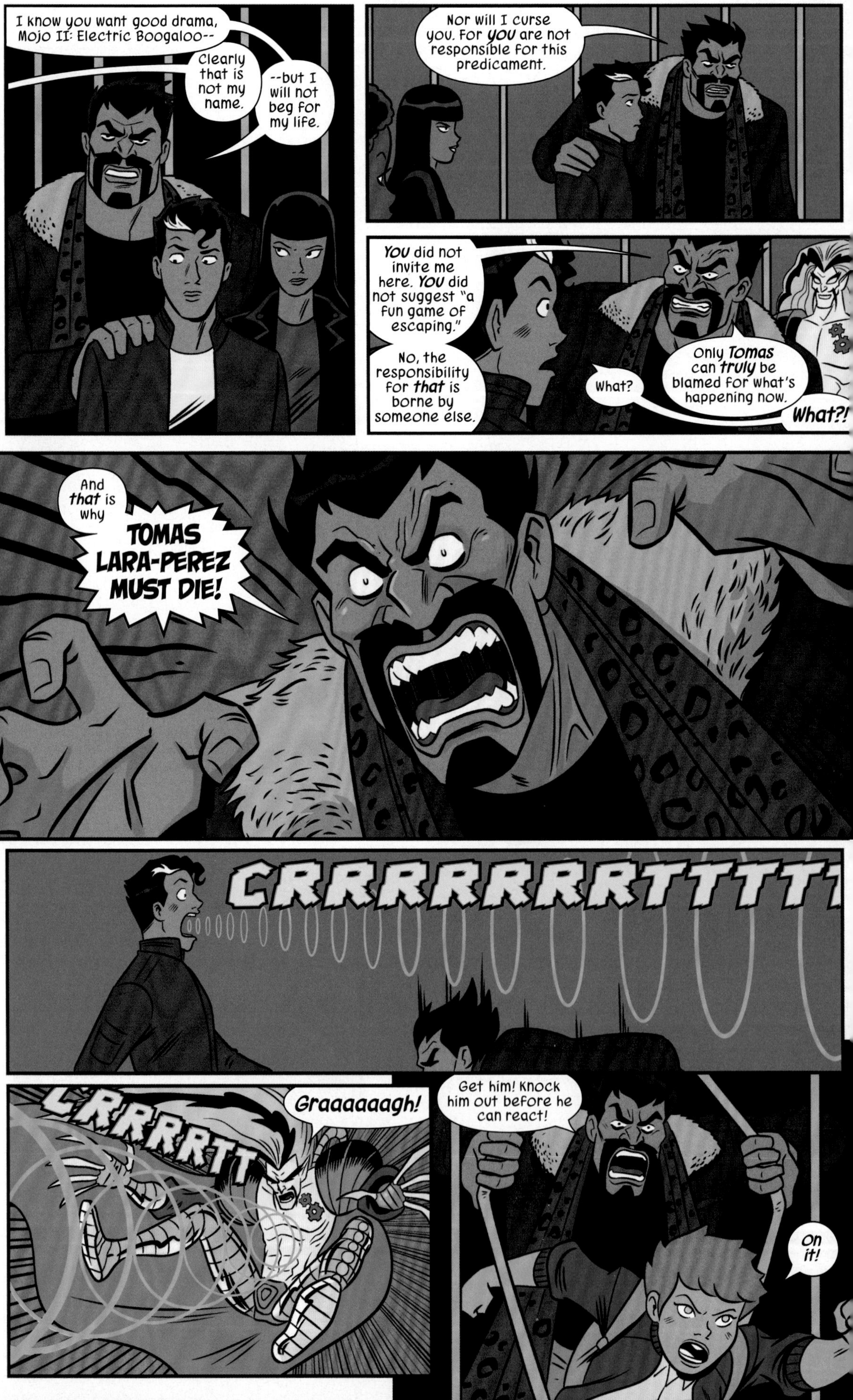
I know you want good drama, Mojo II: Electric Boogaloo--
Clearly that is not my name.
--but I will not beg for my life.
Nor will I curse you. For *you* are not responsible for this predicament.
You did not invite me here. *You* did not suggest "a fun game of escaping."
No, the responsibility for *that* is borne by someone else.
What?
Only *Tomas* can *truly* be blamed for what's happening now.
What?!
And *that* is why
TOMAS LARA-PEREZ MUST DIE!
CRRRRRRRRTTTTT
CRRRRRTTT
Graaaaaagh!
Get him! Knock him out before he can react!
On it!

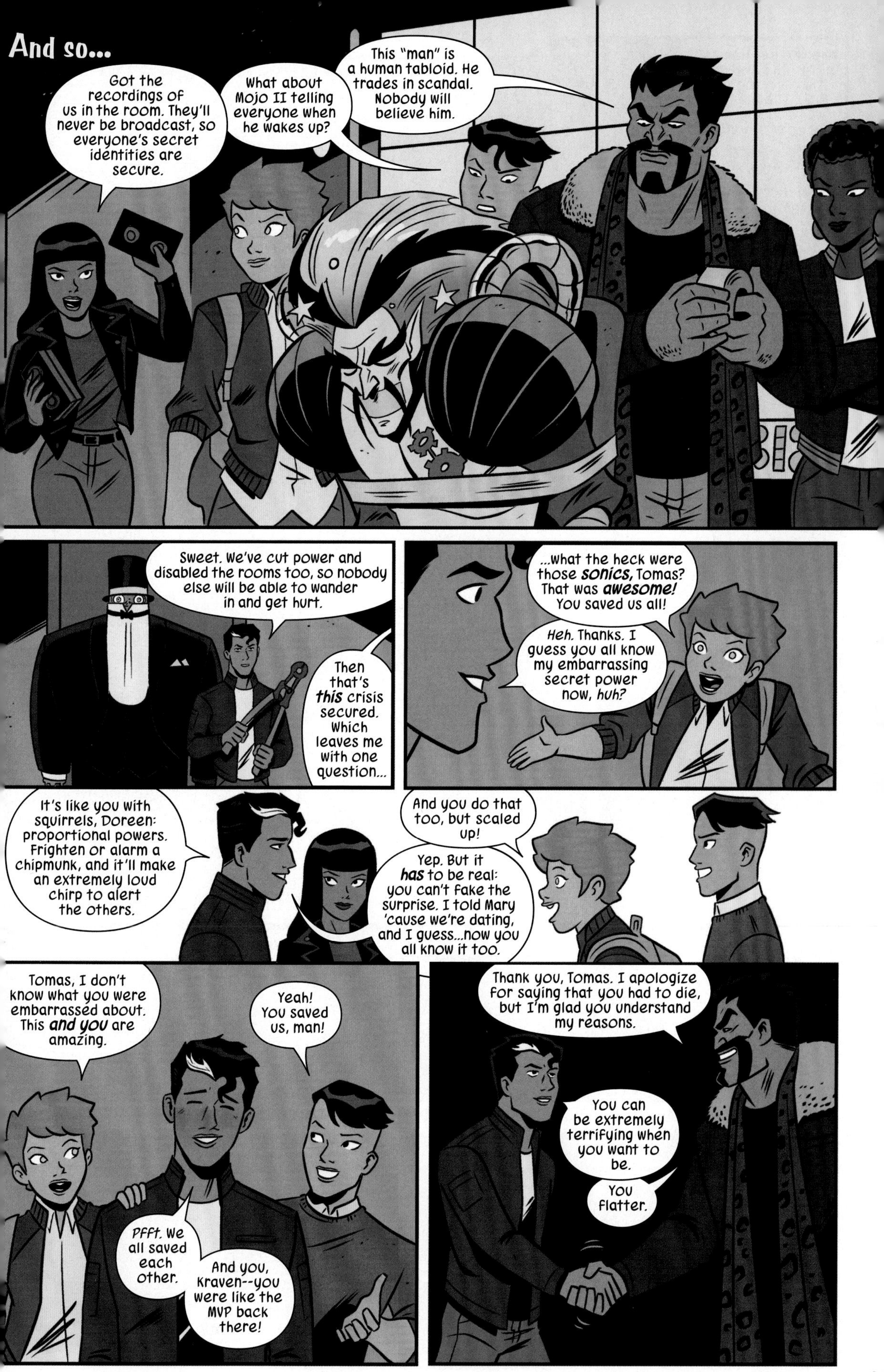
And so...
Got the recordings of us in the room. They'll never be broadcast, so everyone's secret identities are secure.
What about Mojo II telling everyone when he wakes up?
This "man" is a human tabloid. He trades in scandal. Nobody will believe him.
Sweet. We've cut power and disabled the rooms too, so nobody else will be able to wander in and get hurt.
Then that's **this** crisis secured. Which leaves me with one question...
...what the heck were those **sonics,** Tomas? That was **awesome!** You saved us all!
Heh. Thanks. I guess you all know my embarrassing secret power now, *huh?*
It's like you with squirrels, Doreen: proportional powers. Frighten or alarm a chipmunk, and it'll make an extremely loud chirp to alert the others.
And you do that too, but scaled up!
Yep. But it **has** to be real: you can't fake the surprise. I told Mary 'cause we're dating, and I guess...now you all know it too.
Tomas, I don't know what you were embarrassed about. This **and you** are amazing.
Yeah! You saved us, man!
Pfft. We all saved each other.
And you, Kraven--you were like the MVP back there!
Thank you, Tomas. I apologize for saying that you had to die, but I'm glad you understand my reasons.
You can be extremely terrifying when you want to be.
You flatter.

Neither Kraven nor Tomas will mention it, so I will: Kraven's handshake is like a steel trap, and Tomas is doing a terrific job of playing it off like it's no big deal.

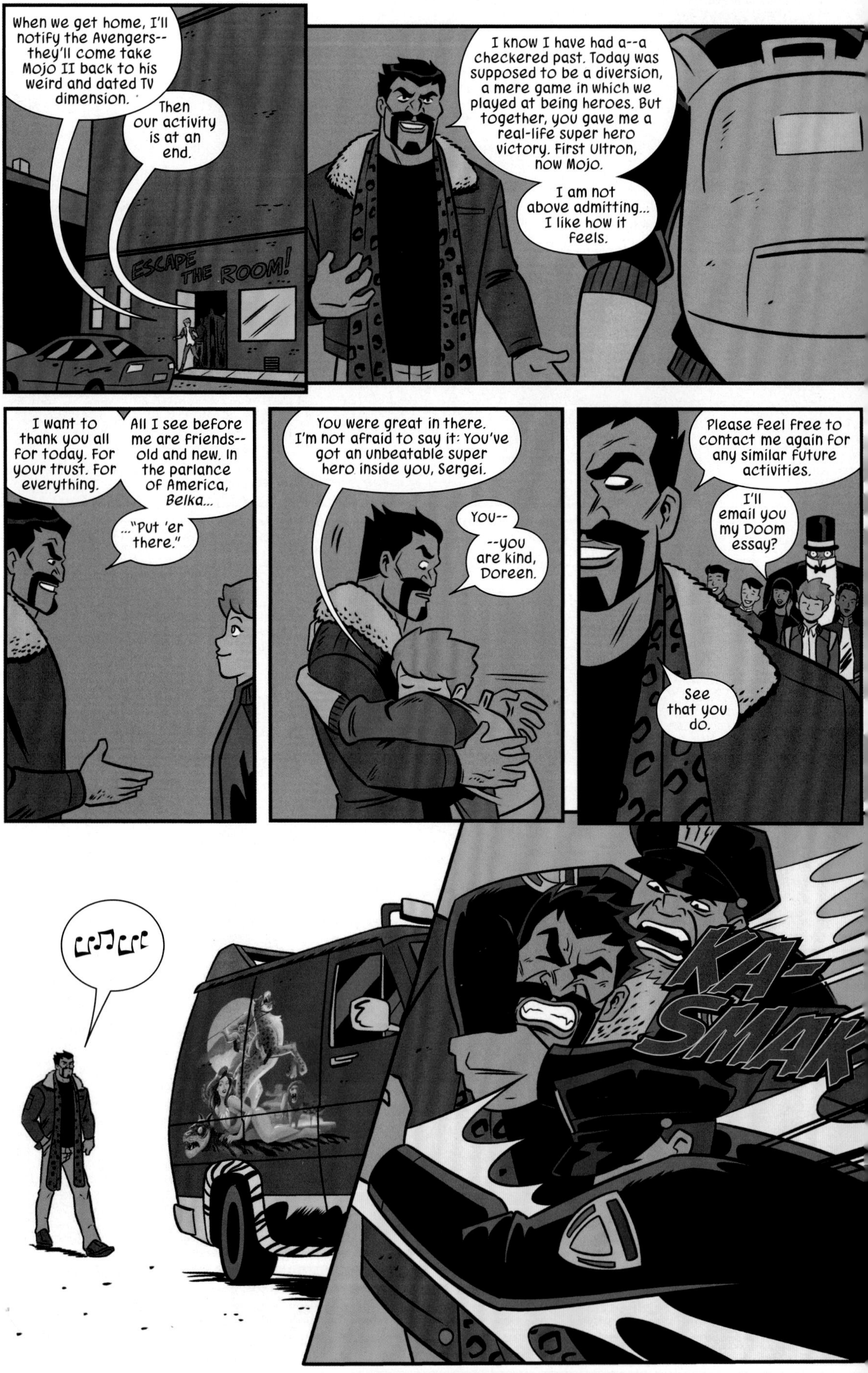

When we get home, I'll notify the Avengers--they'll come take Mojo II back to his weird and dated TV dimension.
Then our activity is at an end.
ESCAPE THE ROOM!
I know I have had a--a checkered past. Today was supposed to be a diversion, a mere game in which we played at being heroes. But together, you gave me a real-life super hero victory. First Ultron, now Mojo.
I am not above admitting... I like how it feels.
I want to thank you all for today. For your trust. For everything.
All I see before me are friends--old and new. In the parlance of America, Belka...
..."Put 'er there."
You were great in there. I'm not afraid to say it: You've got an unbeatable super hero inside you, Sergei.
You--
--you are kind, Doreen.
Please feel free to contact me again for any similar future activities.
I'll email you my Doom essay?
See that you do.
KA-SMAK

This sudden attack is bad news for Kraven, but it's good news for you, the value-loving and page-counting reader who was surprised to discover that this super hero comic seemed to be wrapping up much sooner than usual!

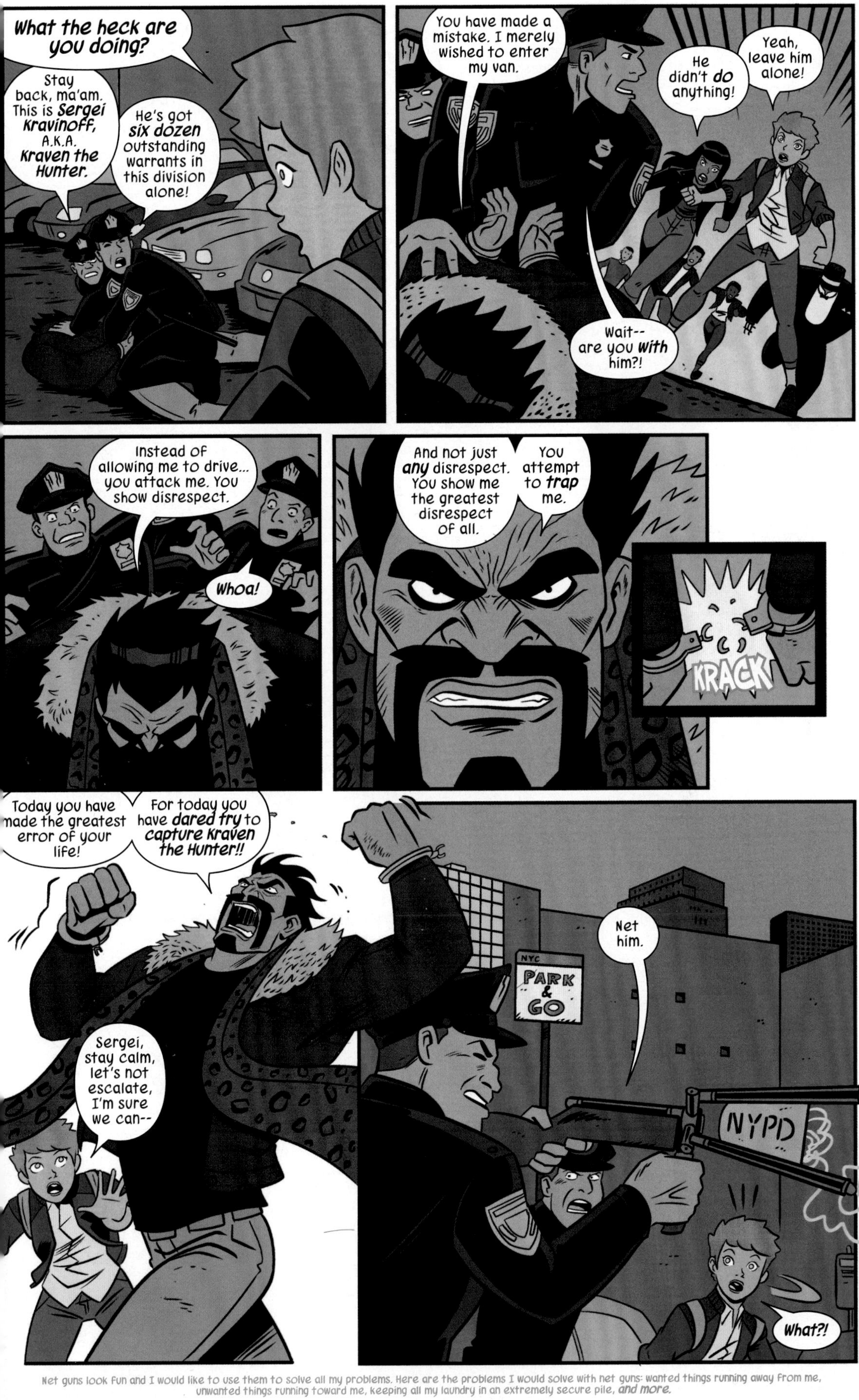
What the heck are you doing?
Stay back, ma'am. This is Sergei Kravinoff, A.K.A. Kraven the Hunter.
He's got six dozen outstanding warrants in this division alone!
You have made a mistake. I merely wished to enter my van.
He didn't do anything!
Yeah, leave him alone!
Wait-- are you with him?!
Instead of allowing me to drive... you attack me. You show disrespect.
Whoa!
And not just any disrespect. You show me the greatest disrespect of all.
You attempt to trap me.
KRACK
Today you have made the greatest error of your life!
For today you have dared try to capture Kraven the Hunter!!
Net him.
NYC
PARK & GO
Sergei, stay calm, let's not escalate, I'm sure we can--
NYPD
What?!

Net guns look fun and I would like to use them to solve all my problems. Here are the problems I would solve with net guns: wanted things running away from me, unwanted things running toward me, keeping all my laundry in an extremely secure pile, *and more.*

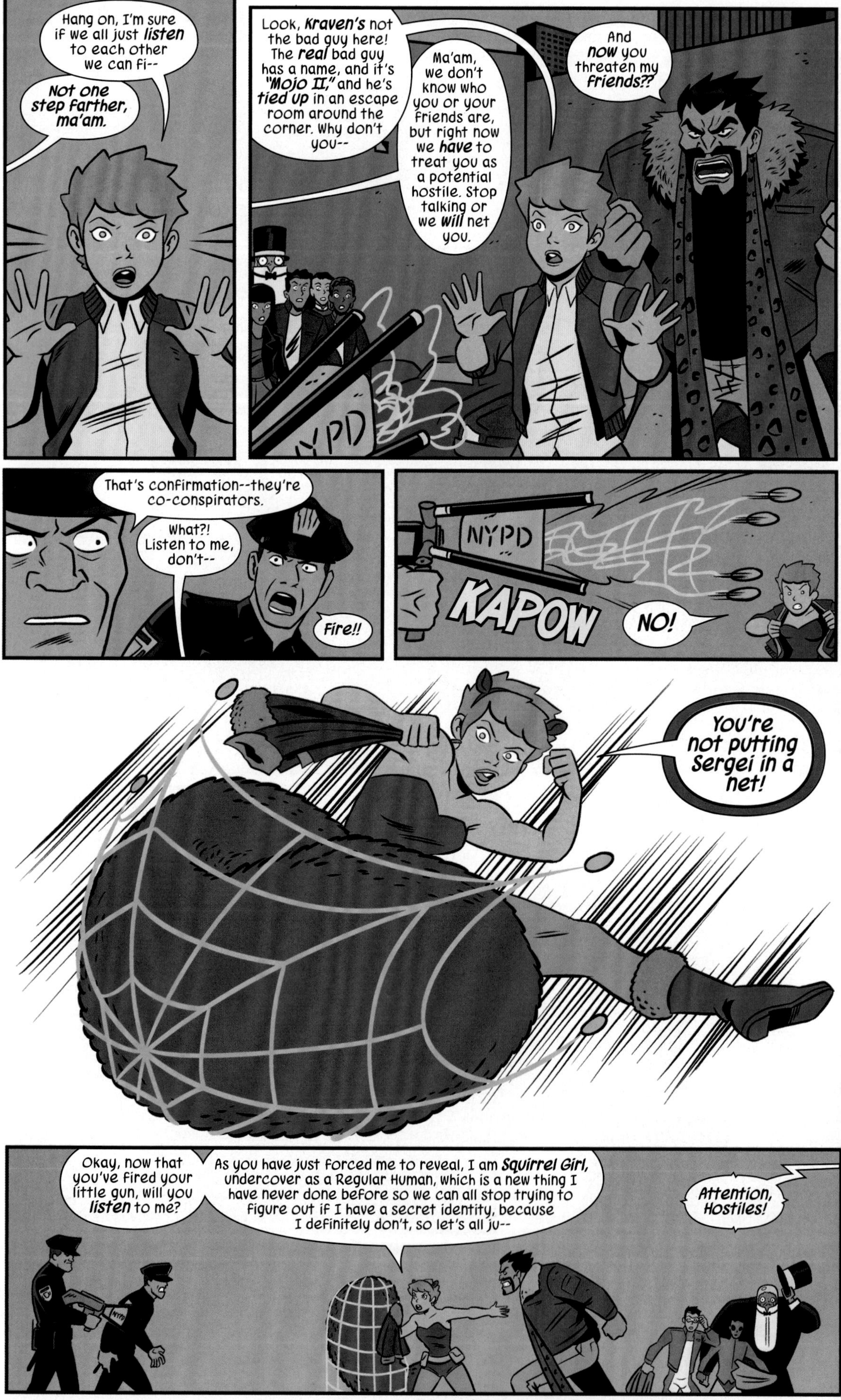
Hang on, I'm sure if we all just listen to each other we can fi--
Not one step farther, ma'am.
Look, Kraven's not the bad guy here! The real bad guy has a name, and it's "Mojo II," and he's tied up in an escape room around the corner. Why don't you--
Ma'am, we don't know who you or your friends are, but right now we have to treat you as a potential hostile. Stop talking or we will net you.
And now you threaten my friends??
NYPD
That's confirmation--they're co-conspirators.
What?! Listen to me, don't--
Fire!!
NYPD
KAPOW
NO!
You're not putting Sergei in a net!
Okay, now that you've fired your little gun, will you listen to me?
As you have just forced me to reveal, I am Squirrel Girl, undercover as a Regular Human, which is a new thing I have never done before so we can all stop trying to figure out if I have a secret identity, because I definitely don't, so let's all ju--
Attention, Hostiles!
NYPD

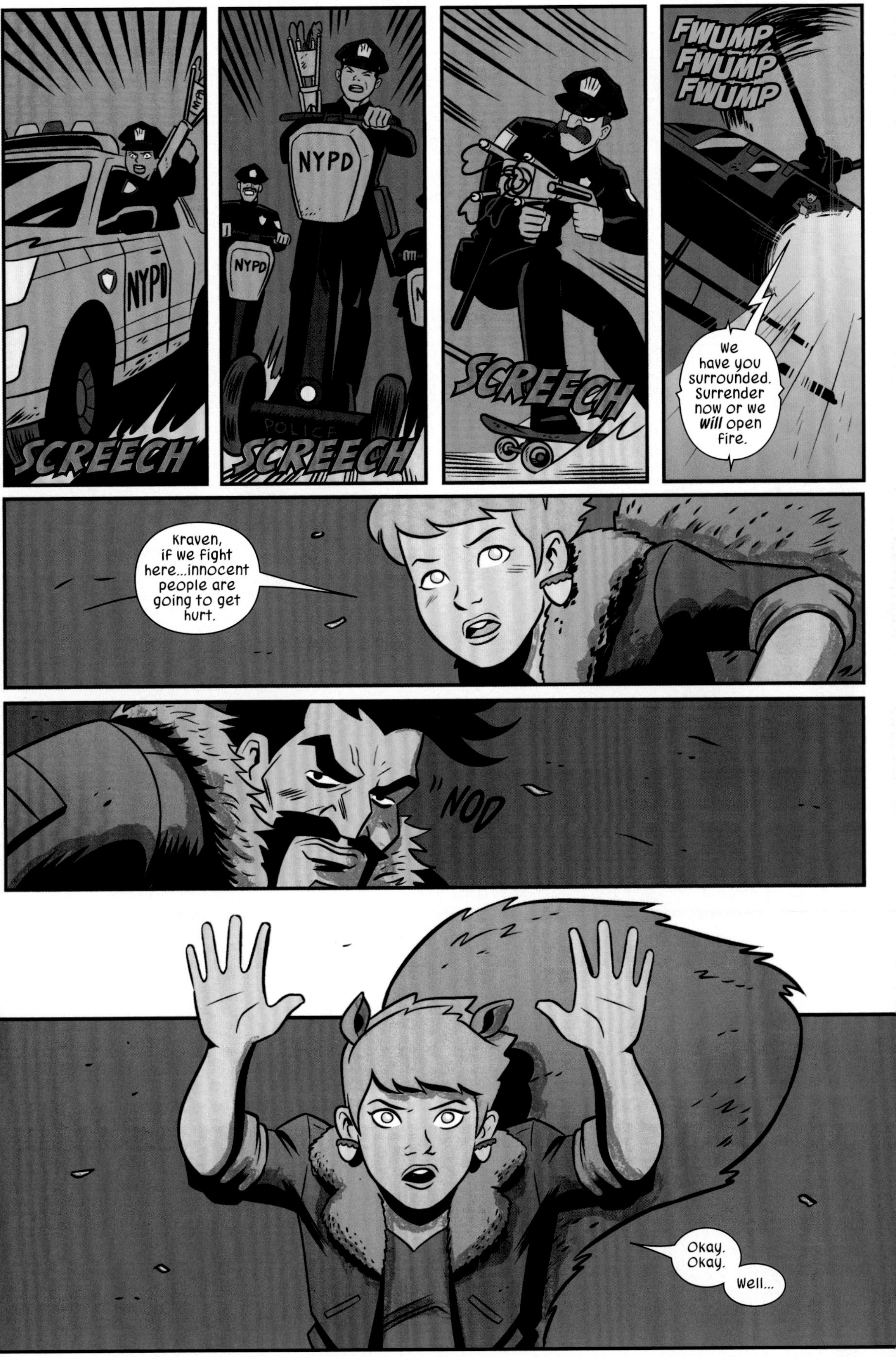
NYPD
SCREECH
NYPD
NYPD
POLICE
SCREECH
SCREECH
FWUMP FWUMP FWUMP
We have you surrounded. Surrender now or we *will* open fire.
Kraven, if we fight here...innocent people are going to get hurt.
NOD
Okay. Okay.
Well...

It seems the new "let all police officers choose their preferred method of wheeled locomotion" program is already paying dividends.

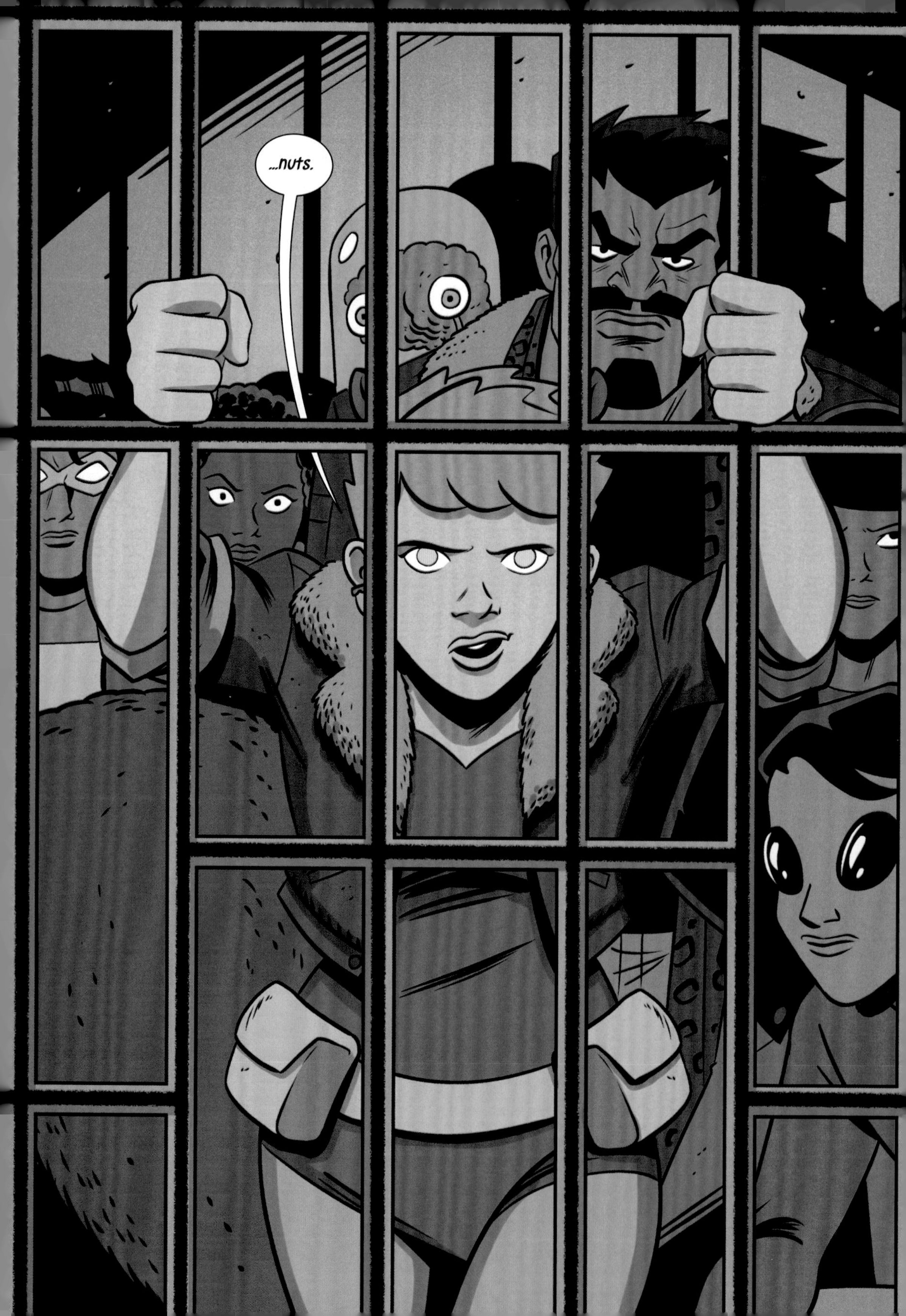
...nuts.

Letters From Nuts

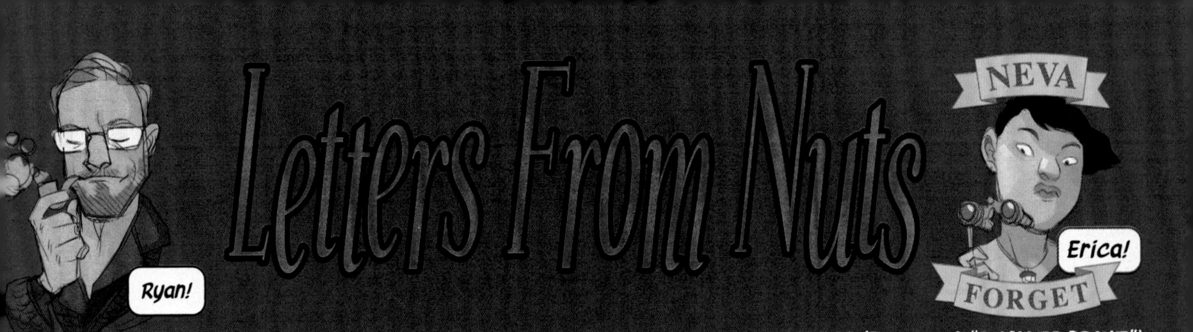
Ryan!
NEVA
FORGET
Erica!

Send letters to mheroes@marvel.com or 135 W 50th St, 7th Floor, New York, NY 10020 (Please mark "OKAY TO PRINT")

I'm just here to say thank you and chitty chuk chu-chuck chitt chuck!!!!!!!!!!!!?

I love you guys.

I am sending along a picture of the next Squirrel Girl character: Hailey Bailey, A.K.A. the Jade Jaguar, age 9.

chutt

Hazel Moody, age 9
Brooklyn, NY

P.S. I have never written to a comic book before!

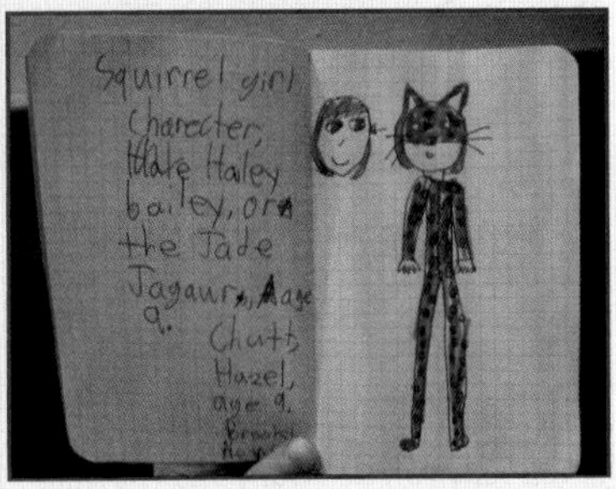
Squirrel girl
charecter,
Haley
bailey, or
the Jade
Jagaur, Age
9.
Chutt
Hazel,
age 9.

RYAN: Hazel, congratulations on both writing into a comic book AND coming up with your own character! I like the Jade Jaguar, and I like how she has green eyes, hinting at her alter ego. Tippy got your message and asked me to write this: "chtt chutt chkkkt chitty"! I have to say, after typing out her message, I agree with it 100%.

Dear Ryan and Erica,

I just want to thank you for THE UNBEATABLE SQUIRREL GIRL. I've been reading comics for well over half my life (since I'm only 22, that's a really impressive way to say "a little over a decade"), and USG has to be the most consistent blast of joy I've ever had the pleasure of reading!

So much so that I use it to help with sadness. I recently lost a close friend and have been fighting my way through the depression that comes with that, and whenever I need a quick burst of happiness, I pick up some SQUIRREL GIRL. I don't want to say that your talking squirrel comic is working on completely eradicating worldwide depression, but it's almost a possibility that there won't be a market for psychiatrists by the time USG #40 comes out. So...way to kill a thriving mental health industry, I guess?

But seriously, it's impossible to feel any sadness when reading SQUIRREL GIRL, and it was already on my favorite comic list before I was hit with some situational depression. It's the comic that takes me the longest to read because I keep having to stop due to laughing too hard. It's the comic that has enough cleverness and wit to bring about the rare, literal "lol." It's the comic whose sheer readability is unmatched by any other. And it's the first comic that's prompted me to write in.

Keep up the great work! (Or don't; I mean, it's your life. Don't let me tell you how to run it. This is really more of a request than a command.)

Sincerely,
Andy K.

P.S. Did you know that there is a group called N.A.S.A. (North American Squirrel Association)? They honestly don't have much to do with squirrels; they're more about helping those with physical disabilities get outdoors. But can you think of how many wacky misunderstandings with the real NASA this could create? Because I'm thinking it's almost certainly close to one.

RYAN: Andy, it's great to get a letter like this, and I'm happy we helped in whatever way we did. One of the great things about being a writer--of comics, prose, websites, anything--is that once you write something, it takes on a life of its own and you don't know what it's going to do or whom it's going to reach. I've met people who have told me the different ways things I've written have affected their lives, and when you reach the point of "we met on a message board because we were fans of you and now we're married and have a kid"--i.e., at the point where there are humans alive on the planet today that wouldn't be there if you weren't--you realize how crazy and interconnected everything is. And writing's just a more visible example of that: just existing in the world and interacting with people every day has the same ripple effects out in the world, so it's always nice for any of us to hear our ripples have been positive. I also like that the timing on your letter comes on an issue that ends with Squirrel Girl in JAIL--not the happiest place to be, generally!--but I promise she'll pull this off. SOMEHOW.

Hi,

Please read this letter from my son for the creative team on UNBEATABLE SQUIRREL GIRL.

Thanks,
Rob

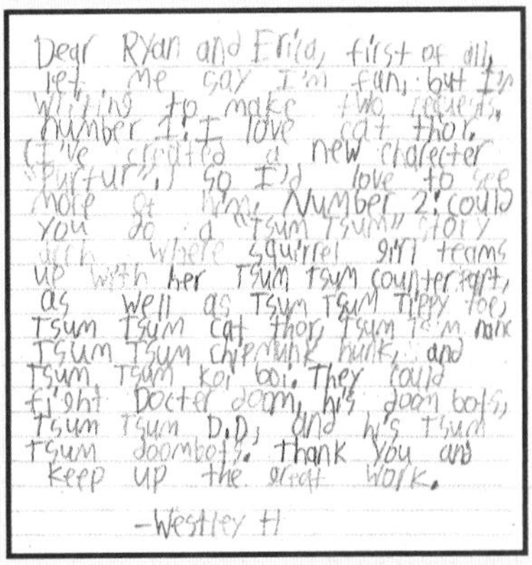

Dear Ryan and Erica, first of all, let me say I'm fan, but I'm writing to make two requests. Number 1: I love cat thor. (I've created a new charecter "Purfur",) so I'd love to see more of him. Number 2: could you do a "Tsum Tsum" story arch where squirrel girl teams up with her Tsum Tsum counterpart, as well as Tsum Tsum Tippy toe, Tsum Tsum cat thor, Tsum Tsum nanc Tsum Tsum chipmunk hunk, and Tsum Tsum koi boi. They could fight Docter doom, his doom bots, Tsum Tsum D.D, and his Tsum Tsum doombots. Thank you and keep up the great work.

-Westley H

RYAN: Westley, I have good news: you are not alone in your love of Cat Thor! I obviously consider him to be the greatest and most dynamic character in Marvel's stable, and I hope that by the time you're an adult, still reading (and maybe--making?) comic books, you will have your choice of the Cat Thor Expanded Cinematic Universe to unwind with. I have a Tsum Tsum Squirrel Girl but have never considered the other characters you invented--I think they'd be great! Doctor Doom wouldn't know what hit him (seriously, he'd be very confused to suddenly be attacked by Tsum Tsum hero duplicates).

Hello,

My dad made me this awesome Squirrel Girl skateboard!

Best,
Zelda Hoffman

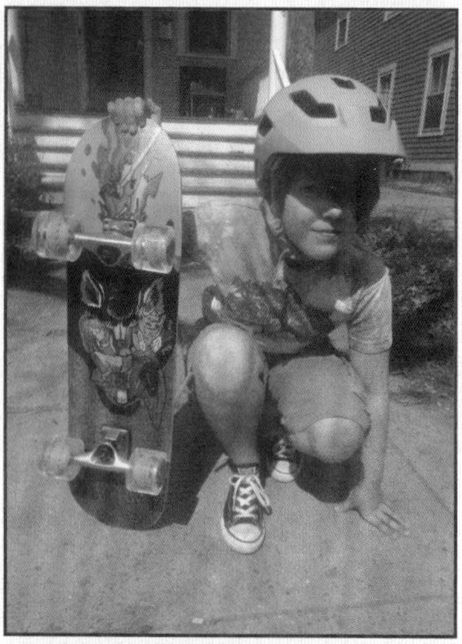

RYAN: Zelda, my props to your dad: That's such a great deck! I also love how your helmet matches the nose of the board. I'm a skateboarder too and my old skateboard had a *T. rex* on it with a dinosaur skull and crossbones underneath. I thought it was the coolest board I ever saw, but that opinion has been RE-EVALUATED, because it didn't say "KICK BUTTS & EAT NUTS" on it. Keep skating: it's fun, it's good for you, and everyone looks awesome on a skateboard! In Toronto once a year all the skaters put on suits and ties and skate downtown in a huge group. We call it the "board meeting."

Dear Erica, Ryan, and the whole SQUIRREL GIRL Team,

I've been hooked on SQUIRREL GIRL since I saw her singing her theme song in a tree in the first (first!) issue, and I just finished Erica's farewell issue, #31. It breaks my heart to see her go, and I just wanted to say thank you so much. Over the past three and a half years, this comic has brought so much joy and laughter to my life. Every single issue has made me laugh out loud, often more than once. Cat Thor! The Kra-Van! Mild-mannered college student Brian Drain! Doreen's date with Sentinel #X-42903-22! Squirrel Girl going undercover dressed as Secret Squirrel! The MOST METAL lesson in binary ever seen! Galactus hates Mondays! Squirrel Girl fighting robot dinosaurs in the Savage Land had LITERALLY EVERYTHING I HAVE EVER WANTED IN A COMIC, and I laughed so hard at Hocky Hoof Hank, the Thor that's literally an actual horse, that my wife had to check on me to make sure I was okay. And through it all, Erica's art was beautiful, hilarious, and unlike anything else on the stands.

Erica, I can't wait to see what you do next. Ryan, you have a loyal reader until we've reached Senior Citizen Nancy and Old Lady Squirrel Girl, for real. Thank you all so much, and keep eating nuts and kicking butts!

Brian Boylan
Columbus, Ohio

RYAN: I'll admit, I was really happy to have the Kra-Van come back in this issue (just before she left the book, Erica and I talked about this story, and the excitement of having the Kra-Van be a plot point was a none-too-small part of this story turning out the way it did). This was a beautiful note, and we sent it along to Erica so she'd see it right away, instead of later on when this issue came out and she could see it there (HI, ERICA). Thank you for such a sweet note, Brian!

Hey Squirrel Team,

With all the emotional punch that last issue packed (I did not cry while reading it to my son, because that would interrupt the flow of the story, but it was a near thing), the part that got me the most was the letters page. I was shocked when I read that Erica is stepping down as artist... I've loved the artwork in each issue just as much as I love the writing (I've been a big fan of talking *T. rexes* for years) and, Erica, it feels like part of the power of Squirrel Girl will be leaving with you. I mean, I know it won't, and I promise I won't cancel my subscription, and I'm sure Mr. Charm will do a fine job in your stead, but--oh, it's just hard to find the right words. It's been a week since I read the news and I still can't think of the right words!

Erica, I hope that wherever your path is headed next will be fantastic, and I hope we still get to see your art out there, and I hope you get lots and lots of letters wishing you well and cheering you on and letting you know how much we'll miss your renditions of Doreen and Nancy arriving in our mailboxes/pull stacks/inboxes/however each month. I am very sure that wherever you go, many nuts will be eaten, and any butts that try to stand in your way will be thoroughly kicked. I wish you all the luck!

Lauren

RYAN: Lauren, I feel you! I was worried about ANYONE else drawing Doreen, but then as soon as Derek sent in his first pencils I was like, "okay, phew, this is actually awesome too, but in a different way." I hope you've been enjoying it, and I thank you for this great note! (We sent it along to Erica directly too, as did we all of these, because when someone sends you something so great about your friend, you let 'em know!)

Dear Ms. Henderson,

(No, seriously, Mr. North, stop reading now. You will get yours soon enough.)

I am still emotional over your leaving SQUIRREL GIRL. But Mr. North gave you a sendoff so spectacular I don't even feel bad about not feeling bad about you not being there next issue.

Even before your reply to my last letter, I had decided to do LEGO versions of both you and Mr. North. LEGO doesn't make freakishly large mini-figures, but I do. I expect to finish them sometime after finals. And I expect that Mr. North will share the images with you if I send them to Marvel. I hope you enjoy them even a fraction as much as I have enjoyed your art all these years.

And while I know that you know that IT IS A HORSE'S TAIL, a picture is worth a thousand words. Even though Hockey Hoof Hank is still a work in progress, I just had to give you a preview. (The face needs to be polished out, and the mane needs some trim work. And a hundred other flaws I am sure I will see after I send this.) Please find enclosed an image of the greatest tail-up of all tales.

Sincerely,
David Oakes

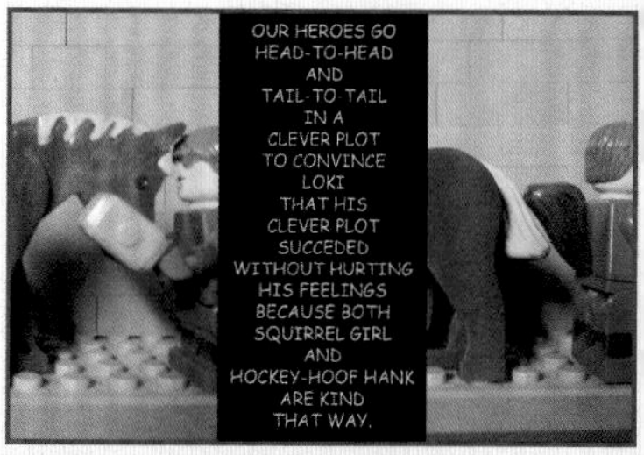
OUR HEROES GO HEAD-TO-HEAD AND TAIL-TO TAIL IN A CLEVER PLOT TO CONVINCE LOKI THAT HIS CLEVER PLOT SUCCEDED WITHOUT HURTING HIS FEELINGS BECAUSE BOTH SQUIRREL GIRL AND HOCKEY-HOOF HANK ARE KIND THAT WAY.

RYAN: As I stopped reading this letter as instructed, I can't really respond, but if I were to hazard a guess I'd say it's awesome and kind and perhaps includes an image of the first fan Hocky Hoof Hank figure? Which I believe is all any of us want out of life??

Next Issue:

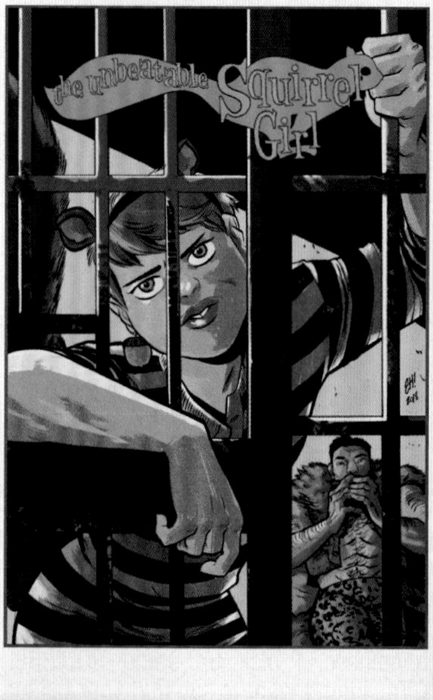
the unbeatable Squirrel Girl

Attention, Squirrel Scouts! Make sure to check out our production blog, **unbeatablesquirrelgirl.tumblr.com**, where we post behind-the-scenes stuff on how the book gets made, along with all sorts of cool things *you* make: fanart, cosplay, whatever!

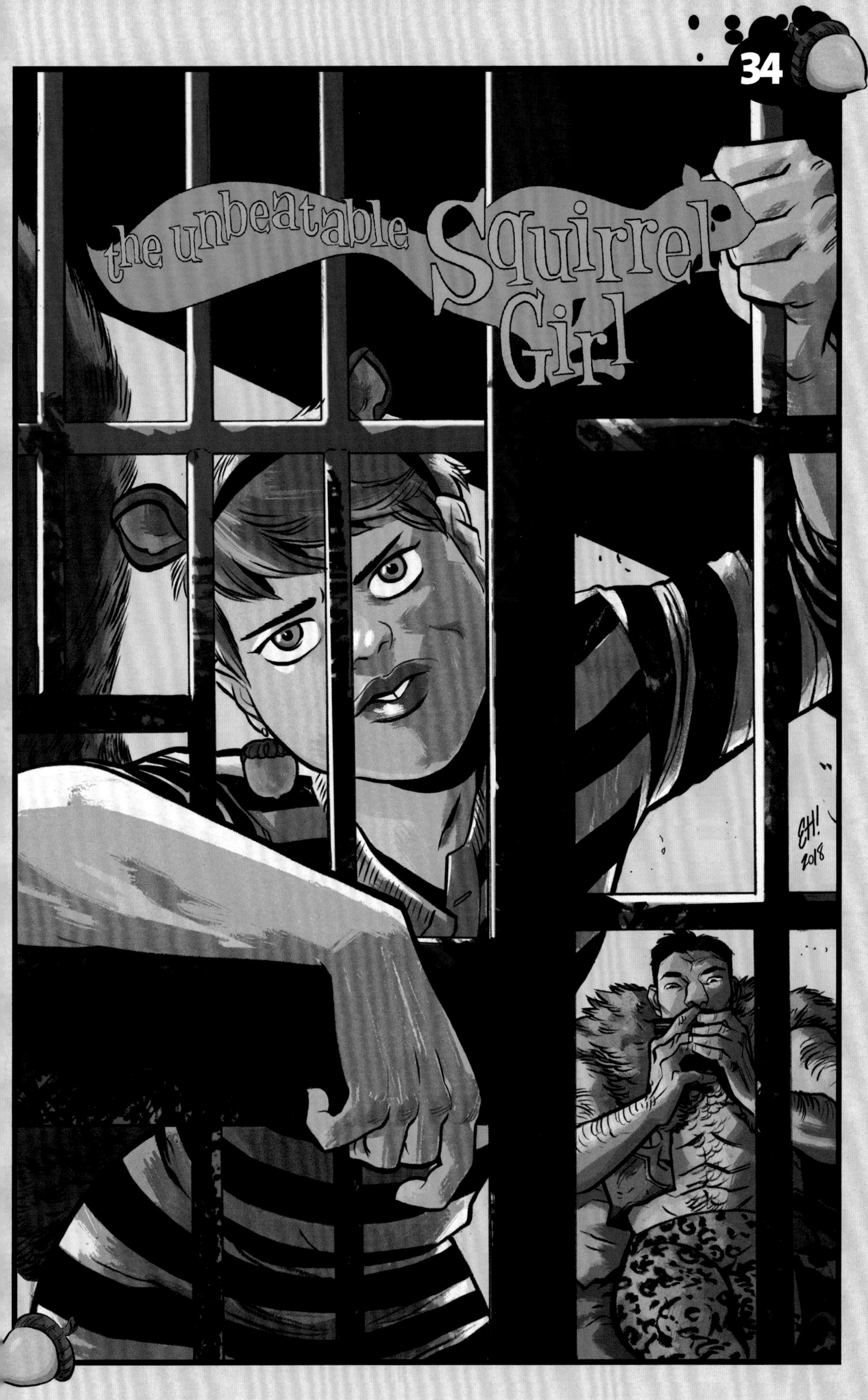
the unbeatable Squirrel Girl
EH! 2018

Doreen Green isn't just a second-year computer science student: she secretly also has all the powers of both squirrel and girl! She uses her amazing abilities to fight crime **and** be as awesome as possible. You know her as...The Unbeatable Squirrel Girl! Find out what she's been up to, with...

Squirrel Girl *in a nutshell*

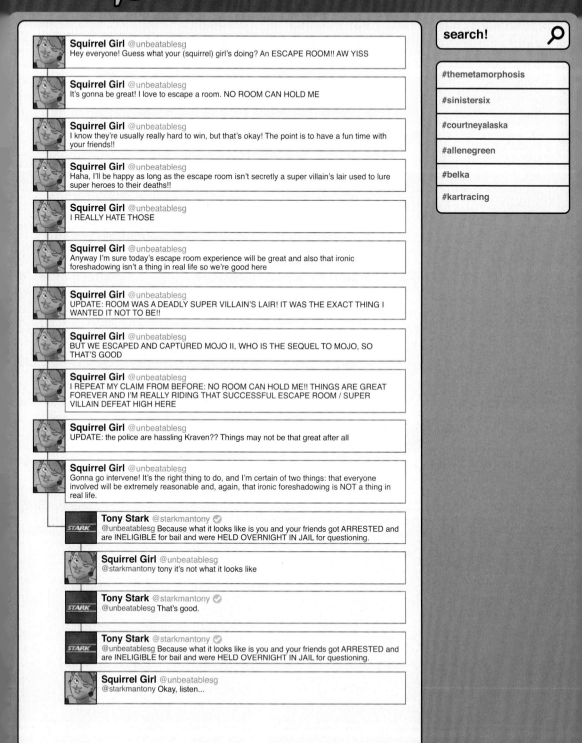

search! 🔍

#themetamorphosis

#sinistersix

#courtneyalaska

#allenegreen

#belka

#kartracing

Squirrel Girl @unbeatablesg
Hey everyone! Guess what your (squirrel) girl's doing? An ESCAPE ROOM!! AW YISS

Squirrel Girl @unbeatablesg
It's gonna be great! I love to escape a room. NO ROOM CAN HOLD ME

Squirrel Girl @unbeatablesg
I know they're usually really hard to win, but that's okay! The point is to have a fun time with your friends!!

Squirrel Girl @unbeatablesg
Haha, I'll be happy as long as the escape room isn't secretly a super villain's lair used to lure super heroes to their deaths!!

Squirrel Girl @unbeatablesg
I REALLY HATE THOSE

Squirrel Girl @unbeatablesg
Anyway I'm sure today's escape room experience will be great and also that ironic foreshadowing isn't a thing in real life so we're good here

Squirrel Girl @unbeatablesg
UPDATE: ROOM WAS A DEADLY SUPER VILLAIN'S LAIR! IT WAS THE EXACT THING I WANTED IT NOT TO BE!!

Squirrel Girl @unbeatablesg
BUT WE ESCAPED AND CAPTURED MOJO II, WHO IS THE SEQUEL TO MOJO, SO THAT'S GOOD

Squirrel Girl @unbeatablesg
I REPEAT MY CLAIM FROM BEFORE: NO ROOM CAN HOLD ME!! THINGS ARE GREAT FOREVER AND I'M REALLY RIDING THAT SUCCESSFUL ESCAPE ROOM / SUPER VILLAIN DEFEAT HIGH HERE

Squirrel Girl @unbeatablesg
UPDATE: the police are hassling Kraven?? Things may not be that great after all

Squirrel Girl @unbeatablesg
Gonna go intervene! It's the right thing to do, and I'm certain of two things: that everyone involved will be extremely reasonable and, again, that ironic foreshadowing is NOT a thing in real life.

Tony Stark @starkmantony ✅
@unbeatablesg Because what it looks like is you and your friends got ARRESTED and are INELIGIBLE for bail and were HELD OVERNIGHT IN JAIL for questioning.

Squirrel Girl @unbeatablesg
@starkmantony tony it's not what it looks like

Tony Stark @starkmantony ✅
@unbeatablesg That's good.

Tony Stark @starkmantony ✅
@unbeatablesg Because what it looks like is you and your friends got ARRESTED and are INELIGIBLE for bail and were HELD OVERNIGHT IN JAIL for questioning.

Squirrel Girl @unbeatablesg
@starkmantony Okay, listen...

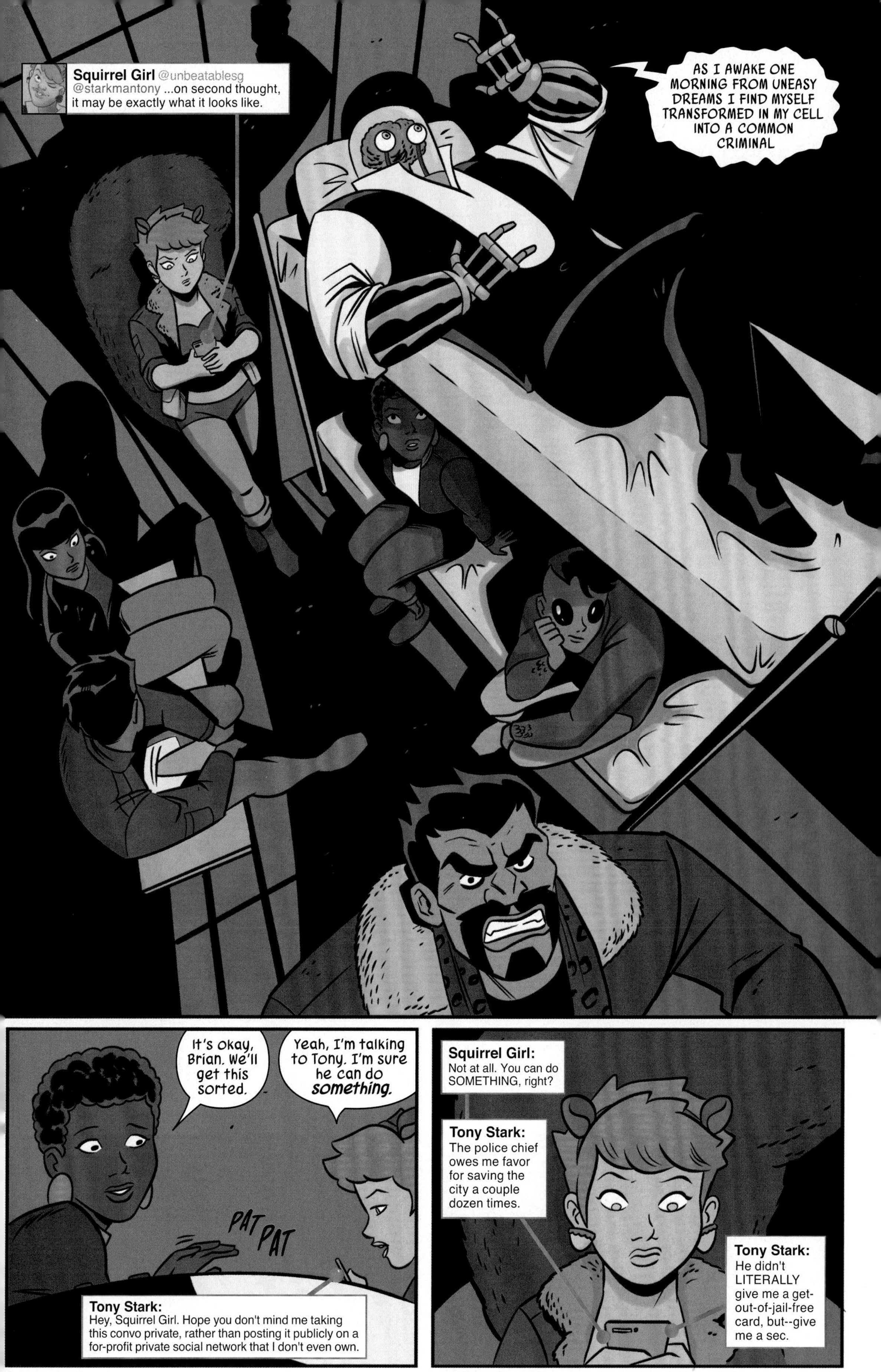
Squirrel Girl @unbeatablesg
@starkmantony ...on second thought, it may be exactly what it looks like.
AS I AWAKE ONE MORNING FROM UNEASY DREAMS I FIND MYSELF TRANSFORMED IN MY CELL INTO A COMMON CRIMINAL
It's okay, Brian. We'll get this sorted.
Yeah, I'm talking to Tony. I'm sure he can do *something.*
PAT PAT
Tony Stark:
Hey, Squirrel Girl. Hope you don't mind me taking this convo private, rather than posting it publicly on a for-profit private social network that I don't even own.
Squirrel Girl:
Not at all. You can do SOMETHING, right?
Tony Stark:
The police chief owes me favor for saving the city a couple dozen times.
Tony Stark:
He didn't LITERALLY give me a get-out-of-jail-free card, but--give me a sec.

Brain Drain is (poorly) quoting Kafka's "The Metamorphosis" there! It's about a man who wakes up and he's transformed into a giant bug. For some reason this does not go well for him, probably because after he wakes up, he ***doesn't*** put on a cape and cowl to fight crime as "Bugman." German modernist literature, man. It ***always*** goes in a different direction.

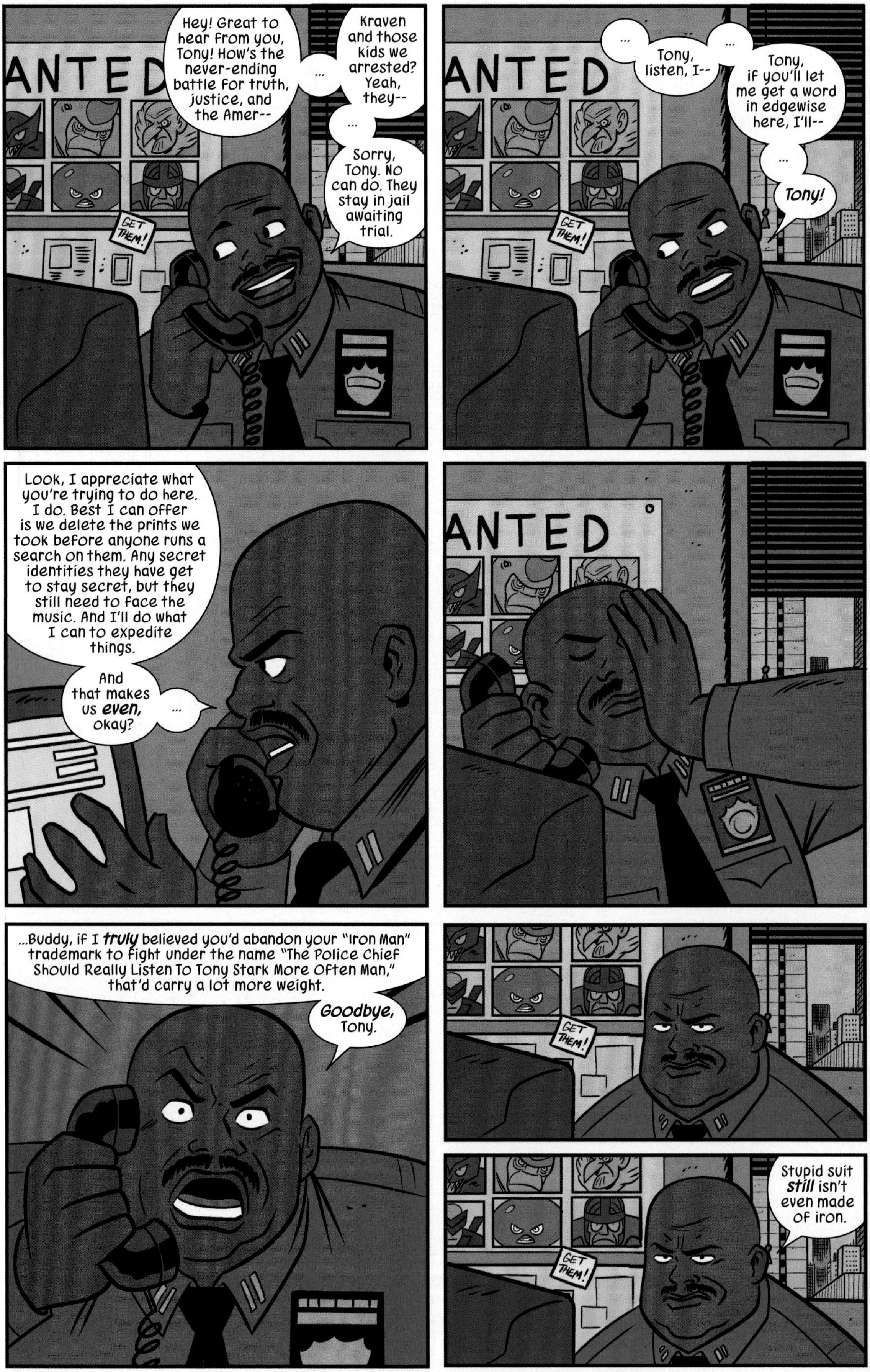
ANTED
GET THEM!
Hey! Great to hear from you, Tony! How's the never-ending battle for truth, justice, and the Amer--
...
Kraven and those kids we arrested? Yeah, they--
...
Sorry, Tony. No can do. They stay in jail awaiting trial.
...
Tony, listen, I--
...
Tony, if you'll let me get a word in edgewise here, I'll--
...
Tony!
Look, I appreciate what you're trying to do here. I do. Best I can offer is we delete the prints we took before anyone runs a search on them. Any secret identities they have get to stay secret, but they still need to face the music. And I'll do what I can to expedite things.
And that makes us *even*, okay?
...
...Buddy, if I *truly* believed you'd abandon your "Iron Man" trademark to fight under the name "The Police Chief Should Really Listen To Tony Stark More Often Man," that'd carry a lot more weight.
Goodbye, Tony.
Stupid suit *still* isn't even made of iron.

In case you're wondering, the cut-off words in Panel 1 weren't going to be "the American way." They were going to be "the American Express credit cards you keep licensing your likeness to; I get their ads in my mail once a week, *Tony*."

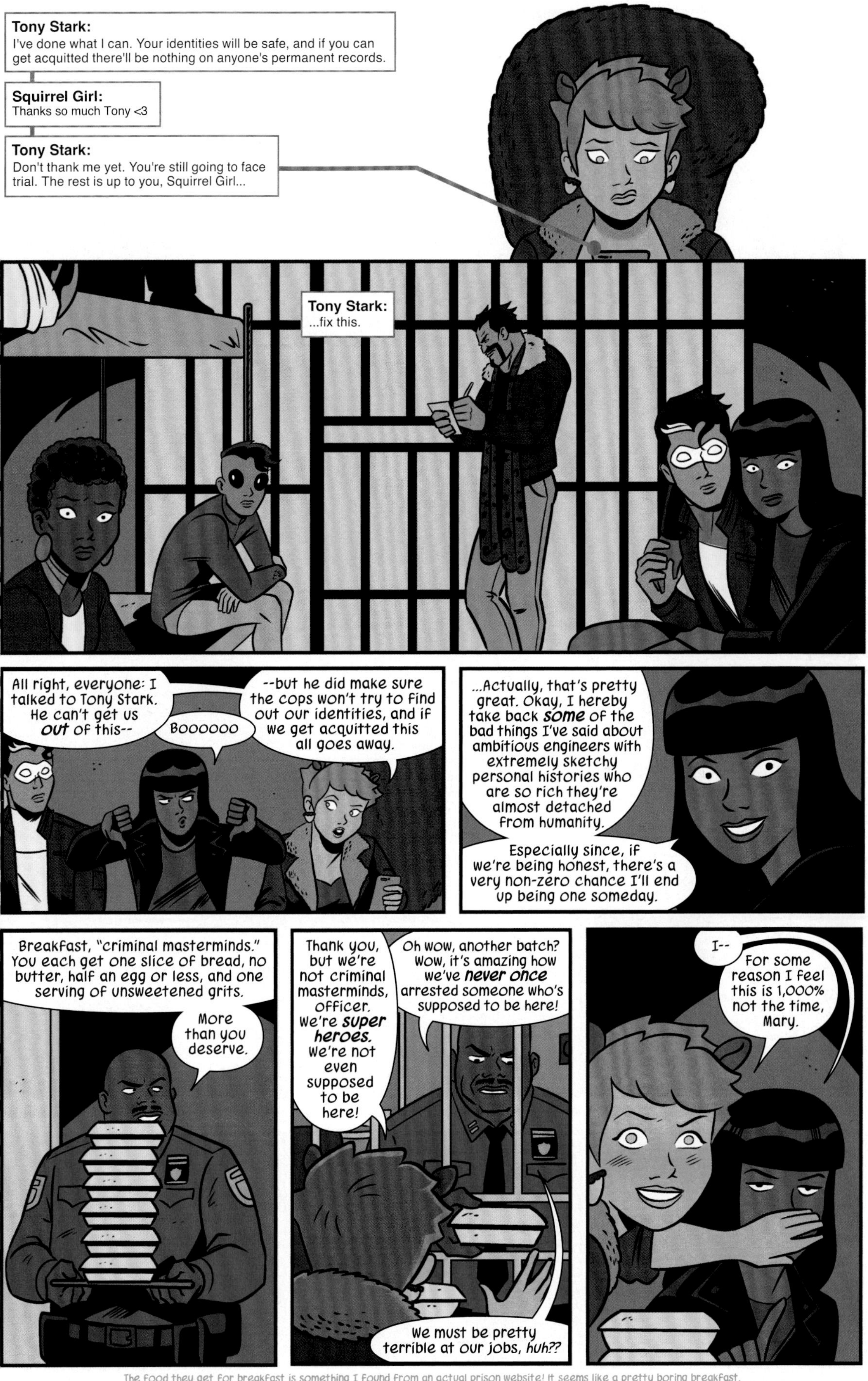
Tony Stark:
I've done what I can. Your identities will be safe, and if you can get acquitted there'll be nothing on anyone's permanent records.
Squirrel Girl:
Thanks so much Tony <3
Tony Stark:
Don't thank me yet. You're still going to face trial. The rest is up to you, Squirrel Girl...
Tony Stark:
...fix this.
All right, everyone: I talked to Tony Stark. He can't get us *out* of this--
Boooooo
--but he did make sure the cops won't try to find out our identities, and if we get acquitted this all goes away.
...Actually, that's pretty great. Okay, I hereby take back *some* of the bad things I've said about ambitious engineers with extremely sketchy personal histories who are so rich they're almost detached from humanity.
Especially since, if we're being honest, there's a very non-zero chance I'll end up being one someday.
Breakfast, "criminal masterminds." You each get one slice of bread, no butter, half an egg or less, and one serving of unsweetened grits.
More than you deserve.
Thank you, but we're not criminal masterminds, officer. We're *super heroes.* We're not even supposed to be here!
Oh wow, another batch? Wow, it's amazing how we've *never once* arrested someone who's supposed to be here!
We must be pretty terrible at our jobs, *huh??*
I--
For some reason I feel this is 1,000% not the time, Mary.

The food they get for breakfast is something I found from an actual prison website! It seems like a pretty boring breakfast. Attention readers! Do not do crimes, because the food is real bad!!

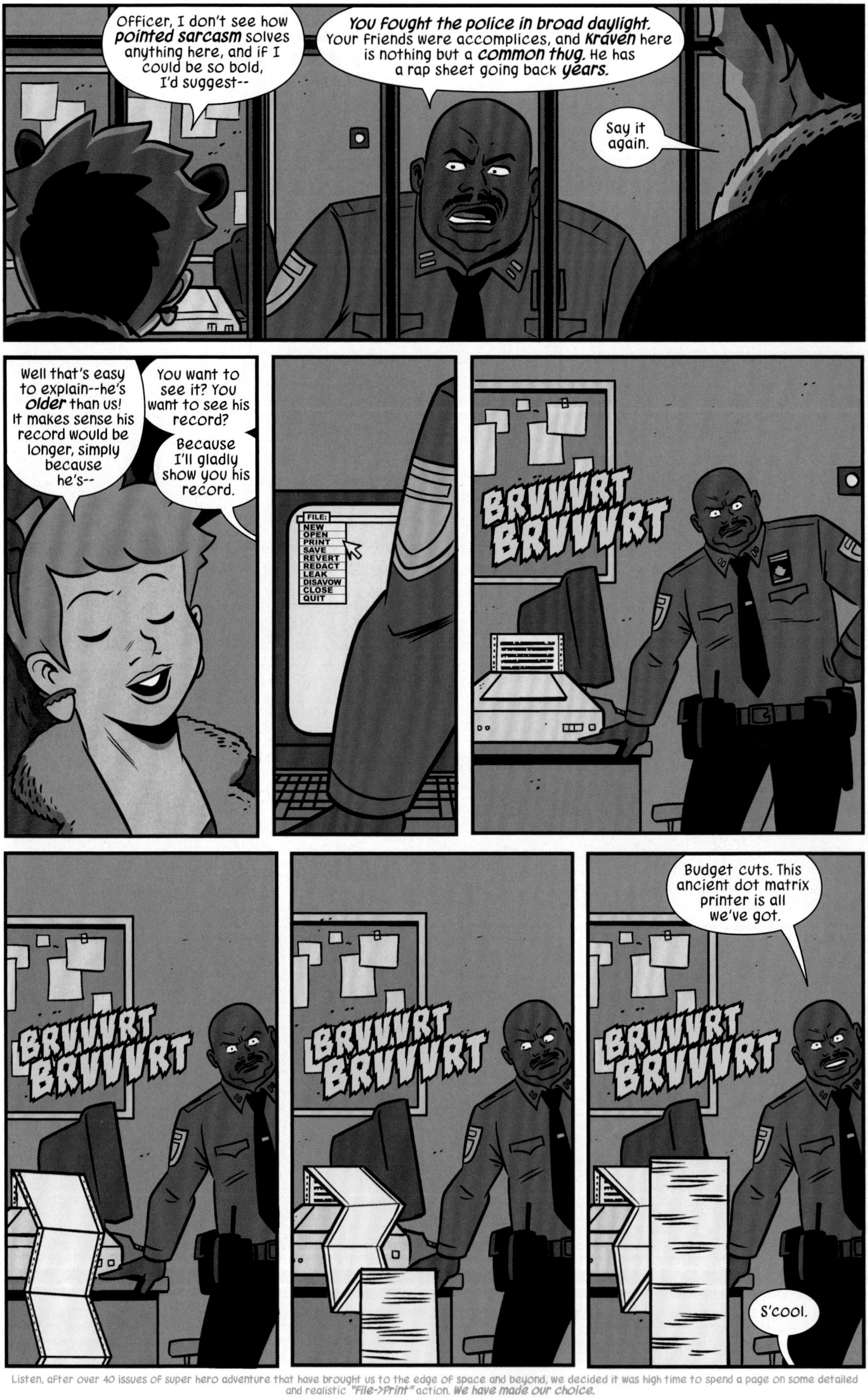
Officer, I don't see how pointed sarcasm solves anything here, and if I could be so bold, I'd suggest--
You fought the police in broad daylight. Your friends were accomplices, and Kraven here is nothing but a common thug. He has a rap sheet going back years.
Say it again.
Well that's easy to explain--he's older than us! It makes sense his record would be longer, simply because he's--
You want to see it? You want to see his record?
Because I'll gladly show you his record.
FILE:
NEW
OPEN
PRINT
SAVE
REVERT
REDACT
LEAK
DISAVOW
CLOSE
QUIT
BRVVVRT BRVVVRT
BRVVVRT BRVVVRT
BRVVVRT BRVVVRT
BRVVVRT BRVVVRT
Budget cuts. This ancient dot matrix printer is all we've got.
S'cool.

Listen, after over 40 issues of super hero adventure that have brought us to the edge of space and beyond, we decided it was high time to spend a page on some detailed and realistic *"File->Print"* action. ***We have made our choice.***

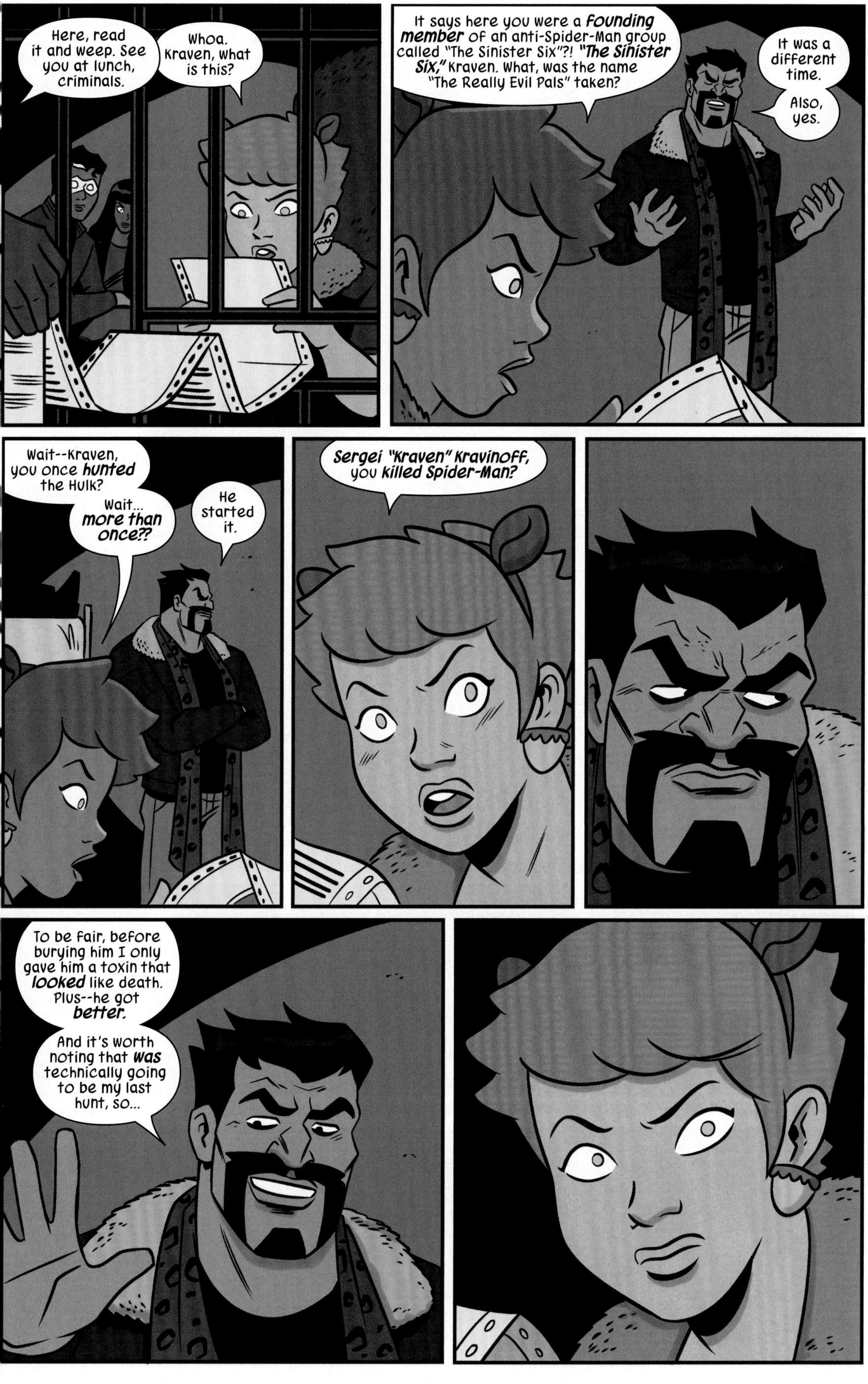
Here, read it and weep. See you at lunch, criminals.
Whoa. Kraven, what is this?
It says here you were a founding member of an anti-Spider-Man group called "The Sinister Six"?! "The Sinister Six," Kraven. What, was the name "The Really Evil Pals" taken?
It was a different time.
Also, yes.
Wait--Kraven, you once hunted the Hulk?
Wait... more than once??
He started it.
Sergei "Kraven" Kravinoff, you killed Spider-Man?
To be fair, before burying him I only gave him a toxin that looked like death. Plus--he got better.
And it's worth noting that was technically going to be my last hunt, so...

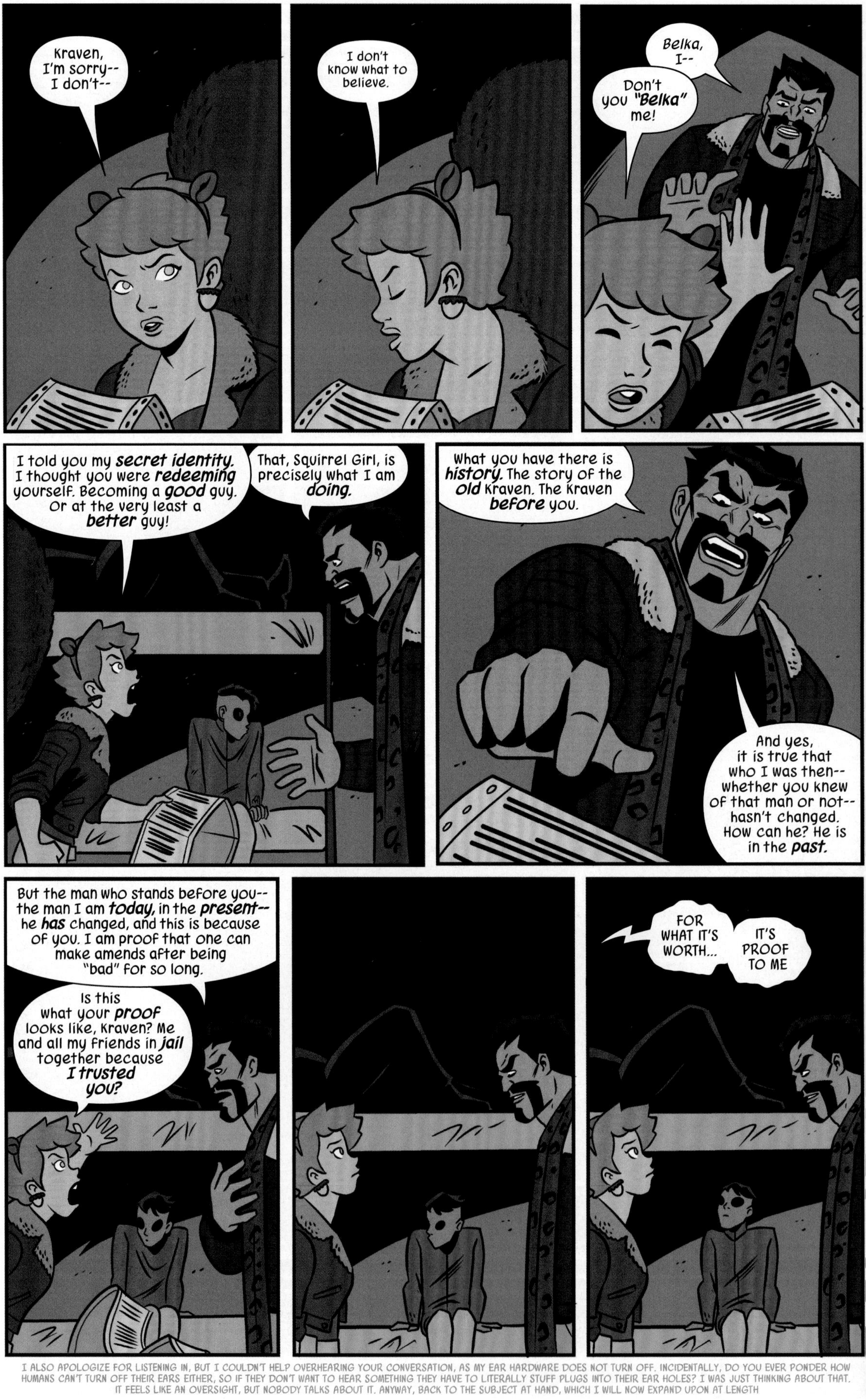

Kraven, I'm sorry-- I don't--
I don't know what to believe.
Belka, I--
Don't you "Belka" me!
I told you my secret identity. I thought you were redeeming yourself. Becoming a good guy. Or at the very least a better guy!
That, Squirrel Girl, is precisely what I am doing.
What you have there is history. The story of the old Kraven. The Kraven before you.
And yes, it is true that who I was then-- whether you knew of that man or not-- hasn't changed. How can he? He is in the past.
But the man who stands before you-- the man I am today, in the present-- he has changed, and this is because of you. I am proof that one can make amends after being "bad" for so long.
Is this what your proof looks like, Kraven? Me and all my friends in jail together because I trusted you?
FOR WHAT IT'S WORTH...
IT'S PROOF TO ME

I ALSO APOLOGIZE FOR LISTENING IN, BUT I COULDN'T HELP OVERHEARING YOUR CONVERSATION, AS MY EAR HARDWARE DOES NOT TURN OFF. INCIDENTALLY, DO YOU EVER PONDER HOW HUMANS CAN'T TURN OFF THEIR EARS EITHER, SO IF THEY DON'T WANT TO HEAR SOMETHING THEY HAVE TO LITERALLY STUFF PLUGS INTO THEIR EAR HOLES? I WAS JUST THINKING ABOUT THAT. IT FEELS LIKE AN OVERSIGHT, BUT NOBODY TALKS ABOUT IT. ANYWAY, BACK TO THE SUBJECT AT HAND, WHICH I WILL NOW EXPAND UPON AT LENGTH

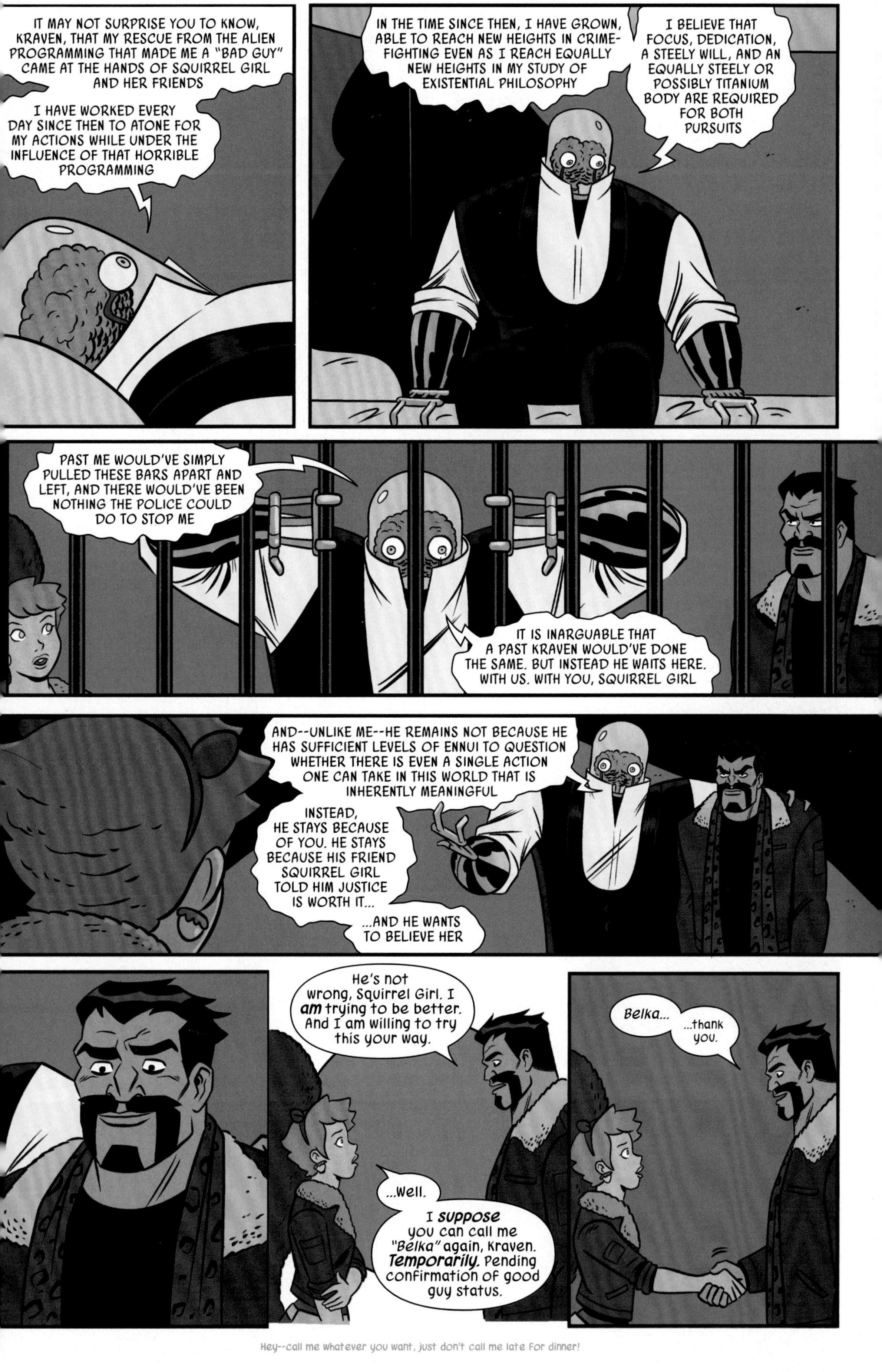
IT MAY NOT SURPRISE YOU TO KNOW, KRAVEN, THAT MY RESCUE FROM THE ALIEN PROGRAMMING THAT MADE ME A "BAD GUY" CAME AT THE HANDS OF SQUIRREL GIRL AND HER FRIENDS
I HAVE WORKED EVERY DAY SINCE THEN TO ATONE FOR MY ACTIONS WHILE UNDER THE INFLUENCE OF THAT HORRIBLE PROGRAMMING
IN THE TIME SINCE THEN, I HAVE GROWN, ABLE TO REACH NEW HEIGHTS IN CRIME-FIGHTING EVEN AS I REACH EQUALLY NEW HEIGHTS IN MY STUDY OF EXISTENTIAL PHILOSOPHY
I BELIEVE THAT FOCUS, DEDICATION, A STEELY WILL, AND AN EQUALLY STEELY OR POSSIBLY TITANIUM BODY ARE REQUIRED FOR BOTH PURSUITS
PAST ME WOULD'VE SIMPLY PULLED THESE BARS APART AND LEFT, AND THERE WOULD'VE BEEN NOTHING THE POLICE COULD DO TO STOP ME
IT IS INARGUABLE THAT A PAST KRAVEN WOULD'VE DONE THE SAME. BUT INSTEAD HE WAITS HERE. WITH US. WITH YOU, SQUIRREL GIRL
AND--UNLIKE ME--HE REMAINS NOT BECAUSE HE HAS SUFFICIENT LEVELS OF ENNUI TO QUESTION WHETHER THERE IS EVEN A SINGLE ACTION ONE CAN TAKE IN THIS WORLD THAT IS INHERENTLY MEANINGFUL
INSTEAD, HE STAYS BECAUSE OF YOU. HE STAYS BECAUSE HIS FRIEND SQUIRREL GIRL TOLD HIM JUSTICE IS WORTH IT...
...AND HE WANTS TO BELIEVE HER
He's not wrong, Squirrel Girl. I **am** trying to be better. And I am willing to try this your way.
...Well.
I **suppose** you can call me "Belka" again, Kraven. **Temporarily.** Pending confirmation of good guy status.
Belka...
...thank you.

Hey--call me whatever you want, just don't call me late for dinner!

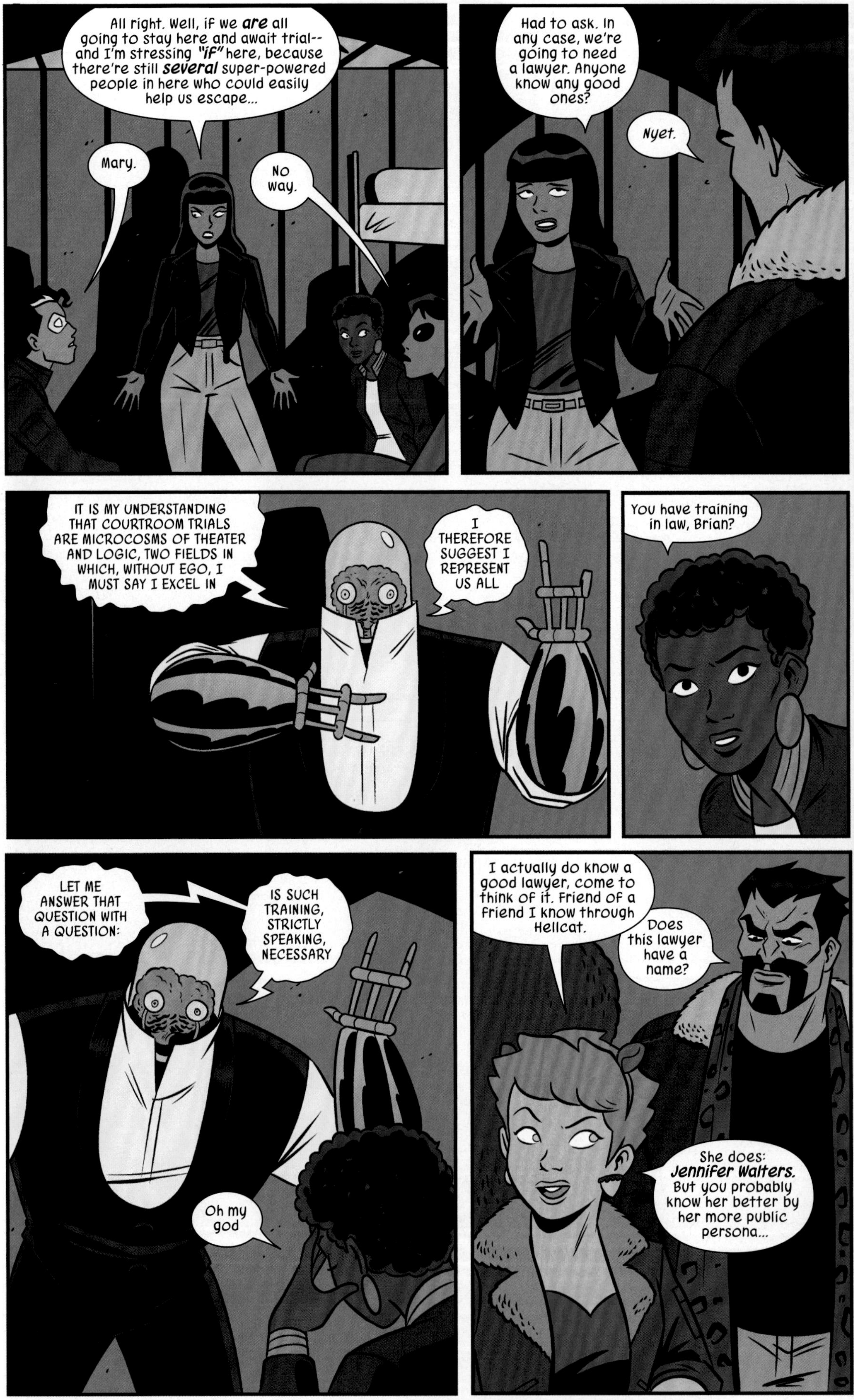

All right. Well, if we **are** all going to stay here and await trial--and I'm stressing *"if"* here, because there're still **several** super-powered people in here who could easily help us escape...
Mary.
No way.
Had to ask. In any case, we're going to need a lawyer. Anyone know any good ones?
Nyet.
IT IS MY UNDERSTANDING THAT COURTROOM TRIALS ARE MICROCOSMS OF THEATER AND LOGIC, TWO FIELDS IN WHICH, WITHOUT EGO, I MUST SAY I EXCEL IN
I THEREFORE SUGGEST I REPRESENT US ALL
You have training in law, Brian?
LET ME ANSWER THAT QUESTION WITH A QUESTION:
IS SUCH TRAINING, STRICTLY SPEAKING, NECESSARY
Oh my god
I actually do know a good lawyer, come to think of it. Friend of a friend I know through Hellcat.
Does this lawyer have a name?
She does: **Jennifer Walters.** But you probably know her better by her more public persona...

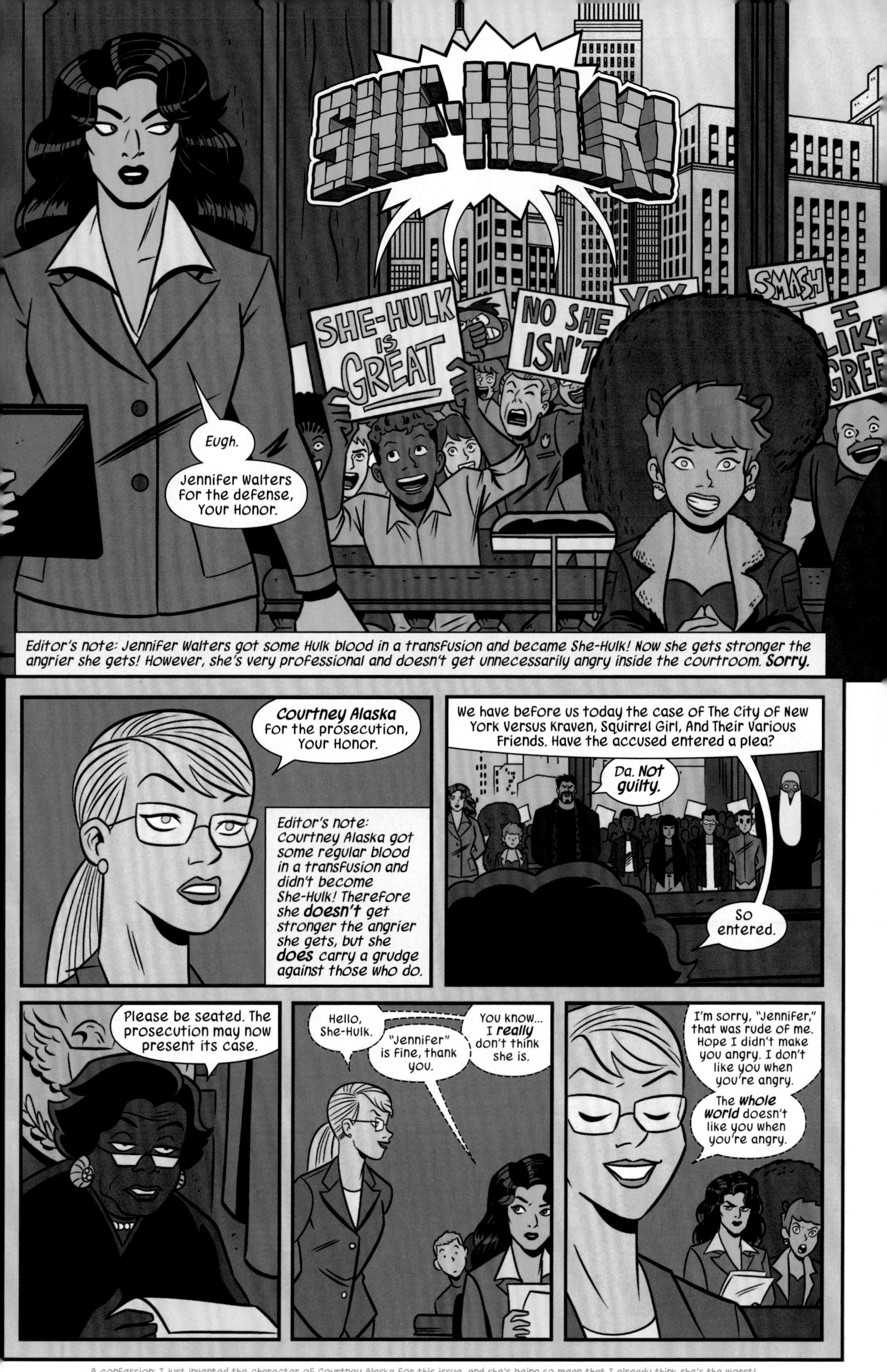
SHE-HULK!
SHE-HULK IS GREAT
NO SHE ISN'T
YAY
SMASH
I LIKE GREE
Eugh.
Jennifer Walters for the defense, Your Honor.
Editor's note: Jennifer Walters got some Hulk blood in a transfusion and became She-Hulk! Now she gets stronger the angrier she gets! However, she's very professional and doesn't get unnecessarily angry inside the courtroom. Sorry.
Courtney Alaska for the prosecution, Your Honor.
Editor's note: Courtney Alaska got some regular blood in a transfusion and didn't become She-Hulk! Therefore she doesn't get stronger the angrier she gets, but she does carry a grudge against those who do.
We have before us today the case of The City of New York Versus Kraven, Squirrel Girl, And Their Various Friends. Have the accused entered a plea?
Da. Not guilty.
So entered.
Please be seated. The prosecution may now present its case.
Hello, She-Hulk.
"Jennifer" is fine, thank you.
You know... I really don't think she is.
I'm sorry, "Jennifer," that was rude of me. Hope I didn't make you angry. I don't like you when you're angry.
The whole world doesn't like you when you're angry.

A confession: I just invented the character of Courtney Alaska for this issue, and she's being so mean that I already think she's the worst! Why you gotta be so mean, Courtney Alaska? Also: if you are going to just be a mean bully, then why did I make your name *so awesome??*

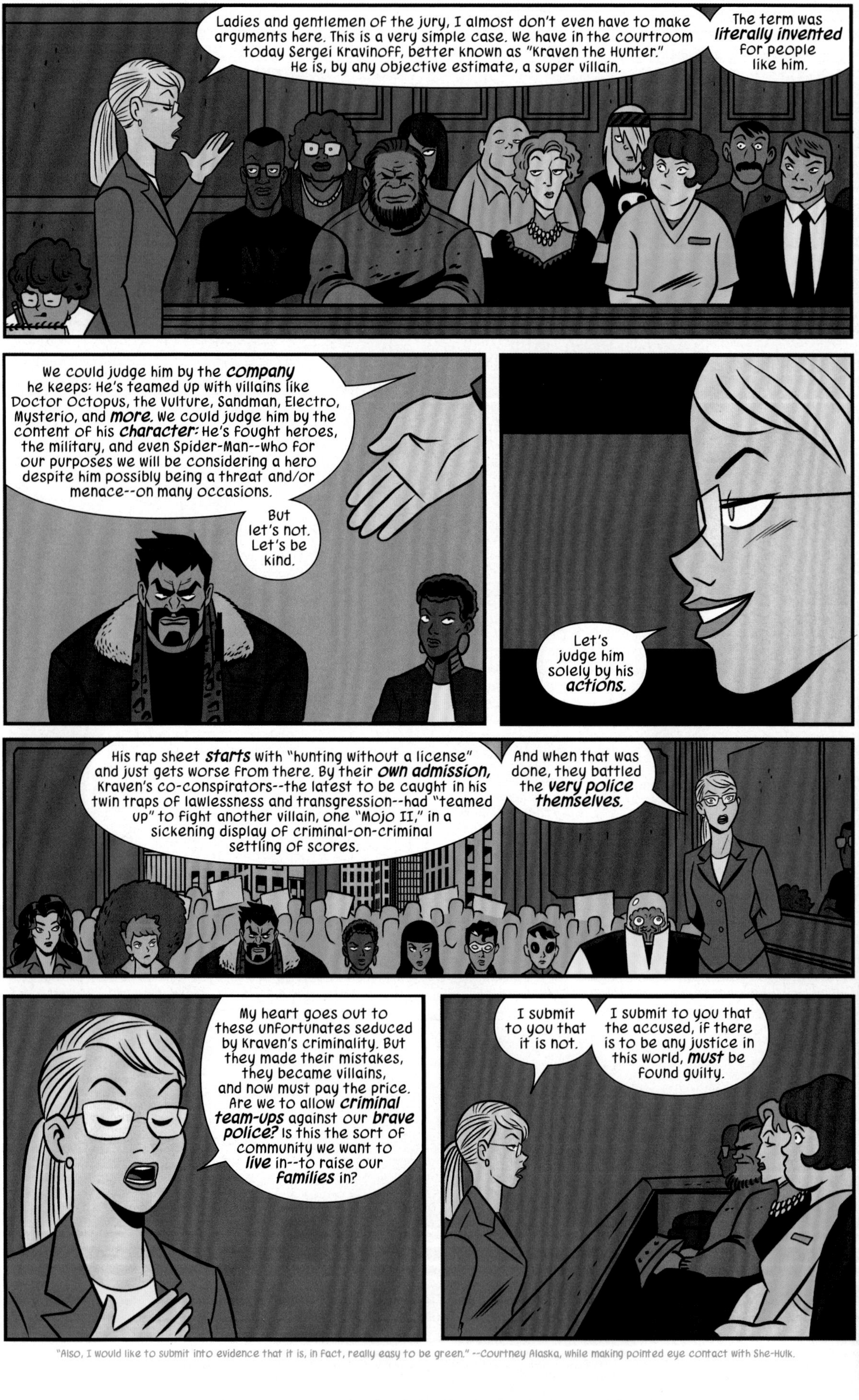
Ladies and gentlemen of the jury, I almost don't even have to make arguments here. This is a very simple case. We have in the courtroom today Sergei Kravinoff, better known as "Kraven the Hunter." He is, by any objective estimate, a super villain.
The term was literally invented for people like him.
We could judge him by the company he keeps: He's teamed up with villains like Doctor Octopus, the Vulture, Sandman, Electro, Mysterio, and more. We could judge him by the content of his character: He's fought heroes, the military, and even Spider-Man--who for our purposes we will be considering a hero despite him possibly being a threat and/or menace--on many occasions.
But let's not. Let's be kind.
Let's judge him solely by his actions.
His rap sheet starts with "hunting without a license" and just gets worse from there. By their own admission, Kraven's co-conspirators--the latest to be caught in his twin traps of lawlessness and transgression--had "teamed up" to fight another villain, one "Mojo II," in a sickening display of criminal-on-criminal settling of scores.
And when that was done, they battled the very police themselves.
My heart goes out to these unfortunates seduced by Kraven's criminality. But they made their mistakes, they became villains, and now must pay the price. Are we to allow criminal team-ups against our brave police? Is this the sort of community we want to live in--to raise our families in?
I submit to you that it is not.
I submit to you that the accused, if there is to be any justice in this world, must be found guilty.

"Also, I would like to submit into evidence that it is, in fact, really easy to be green." --Courtney Alaska, while making pointed eye contact with She-Hulk.

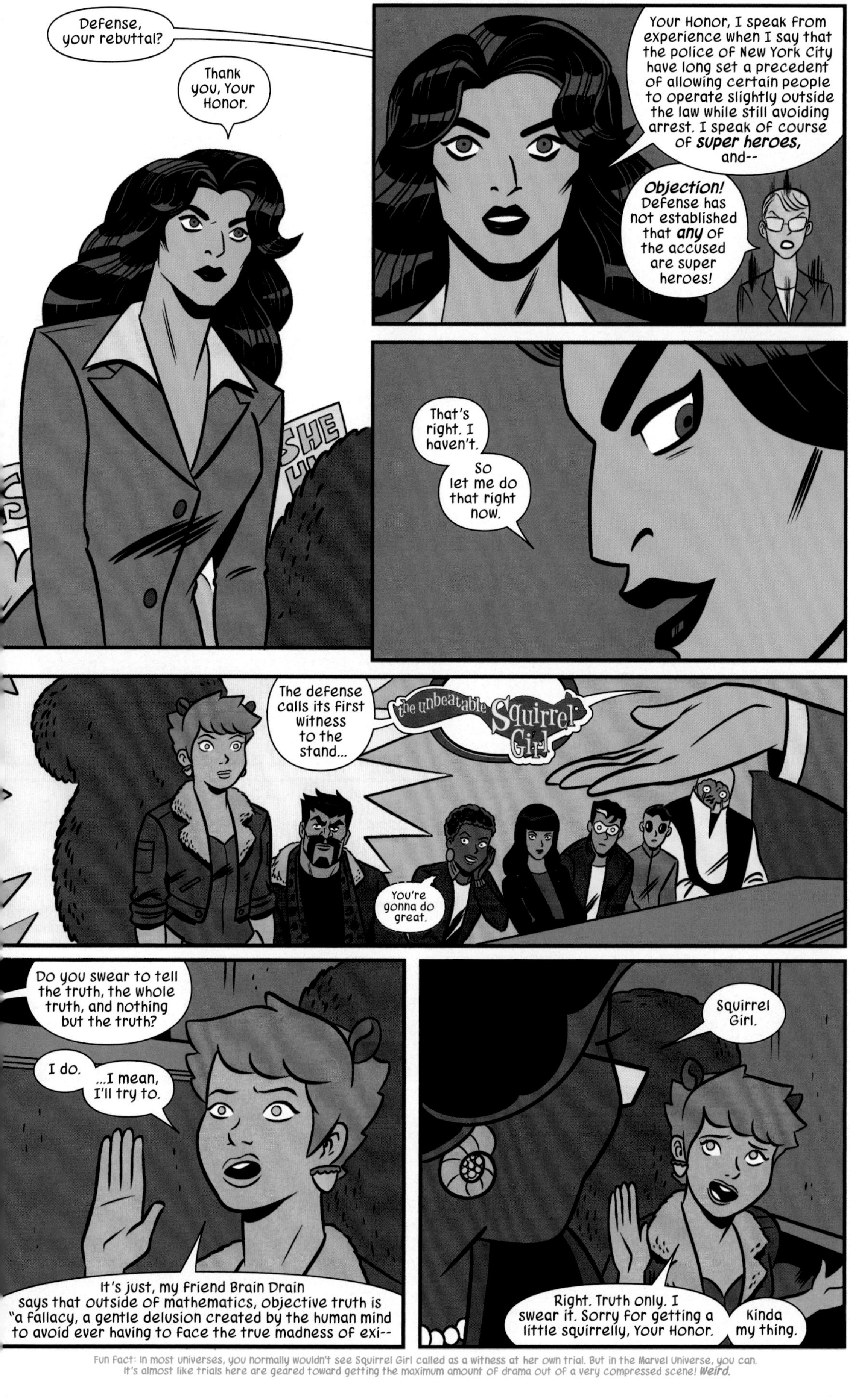
Defense, your rebuttal?
Thank you, Your Honor.
Your Honor, I speak from experience when I say that the police of New York City have long set a precedent of allowing certain people to operate slightly outside the law while still avoiding arrest. I speak of course of **super heroes,** and--
Objection! Defense has not established that ***any*** of the accused are super heroes!
That's right. I haven't.
So let me do that right now.
The defense calls its first witness to the stand...
the unbeatable Squirrel Girl
You're gonna do great.
Do you swear to tell the truth, the whole truth, and nothing but the truth?
I do.
...I mean, I'll try to.
It's just, my friend Brain Drain says that outside of mathematics, objective truth is "a fallacy, a gentle delusion created by the human mind to avoid ever having to face the true madness of exi--
Squirrel Girl.
Right. Truth only. I swear it. Sorry for getting a little squirrelly, Your Honor.
Kinda my thing.

Fun Fact: In most universes, you normally wouldn't see Squirrel Girl called as a witness at her own trial. But in the Marvel Universe, you can. It's almost like trials here are geared toward getting the maximum amount of drama out of a very compressed scene! ***Weird.***

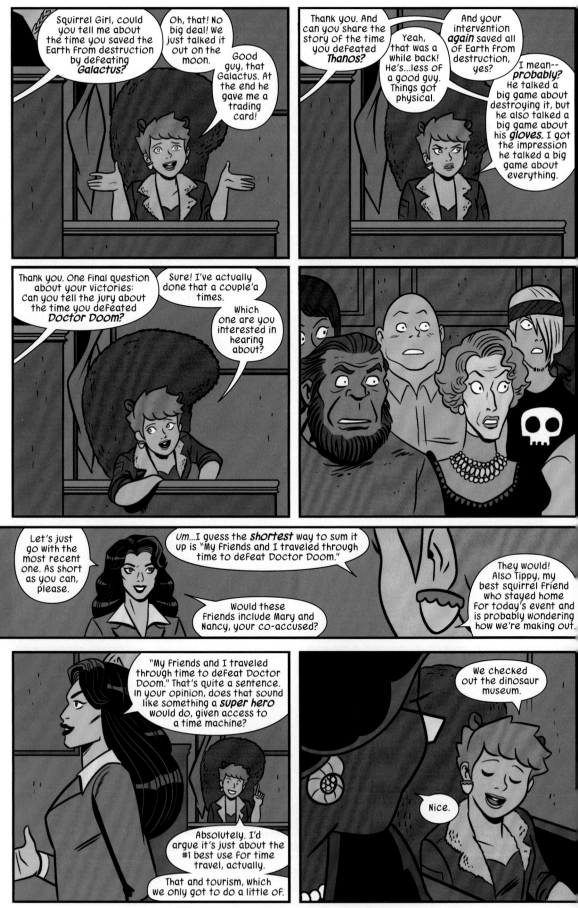

Squirrel Girl, could you tell me about the time you saved the Earth from destruction by defeating *Galactus*?

Oh, that! No big deal! We just talked it out on the moon.

Good guy, that Galactus. At the end he gave me a trading card!

Thank you. And can you share the story of the time you defeated *Thanos*?

Yeah, that was a while back! He's...less of a good guy. Things got physical.

And your intervention *again* saved all of Earth from destruction, yes?

I mean-- *probably?* He talked a big game about destroying it, but he also talked a big game about his *gloves.* I got the impression he talked a big game about everything.

Thank you. One final question about your victories: Can you tell the jury about the time you defeated *Doctor Doom?*

Sure! I've actually done that a couple'a times.

Which one are you interested in hearing about?

Let's just go with the most recent one. As short as you can, please.

Um...I guess the *shortest* way to sum it up is "My friends and I traveled through time to defeat Doctor Doom."

Would these friends include Mary and Nancy, your co-accused?

They would! Also Tippy, my best squirrel friend who stayed home for today's event and is probably wondering how we're making out.

"My friends and I traveled through time to defeat Doctor Doom." That's quite a sentence. In your opinion, does that sound like something a *super hero* would do, given access to a time machine?

Absolutely. I'd argue it's just about the #1 best use for time travel, actually.

That and tourism, which we only got to do a little of.

We checked out the dinosaur museum.

Nice.

Here's an *objective truth* for you: Given even the smallest opportunity, I will never not dunk on Thanos. Hah! What a tool!

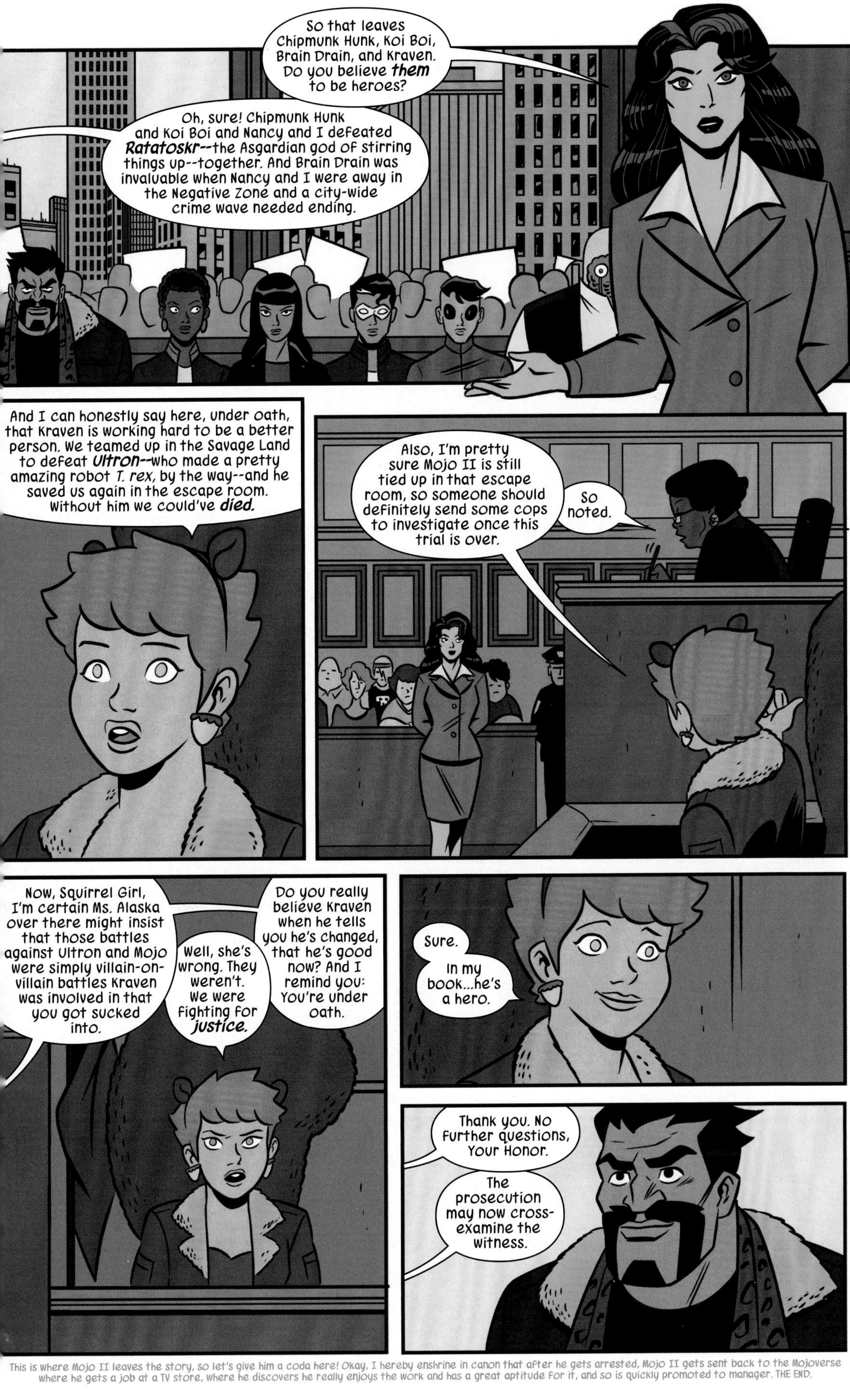
So that leaves Chipmunk Hunk, Koi Boi, Brain Drain, and Kraven. Do you believe *them* to be heroes?
Oh, sure! Chipmunk Hunk and Koi Boi and Nancy and I defeated *Ratatoskr*--the Asgardian god of stirring things up--together. And Brain Drain was invaluable when Nancy and I were away in the Negative Zone and a city-wide crime wave needed ending.
And I can honestly say here, under oath, that Kraven is working hard to be a better person. We teamed up in the Savage Land to defeat *Ultron*--who made a pretty amazing robot *T. rex*, by the way--and he saved us again in the escape room. Without him we could've *died.*
Also, I'm pretty sure Mojo II is still tied up in that escape room, so someone should definitely send some cops to investigate once this trial is over.
So noted.
Now, Squirrel Girl, I'm certain Ms. Alaska over there might insist that those battles against Ultron and Mojo were simply villain-on-villain battles Kraven was involved in that you got sucked into.
Well, she's wrong. They weren't. We were fighting for *justice.*
Do you really believe Kraven when he tells you he's changed, that he's good now? And I remind you: You're under oath.
Sure.
In my book...he's a hero.
Thank you. No further questions, Your Honor.
The prosecution may now cross-examine the witness.

This is where Mojo II leaves the story, so let's give him a coda here! Okay, I hereby enshrine in canon that after he gets arrested, Mojo II gets sent back to the Mojoverse where he gets a job at a TV store, where he discovers he really enjoys the work and has a great aptitude for it, and so is quickly promoted to manager. THE END.

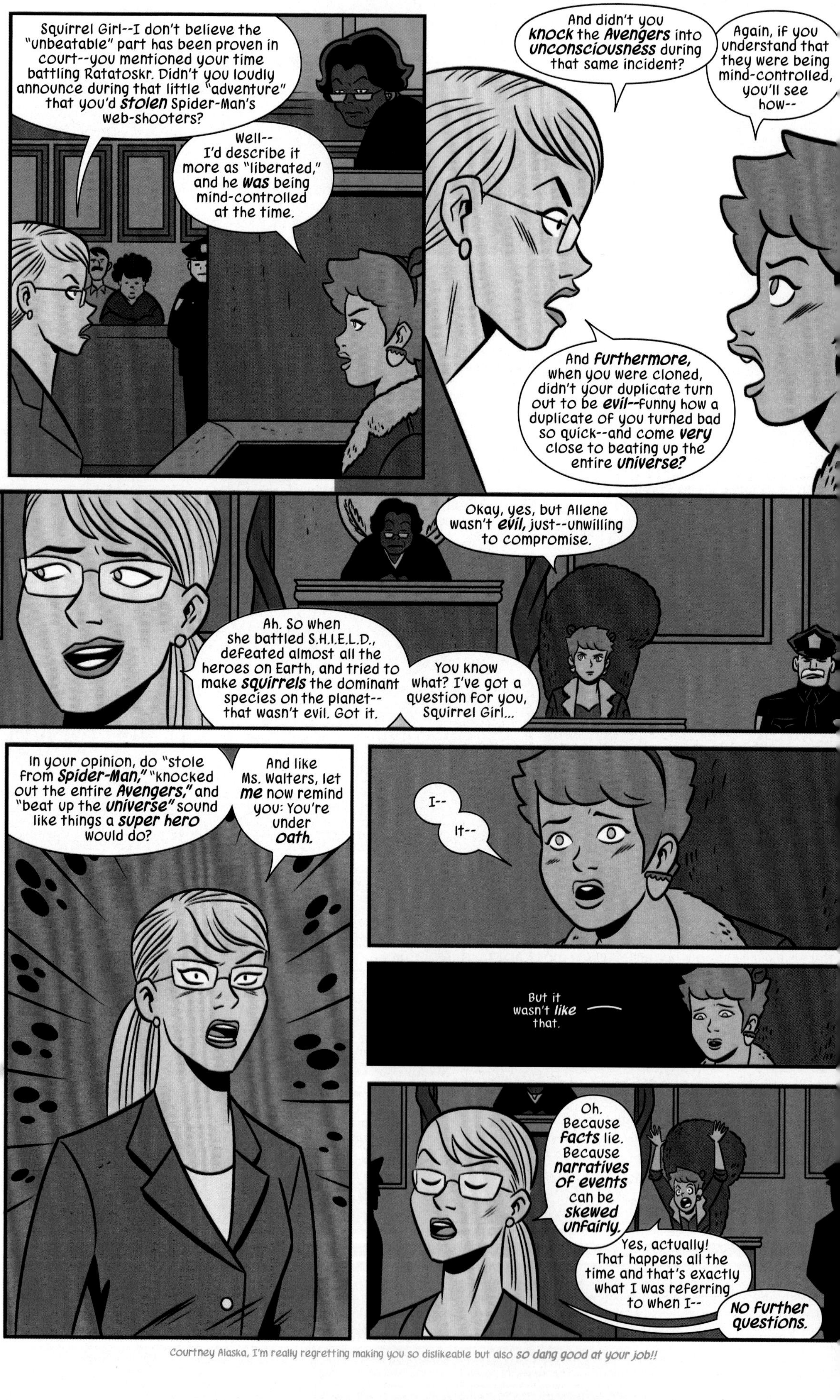
Squirrel Girl--I don't believe the "unbeatable" part has been proven in court--you mentioned your time battling Ratatoskr. Didn't you loudly announce during that little "adventure" that you'd stolen Spider-Man's web-shooters?
Well-- I'd describe it more as "liberated," and he was being mind-controlled at the time.
And didn't you knock the Avengers into unconsciousness during that same incident?
Again, if you understand that they were being mind-controlled, you'll see how--
And furthermore, when you were cloned, didn't your duplicate turn out to be evil--funny how a duplicate of you turned bad so quick--and come very close to beating up the entire universe?
Okay, yes, but Allene wasn't evil, just--unwilling to compromise.
Ah. So when she battled S.H.I.E.L.D., defeated almost all the heroes on Earth, and tried to make squirrels the dominant species on the planet--that wasn't evil. Got it.
You know what? I've got a question for you, Squirrel Girl...
In your opinion, do "stole from Spider-Man," "knocked out the entire Avengers," and "beat up the universe" sound like things a super hero would do?
And like Ms. Walters, let me now remind you: You're under oath.
I--
It--
But it wasn't like that.
Oh. Because facts lie. Because narratives of events can be skewed unfairly.
Yes, actually! That happens all the time and that's exactly what I was referring to when I--
No further questions.

Courtney Alaska, I'm really regretting making you so dislikeable but also *so dang good at your job!!*

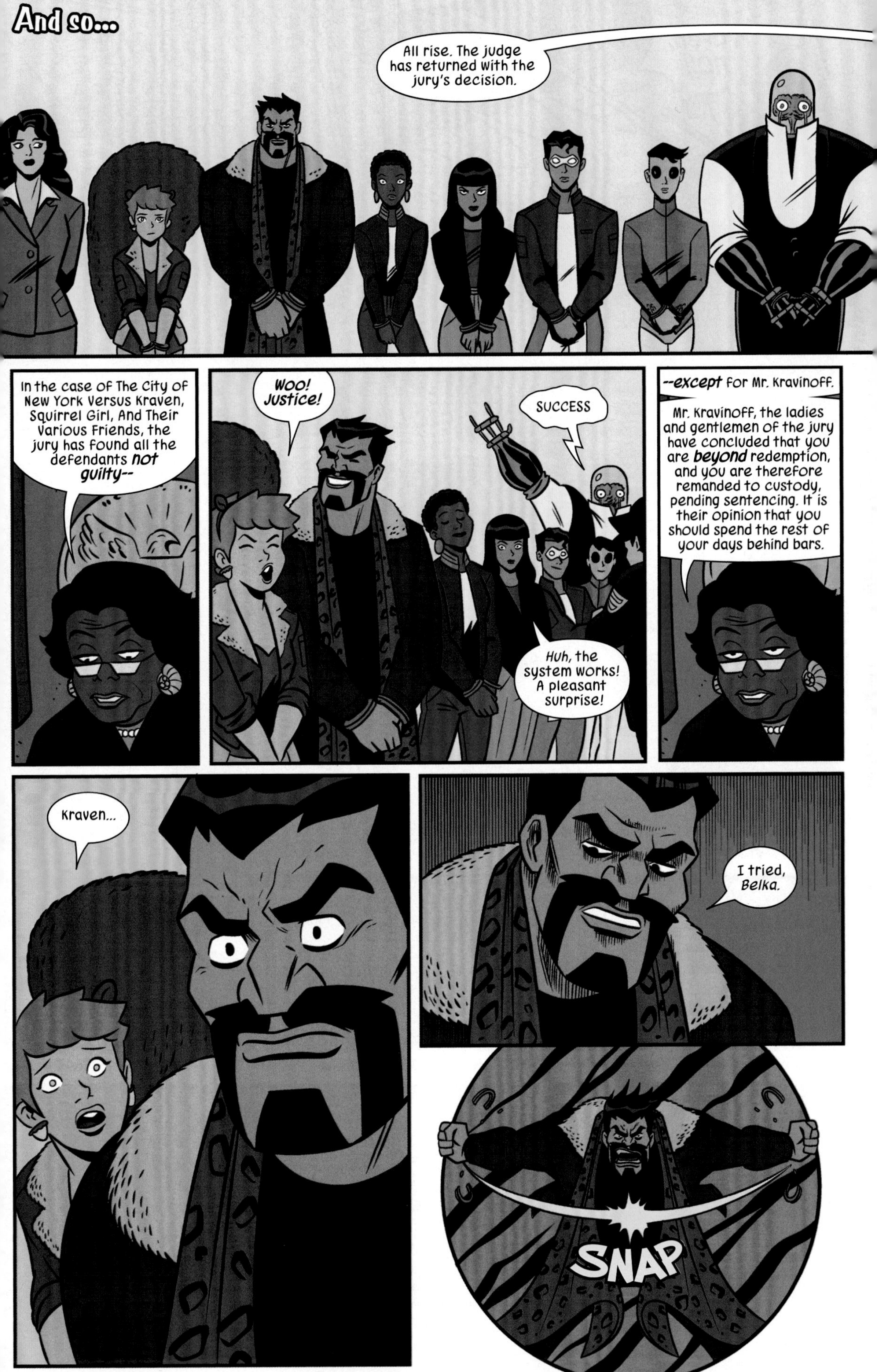
And so...
All rise. The judge has returned with the jury's decision.
In the case of The City of New York Versus Kraven, Squirrel Girl, And Their Various Friends, the jury has found all the defendants *not guilty*--
Woo! Justice!
SUCCESS
Huh, the system works! A pleasant surprise!
--*except* for Mr. Kravinoff.
Mr. Kravinoff, the ladies and gentlemen of the jury have concluded that you are *beyond* redemption, and you are therefore remanded to custody, pending sentencing. It is their opinion that you should spend the rest of your days behind bars.
Kraven...
I tried, Belka.
SNAP

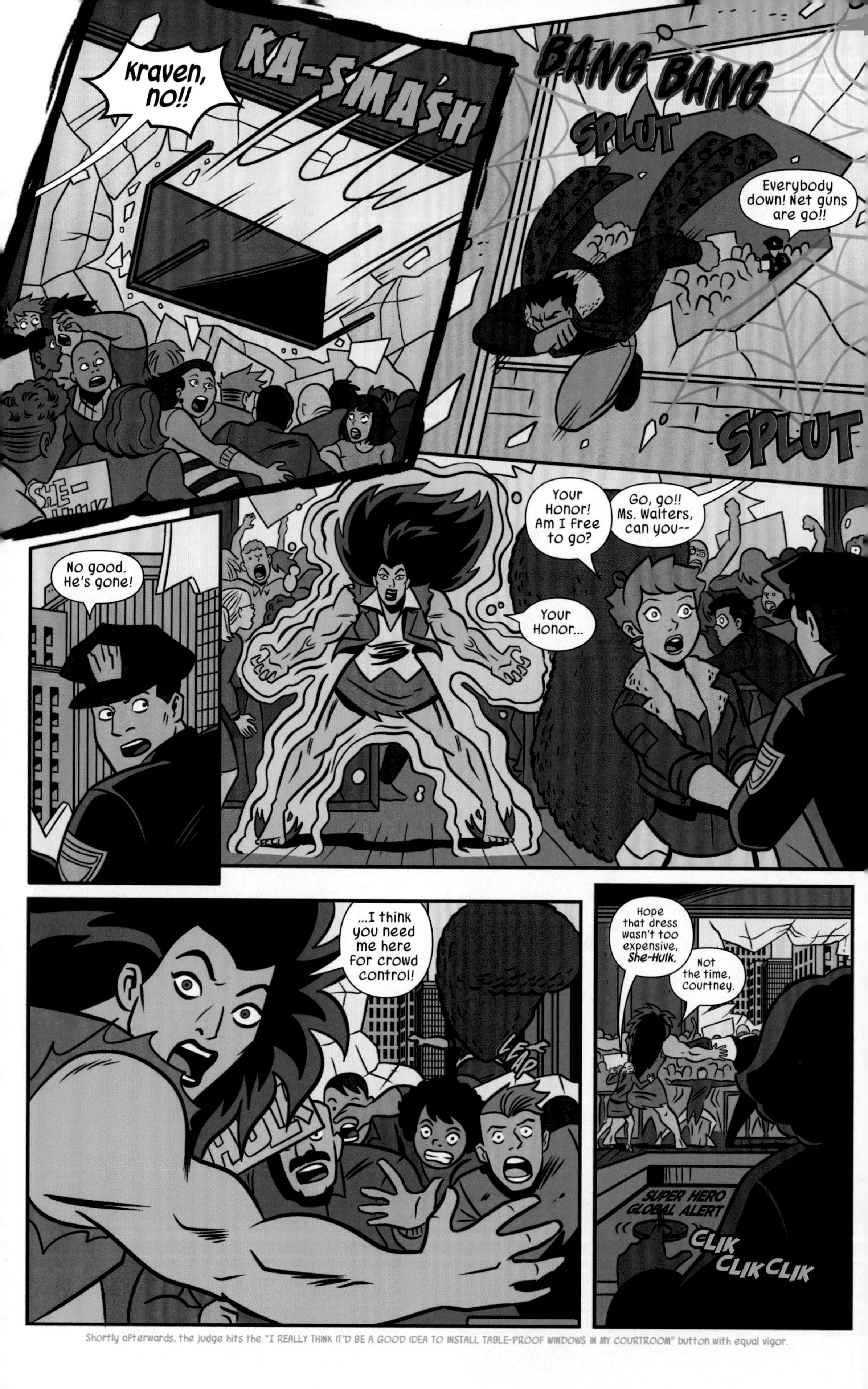
Kraven, no!!
KA-SMASH
SHE-HULK
BANG BANG
SPLUT
Everybody down! Net guns are go!!
SPLUT
No good. He's gone!
Your Honor...
Your Honor! Am I free to go?
Go, go!! Ms. Walters, can you--
...I think you need me here for crowd control!
LEAP
Hope that dress wasn't too expensive, She-Hulk.
Not the time, Courtney.
SUPER HERO GLOBAL ALERT
CLIK CLIK CLIK

Shortly afterwards, the judge hits the "I REALLY THINK IT'D BE A GOOD IDEA TO INSTALL TABLE-PROOF WINDOWS IN MY COURTROOM" button with equal vigor.

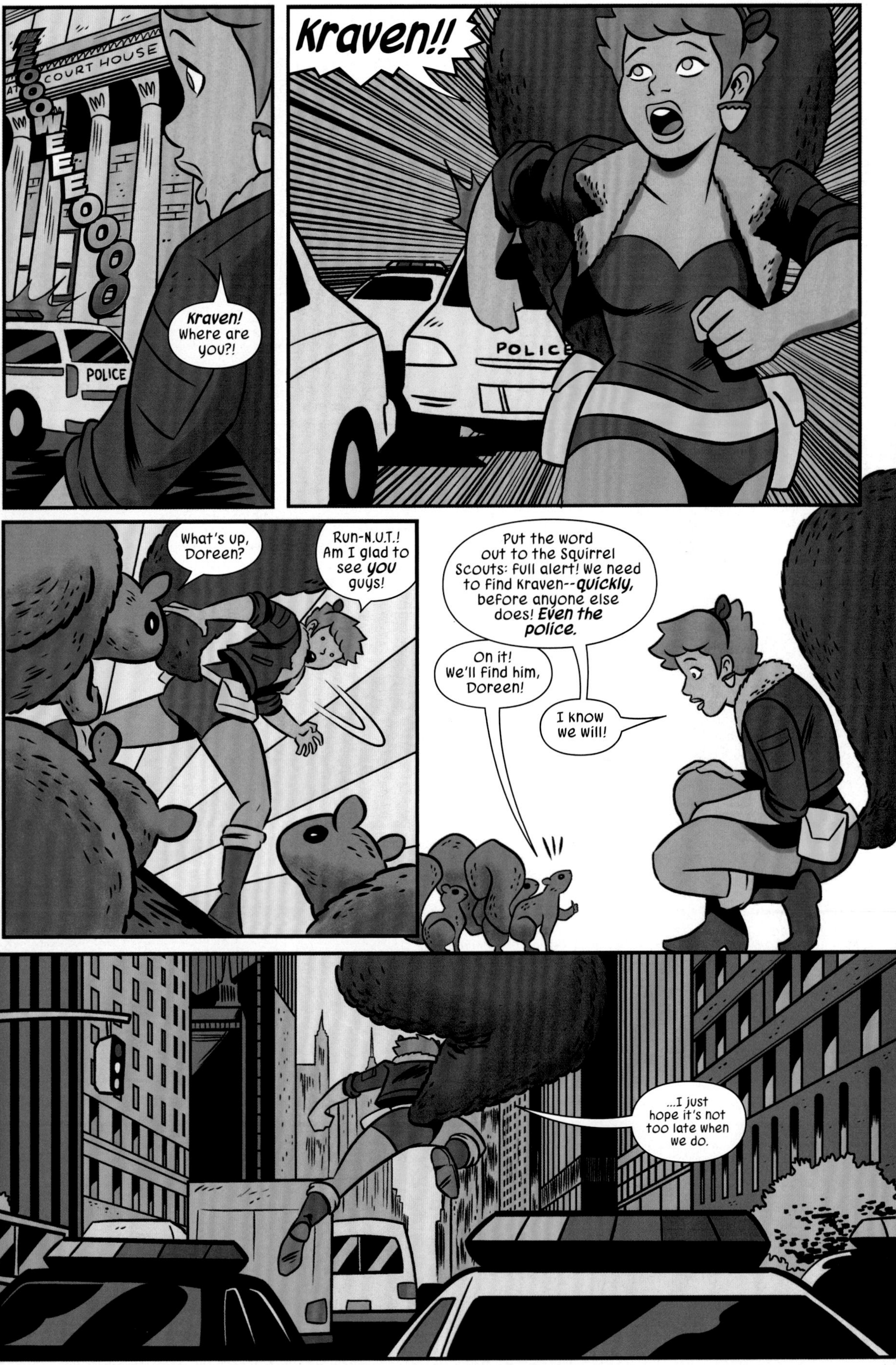
WEEOOOWEEEOOOOO
AT COURT HOUSE
POLICE
Kraven! Where are you?!
Kraven!!
POLICE
What's up, Doreen?
RUN-N.U.T.! Am I glad to see *you* guys!
Put the word out to the Squirrel Scouts: full alert! We need to find Kraven--*quickly,* before anyone else does! *Even the police.*
On it! We'll find him, Doreen!
I know we will!
...I just hope it's not too late when we do.

In case you're wondering, yes, Run-N.U.T. *has* dropped some killer tracks. You may be wondering how three squirrels manage to sneak into a studio to get albums recorded without being noticed, and they will be the first to admit: it's tricky.

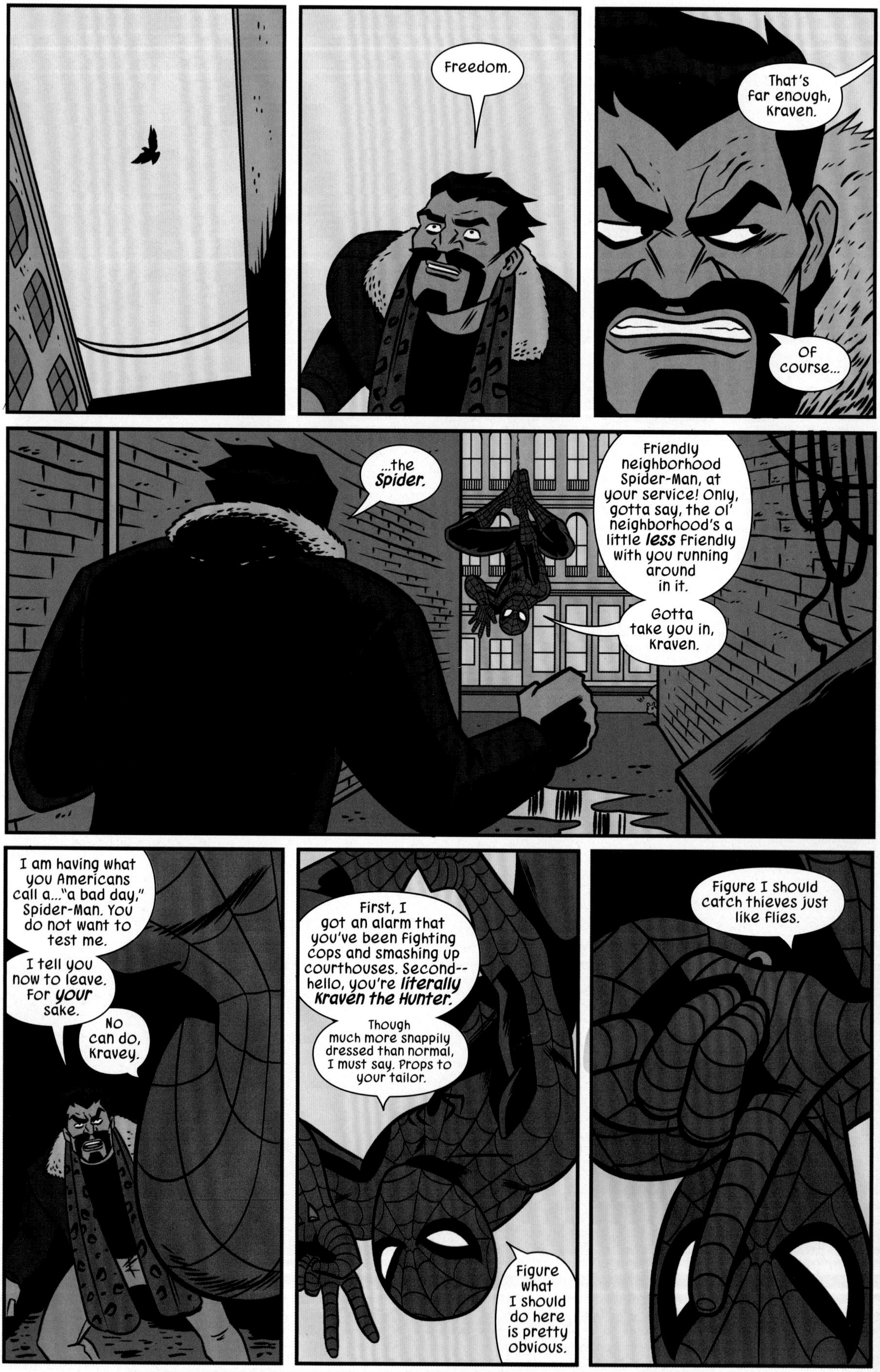
Freedom.
That's far enough, Kraven.
Of course...
...the Spider.
Friendly neighborhood Spider-Man, at your service! Only, gotta say, the ol' neighborhood's a little less friendly with you running around in it.
Gotta take you in, Kraven.
I am having what you Americans call a..."a bad day," Spider-Man. You do not want to test me.
I tell you now to leave. For your sake.
No can do, Kravey.
First, I got an alarm that you've been fighting cops and smashing up courthouses. Second--hello, you're literally Kraven the Hunter.
Though much more snappily dressed than normal, I must say. Props to your tailor.
Figure what I should do here is pretty obvious.
Figure I should catch thieves just like flies.

SPIDER-MAN, HOW MANY TIMES HAVE YOU USED THAT LINE BEFORE? HOW MANY TIMES HAVE YOU USED THAT LINE TODAY ALONE, SPIDER-MAN.

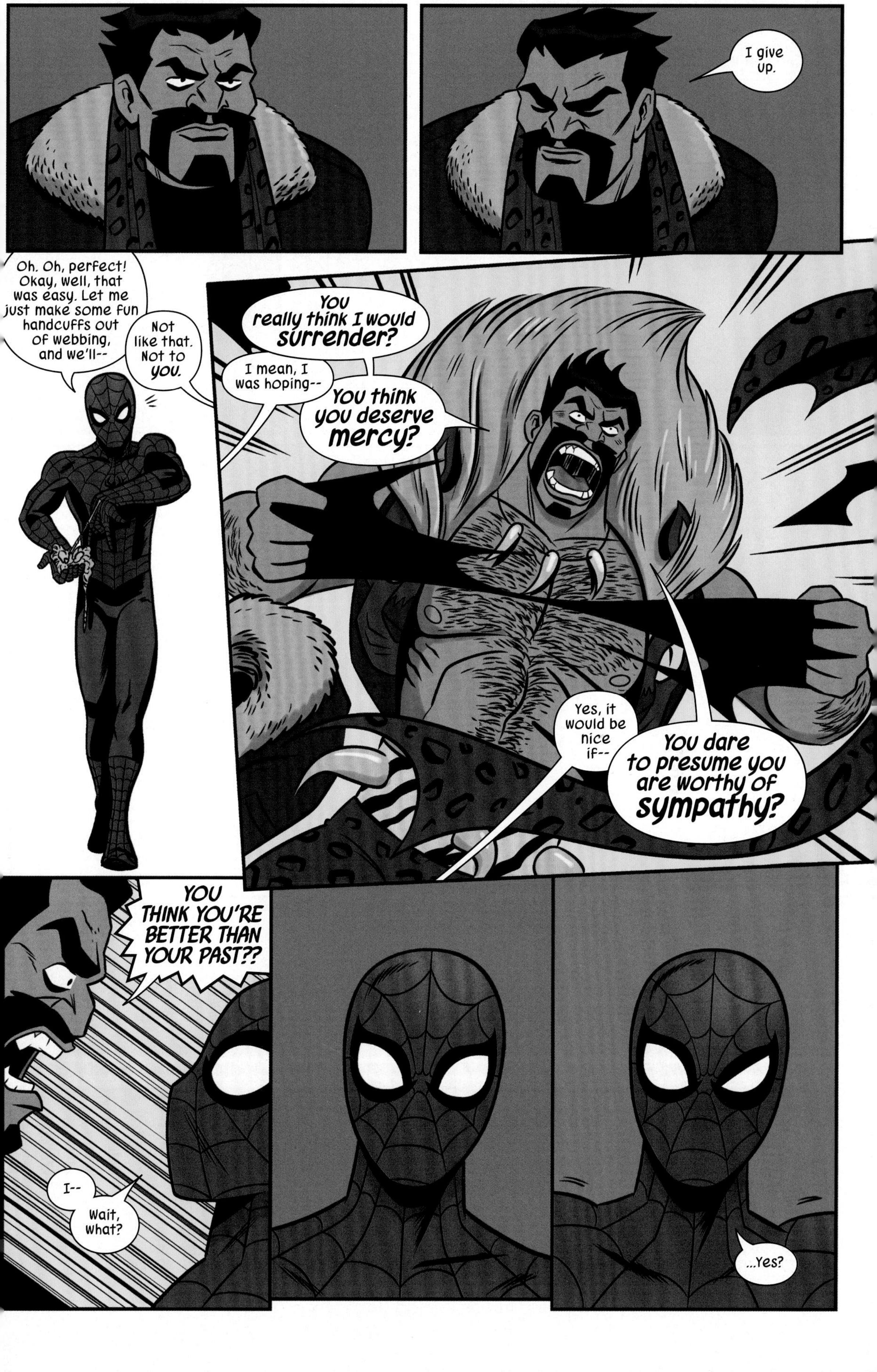
I give up.
Oh. Oh, perfect! Okay, well, that was easy. Let me just make some fun handcuffs out of webbing, and we'll--
Not like that. Not to you.
You really think I would surrender?
I mean, I was hoping--
You think you deserve mercy?
Yes, it would be nice if--
You dare to presume you are worthy of sympathy?
YOU THINK YOU'RE BETTER THAN YOUR PAST??
I--
Wait, what?
...Yes?

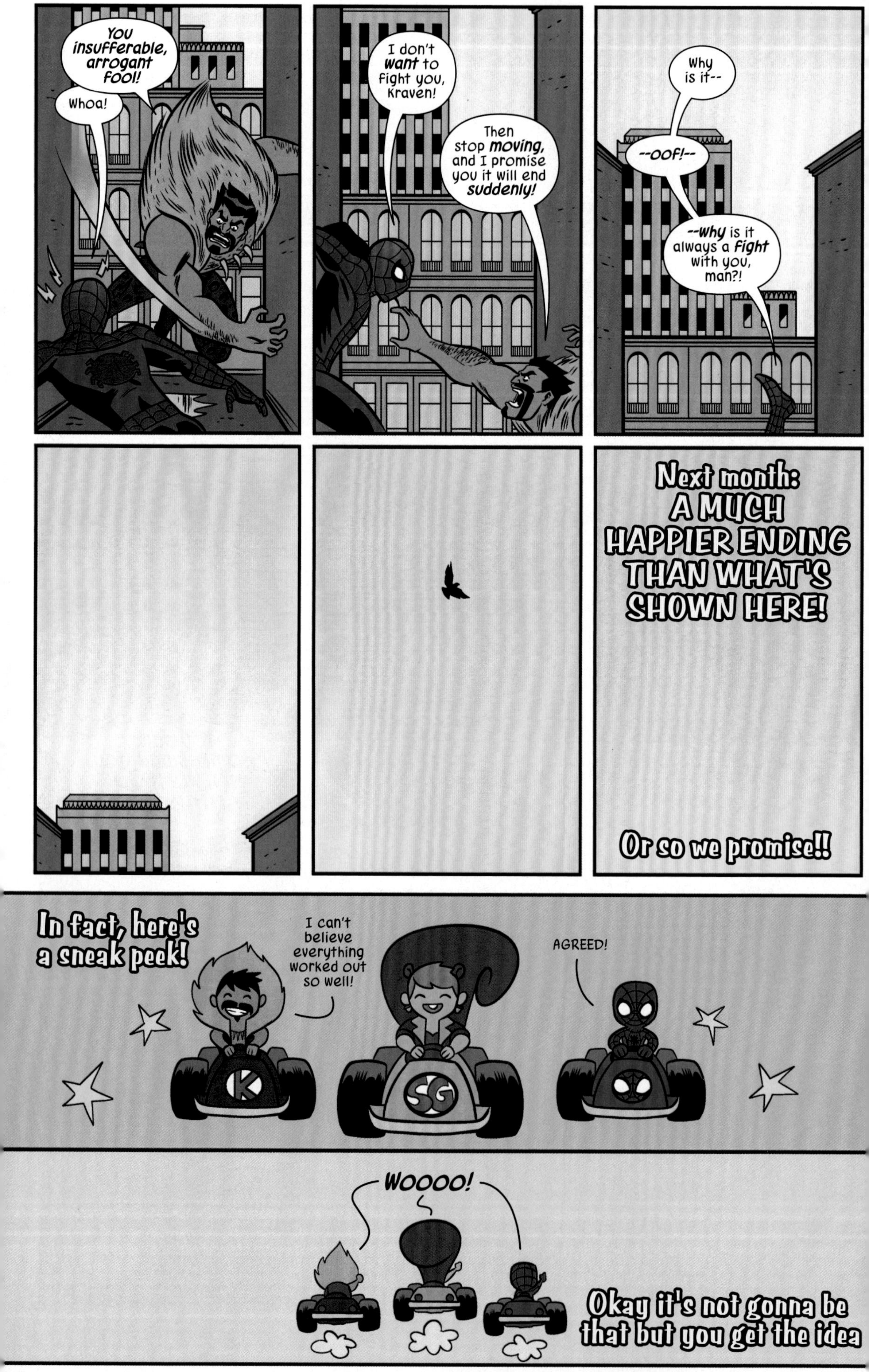
You insufferable, arrogant fool!
Whoa!
I don't want to fight you, Kraven!
Then stop moving, and I promise you it will end suddenly!
Why is it--
--OOF!--
--why is it always a fight with you, man?!
Next month: A MUCH HAPPIER ENDING THAN WHAT'S SHOWN HERE!
Or so we promise!!
In fact, here's a sneak peek!
I can't believe everything worked out so well!
AGREED!
WOOOO!
Okay it's not gonna be that but you get the idea

Letters From Nuts

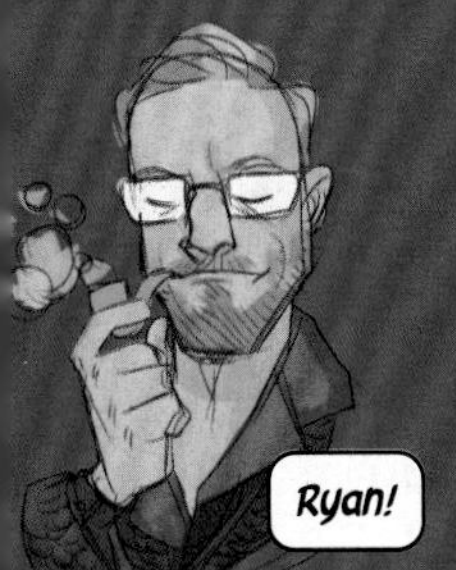
Ryan!

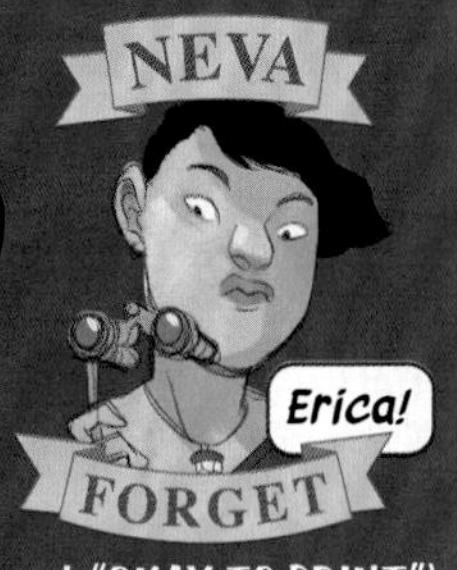
NEVA
Erica!
FORGET

Send letters to mheroes@marvel.com or 135 W 50th St, 7th Floor, New York, NY 10020 (Please mark "OKAY TO PRINT")

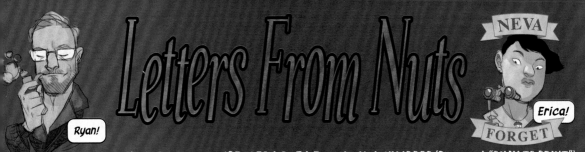

If comics are meant to awaken the imagination, then UNBEATABLE SQUIRREL GIRL #31 meets that challenge. The storyline is epic in scope. Humor pops up everywhere. Tenderness surfaces where it counts.

Erica's departure from the book was especially moving, as it closed an edition that dealt with a lifetime of work and accomplishment.

If there were ever a single comic book issue that lives up to its brand name, it's UNBEATABLE SQUIRREL GIRL #31.

Ivan Borodin
Los Angeles

RYAN: Ivan, thank you so much--that's exactly what we were shooting for, so it's great to hear it hit the mark for you. I have to confess that the theme of dealing with a lifetime of work and accomplishment wasn't something I had in mind when I wrote it, but it's funny how things surface when you're writing! I'm so glad we could see Erica out on a story that worked in that way.

Hello Ryan and Erica,

I saw Ciro's letter a while ago about the (really cool) Squirrel Girl figurine they made, and I have found an actual (official) Squirrel Girl figurine (It's a Funko Pop though)! She even comes with Tippy Toe!

I'm not sure if this was what you (Ryan) were looking for, but I'm so excited for you and other Squirrel Scouts to see it because this is like the first official Squirrel Girl thing I've personally seen! I also have some questions about Doreen.

1. Does she still have her Avengers bed sheets? (from *Squirrel Meets World)*

2. What is her favorite (non-nut) food?

3. How does she feel about pineapple on pizza?

Thanks for reading!
Cora (one of the biggest squirrel girl fans out there!)

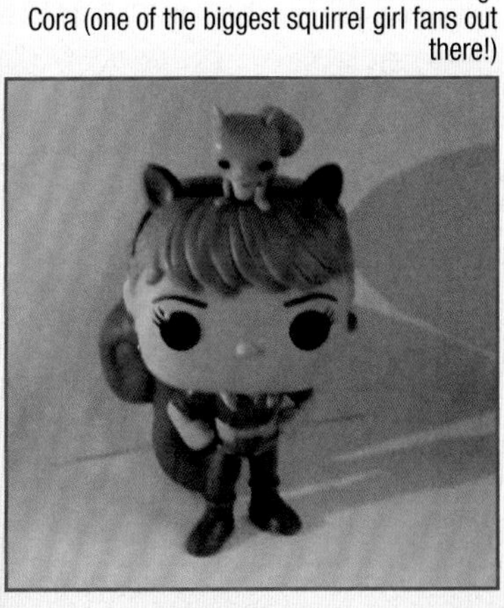

RYAN: Fun fact: That Squirrel Girl figure sits on my desk and watches me work every day alongside Tippy and a half-squirrel half-*T. rex* figure that a friend 3-D printed for me! I'm afraid I must now admit it: my desk is extremely awesome. To answer your questions:

1. She does! Well, they're not the SAME bed sheets, but she's cycled in new Avengers-branded merchandise over the years.

2. Recently she is big into that thing where you cook cauliflower with buffalo wing sauce to make crunchy vegetarian buffalo wings. In a startling coincidence, so am I.

3. This question is actually answered in the comics! Check out the brand new MARVEL RISING crossover--OUT NOW--and you'll find the answer to this question, as well as an entire adventure in which Squirrel Girl and Ms. Marvel meet for the first time, entirely unrelated to this question!!

Team Sciuridae,

I've been a Spidey fan for over 50 years and always thought Kraven was a great villain. And now, thanks to you guys, he's also a great hero. (And the owner of a sweet ride. Who knew?)

I would absolutely read Stone-Cold Kickin' It with Sergei Kravinoff. Ryan, get working on that, please.

I read a lot of comics each month and I've got to thank you for SQUIRREL GIRL. The adventures of Doreen and company make me smile more than any other book I get. (Which I guess isn't that hard to do since I read a lot of depressing stuff, but still...thanks! It's a great book! You guys rock! Take care, Erica!)

Make Mine Marvel!
Rob Shelor, P.M.M., F.F.F.
Roanoke, VA

RYAN: Hey, Rob--thank you! And as a guy who is Interested In Hearing What Kraven Is Up To, I'm super glad you got to read this issue in particular. I'm really into Street Clothes Kraven--that style! That confident, graceful choice in clothing! And now, along with Stone-Cold Kickin' It With Sergei Kravinoff, I would 100% like to see a Marvel Street Clothes Issue--like the old Swimsuit Issues, but full of fashion-forward civilian clothes. As the writer of comics, it's already done: "Everyone wears cool street clothes." There. Done. Marvel, make it happen, thanks in advance!

BOOM--Mystery Escape Room operator in Squirrel Girl. I proclaim this BOOM and Jim Lee art fit to print.

Nolan

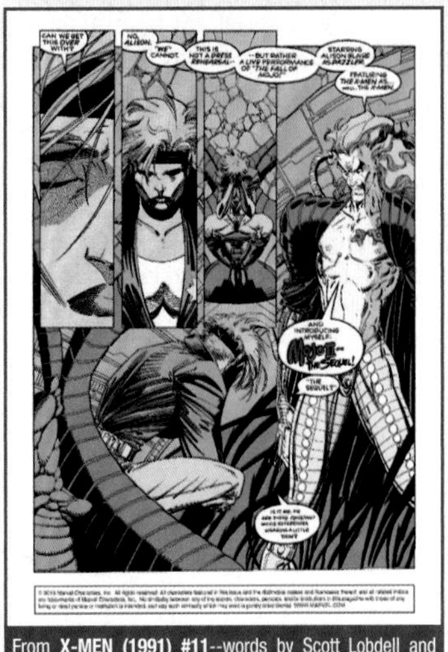
CAN WE GET THIS OVER WITH?
NO, ALISON.
"WE" CANNOT.
THIS IS NOT A DRESS REHEARSAL--
--BUT RATHER A LIVE PERFORMANCE OF "THE FALL OF MOJO!"
STARRING ALISON BLAIRE AS DAZZLER,
FEATURING THE X-MEN AS... WELL, THE X-MEN!
AND INTRODUCING MYSELF: MOJO II-- THE SEQUEL!
"THE SEQUEL?"

From **X-MEN (1991) #11**--words by Scott Lobdell and Jim Lee, and art by Jim Lee, Bob Wiacek, and Marie Javins.

RYAN: You think you're picking an obscure '90s character who hasn't been seen or heard from in almost 30 years, you wrap him in a mummy-style disguise, and STILL someone pieces together the clues and figures it out before the big reveal. Well done! I'm sincerely impressed, Nolan, and I hereby declare you "The #1 Fan of Mojo II: The Sequel"! This award comes with a sturdy handshake, should ever we meet. Enjoy!

Dear Ryan, Derek, Rico, Travis (and Erica!),

I was (and am) bummed that Erica will no longer be providing the interior art for UNBEATABLE SQUIRREL GIRL, but nearly suffered emotional whiplash from the exciting news that Derek Charm would be taking over! I love Ryan and Derek's work on *Jughead,* so I had high expectations for USG #32--and they were exceeded!

Derek's sense of action layout and cartooniness is somewhat similar to Erica's, such that with Rico's colors & Travis' lettering, the art transition was nearly seamless. So far, all I've heard is that Derek will providing art for this story arc, but I hope he will stay on the title permanently. C'mon, Marvel--Make Mine Derek!

As to a guess about the mystery villain... the facial hair outside the Mummy costume suggests the Mandarin, but that escape room has such a Murderworld vibe, so I'm gonna say this dastardly deathtrap is the brainchild of Arcade, cosplaying as the Mandarin, disguised as a mummy. Right or wrong, that's the most *fun* guess I can come up with.

With some recent Free Comic Book Day purchases, I now have a complete run of Erica's work on USG all ready to share with my daughter, who is expected to be born in June (and we're already acclimating her to

Ryan's bottom-of-the-page jokes while she's in utero). Thanks to all y'all for crafting such wonderful stories for me and my family.

Until Doreen Goes Paleo,
Craig E. Bacon
Irmo, SC

RYAN: Craig, this was an EXCELLENT guess, especially since at the earliest points in the story it was going to involve Arcade, until Mojo II reared his peak-'90s head. And the idea that the villain would be Arcade who is cosplaying as someone else for no particular reason--like he decided to pull off an evil scheme on his way to the local con--is pretty great.

Congratulations on the upcoming birth of your daughter, and I'm glad you're keeping her entertained in the womb! You'll still have to teach her spoken language, then written language, then the visual language of comics--but once she has all that, having a stack of comics at the end to read is going to make all that education TOTALLY worth it. Also, literacy has other uses, too. I GUESS.

Dear Erica and Ryan,

Just had to share the Mother's Day present my son made for me this year--my very own SQUIRREL GIRL minicomic, featuring Squirl [sic] Mom! Thanks so much for your comic, we're all big fans.

Margaret Gwyn
Victoria, BC

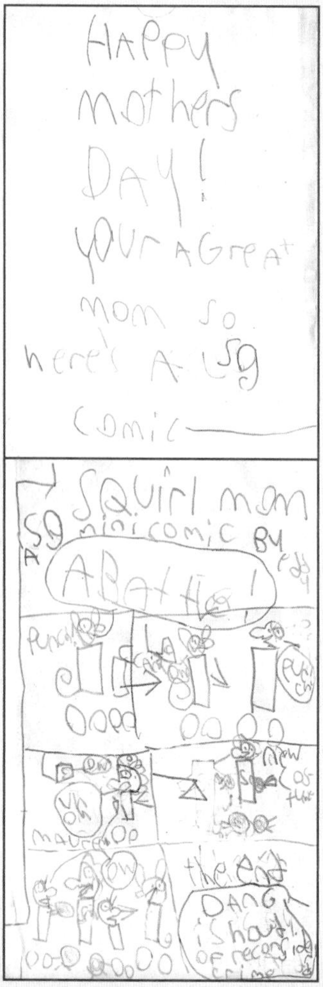

TRANSCRIPTION:

SQUIRL MOM
A SG minicomic by Eddy
"A Battle!" <spoken from off-panel>

Panel 1: <Squirrel Girl punches a bad guy.>
Squirrel Girl: "A Battle!"
Sound effect: Punch!

Panel 2: <A bad guy punches Squirrel Girl. A camera, labeled "Cam," watches the action from the top right corner.>
Bad Guy: "Punch!"
Squirrel Girl: "Ow"

Panel 3: <Maureen Green, labeled "Maureen," watches the battle from her camera.>
Squirrel Girl, from camera: "Ow"
Maureen: "Uh oh"

Panel 4: <Maureen is in a room with an empty hanger. She's changed into a costume with "SM" on the front.>
Sound effect: "New costume"

Panel 5: <Squirrel Mom and Squirrel Girl each punch the bad guy.>
Bad Guy: "Ow"

Panel 6:
The end
Bad Guy, off-panel: "Dang I should of reconsidered crime"

RYAN: Margaret, this is so great! We shared this with Erica, too, and she loved it as much as we did. It's got everything: conflict, team-ups and the origin of a new hero, Squirrel Mom. I love it. You've got a budding cartoonist in your house!

Did you miss out on Squirrel Girl and her friends' adventures and victories over Galactus, Thanos, Doctor Doom, Ratatoskr, Ultron, the Negative Zone, and a city-wide crime wave? Well GOOD NEWS: You can catch up in any bookstore! Just look for:

THE UNBEATABLE SQUIRREL GIRL VOL. 1: SQUIRREL GIRL -- for good times with Galactus

THE UNBEATABLE SQUIRREL GIRL & THE GREAT LAKES AVENGERS -- for Squirrel Girl's defeat of that jerk Thanos AND her very first defeat of Doctor Doom!

THE UNBEATABLE SQUIRREL GIRL VOL. 3: SQUIRREL, YOU REALLY GOT ME NOW -- for her LATEST defeat of the very same Doctor Doom!

THE UNBEATABLE SQUIRREL GIRL VOL. 2: SQUIRREL YOU KNOW IT'S TRUE -- for Ratatoskr's rodent schemes!

THE UNBEATABLE SQUIRREL GIRL VOL. 7: I'VE BEEN WAITING FOR A SQUIRREL LIKE YOU -- for a team-up with Kraven against a dinosaur Ultron!

THE UNBEATABLE SQUIRREL GIRL BEATS UP THE MARVEL UNIVERSE OGN -- for the scoop on Allene Green, Squirrel Girl's not-evil-but-misguided clone who now lives in the Negative Zone!

THE UNBEATABLE SQUIRREL GIRL VOL. 6: WHO RUN THE WORLD? SQUIRRELS -- for Brain Drain, Koi Boy, and Chipmunk Hunk's solo night defending all of New York!

And for those of you waiting on that Ms. Marvel/Squirrel Girl crossover, catch up on the MARVEL RISING event! MARVEL RISING: ALPHA and MARVEL RISING: SQUIRREL GIRL/MS. MARVEL are already on shelves. Don't miss MARVEL RISING: MS. MARVEL/SQUIRREL GIRL, on sale August 1!

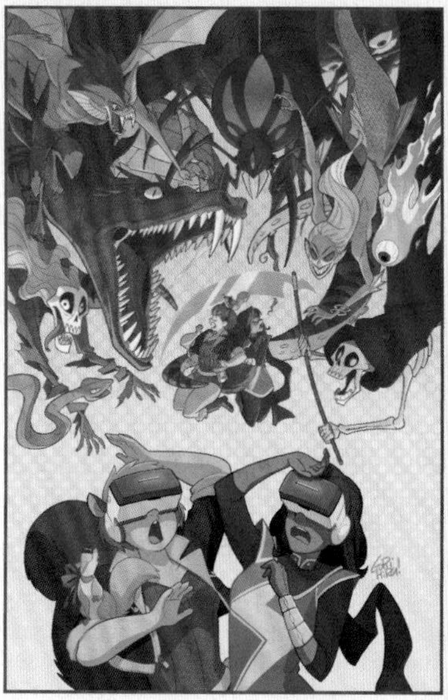

Next Issue:

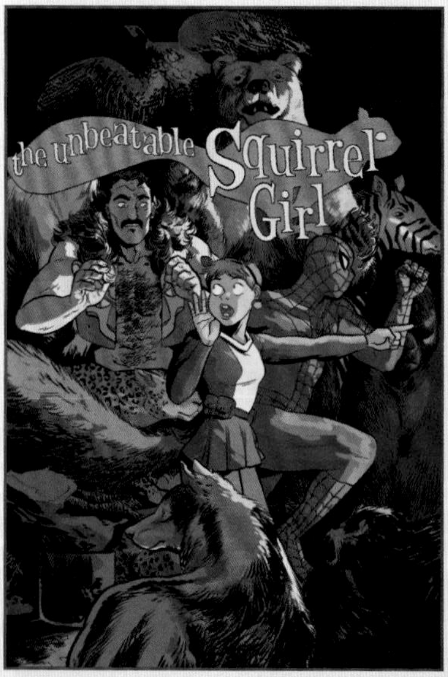

Attention, Squirrel Scouts! Make sure to check out our production blog, **unbeatablesquirrelgirl.tumblr.com**, where we post behind-the-scenes stuff on how the book gets made, along with all sorts of cool things *you* make: fanart, cosplay, whatever!

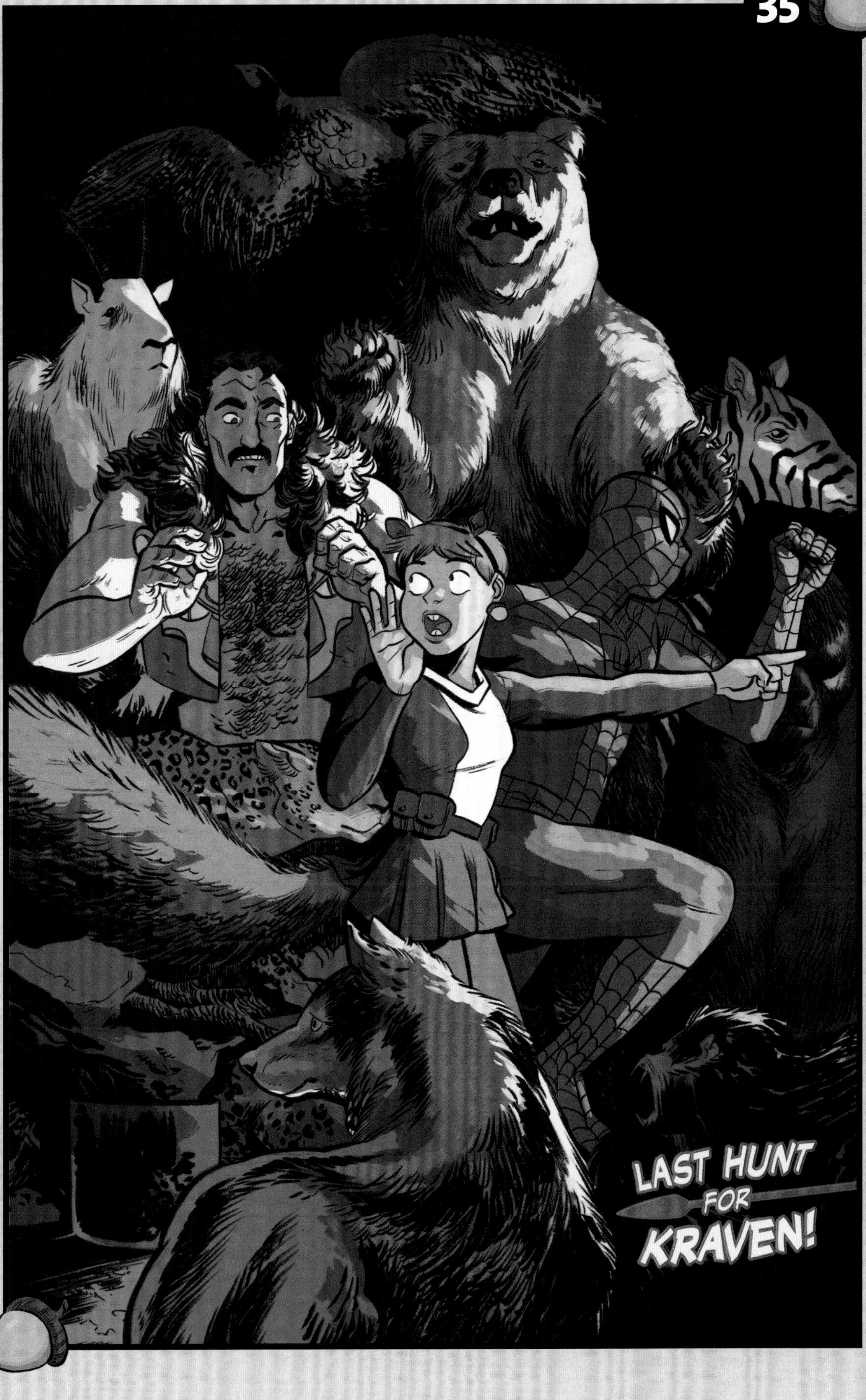
LAST HUNT
FOR
KRAVEN!

Doreen Green isn't just a second-year computer science student: she secretly also has all the powers of both squirrel and girl! She uses her amazing abilities to fight crime **and** be as awesome as possible. You know her as...The Unbeatable Squirrel Girl! Find out what she's been up to, with...

Squirrel Girl *in a nutshell*

search! 🔍

#rocketfists

#thewhisper

#toomuchwebbing

#frenchnationalconvention

#parboiledrice

#belka

Squirrel Girl @unbeatablesg
I GOT ARRESTED BY THE POLICE?? LIKE IF YOU THINK I SHOULD DEFINITELY GO FREE, RT IF YOU THINK I SHOULD DEFINITELY GO FREE AND ALSO THE POLICE SHOULD BUY ME SOME NICE CHOCOLATE-COVERED ALMONDS AS AN APOLOGY

Squirrel Girl @unbeatablesg
also all my friends got arrested too so the previous tweet applies to them as well, including @unshavenkraven!!

Squirrel Girl @unbeatablesg
@NYPDNews yo how many rts for a girl to earn a "get out of jail free" card

Squirrel Girl @unbeatablesg
UPDATE: I have been informed by a VERY sassy police officer that "RTs are not admissible in court" so thank you all for the RTs but I think this is going to trial!! Will they let me post to social media in the courtroom? Sources say: man, hopefully!

Squirrel Girl @unbeatablesg
THE TRIAL OF SQUIRREL GIRL HAS BEGUN!! And thus, so too begins...THE LIVE-TWEET OF THE TRIAL OF SQUIRREL GIRL

Squirrel Girl @unbeatablesg
omg the prosecutor is...REALLY MEAN?? like not in a prosecutorial sense, but in a "she sassed my lawyer with a personal attack right to her face!" p.s. my lawyer is Jennifer Walters A.K.A. She-Hulk and she's the BEST

Squirrel Girl @unbeatablesg
is the prosecutor playing 252-dimensional chess and trying to unnerve me...or is she just a jerk?? either way BAD NEWS FOR HER: I've studied all the way up to 299-dimensional chess, so NERVES OF STEEL right here

Squirrel Girl @unbeatablesg
i'm going on the stand now wish me luck!!

Squirrel Girl @unbeatablesg
okay so

Squirrel Girl @unbeatablesg
my time on the stand went--okay, I think?? I talked about all the super villains I defeated and the jury seemed impressed with the ol' "defeated Doctor Doom more than once" thing. I *think* they think I'm a hero and not a super villain who belongs in jail forever??

Squirrel Girl @unbeatablesg
not sure I nailed it with the prosecutor but I did tell the truth the whole truth and nothing but the truth!

Squirrel Girl @unbeatablesg
waiting for the jury to decide our fate now...

Squirrel Girl @unbeatablesg
any minute now...

Squirrel Girl @unbeatablesg
they're coming back into the courtroom! ahhhhhh so anxious!

Squirrel Girl @unbeatablesg
NOT GUILTY!!!!!!!!

Squirrel Girl @unbeatablesg
wait--not guilty except for KRAVEN?! he's not gonna take this well, he's

Squirrel Girl @unbeatablesg
UPDATE KRAVEN HAS ESCAPED COURT AND ALL OF NYC IS ON HIS TAIL

Squirrel Girl @unbeatablesg
SOMETHING BAD IS ABOUT TO HAPPEN IF I DON'T FIND HIM FIRST!!

Squirrel Girl @unbeatablesg
THE LIVE-TWEET OF THE TRIAL OF SQUIRREL GIRL IS CONCLUDED, I GOTTA GO SAVE MY FRIEND

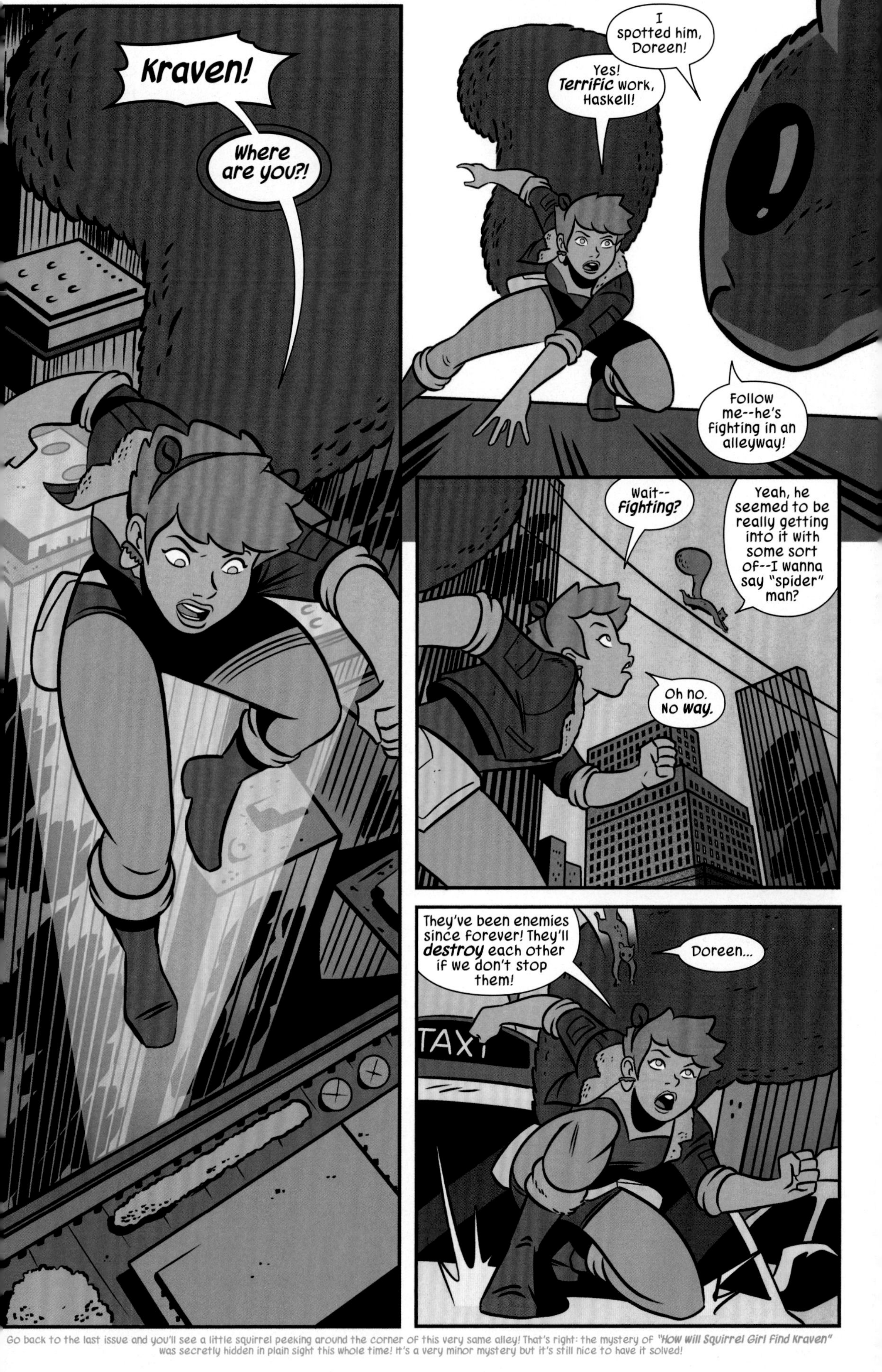
Kraven!
Where are you?!
I spotted him, Doreen!
Yes! Terrific work, Haskell!
Follow me--he's fighting in an alleyway!
Wait-- fighting?
Yeah, he seemed to be really getting into it with some sort of--I wanna say "spider" man?
Oh no. No way.
They've been enemies since forever! They'll destroy each other if we don't stop them!
Doreen...
TAXI

Go back to the last issue and you'll see a little squirrel peeking around the corner of this very same alley! That's right: the mystery of *"How will Squirrel Girl Find Kraven"* was secretly hidden in plain sight this whole time! It's a very minor mystery but it's still nice to have it solved!

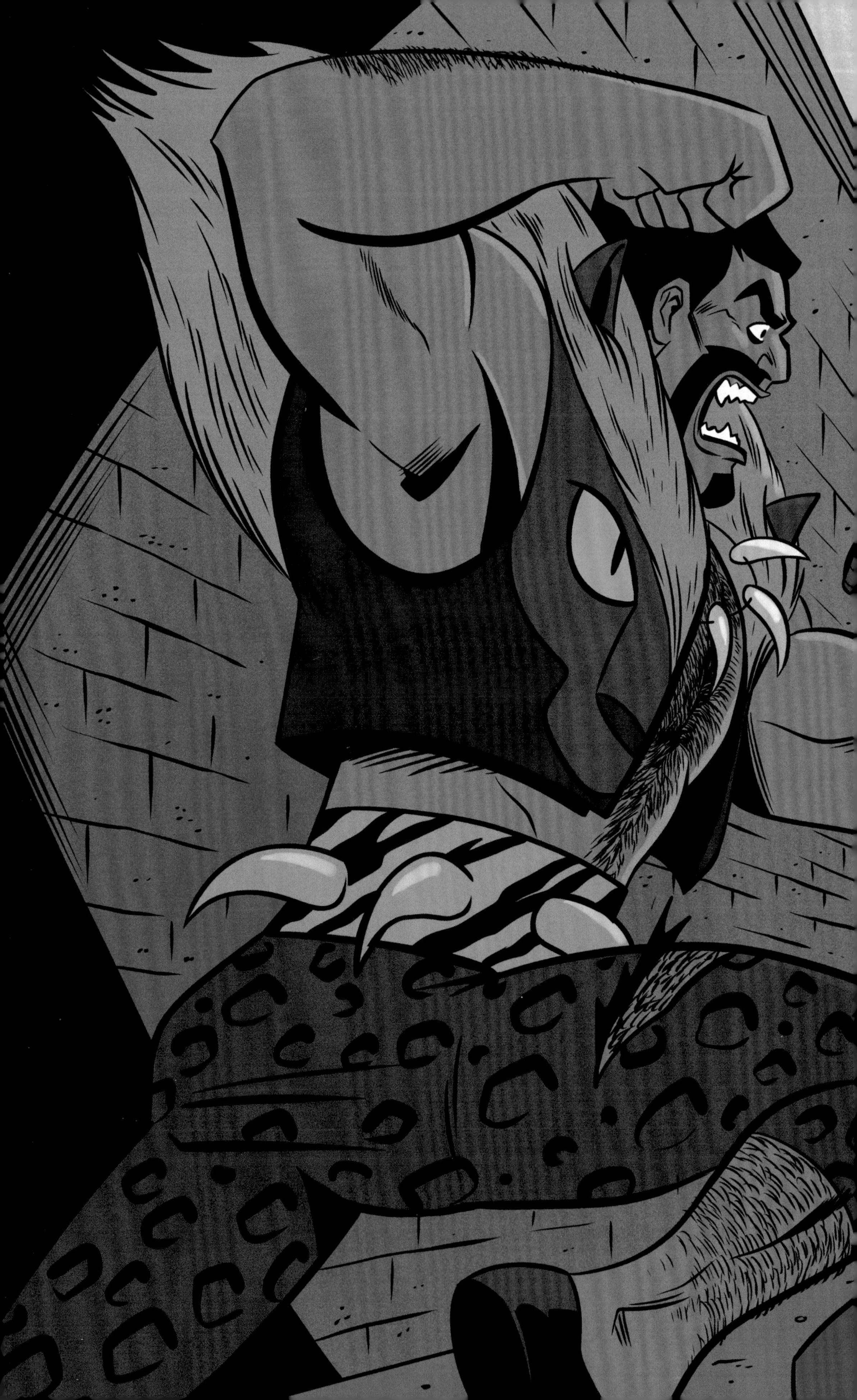

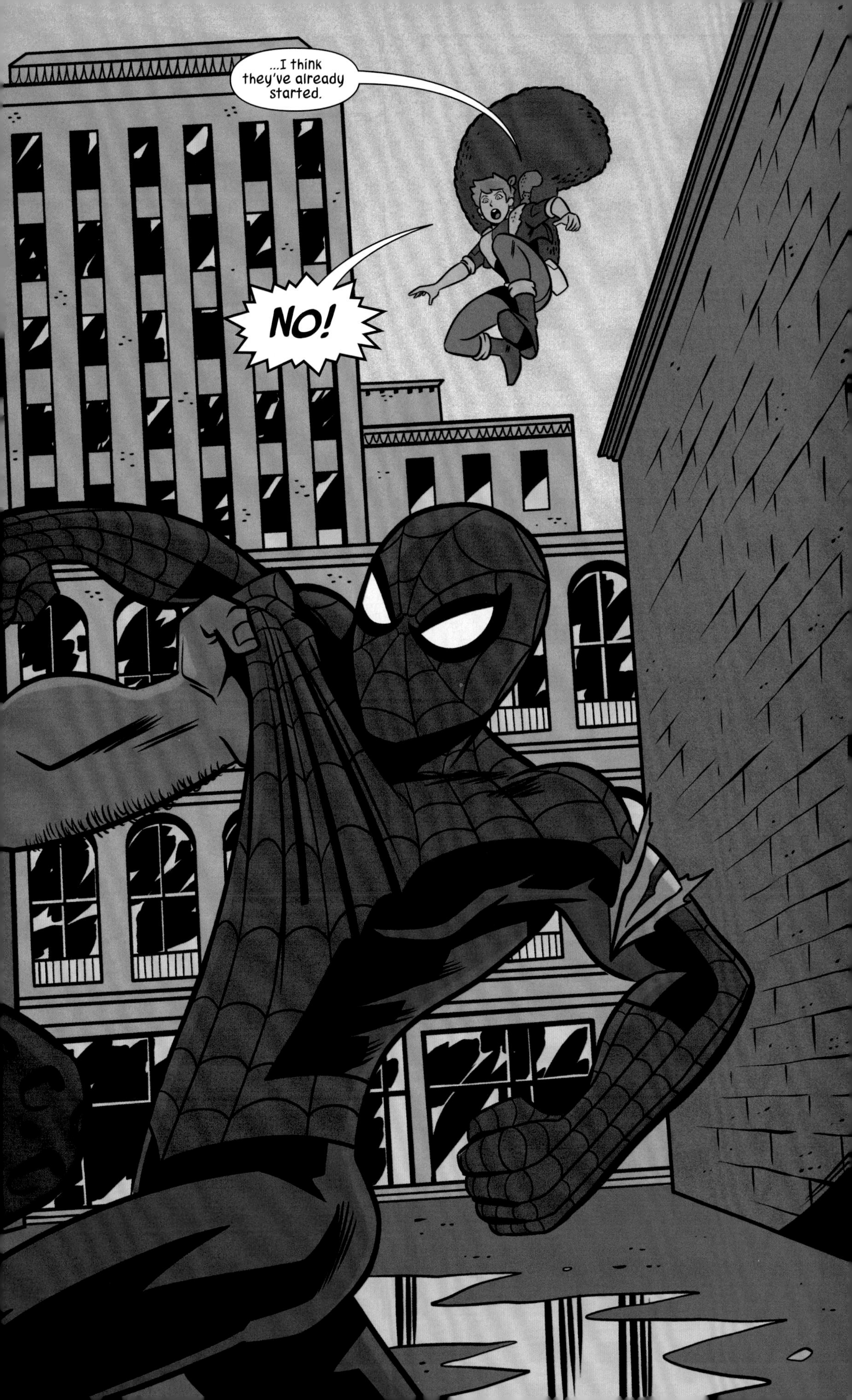
...I think they've already started.
NO!

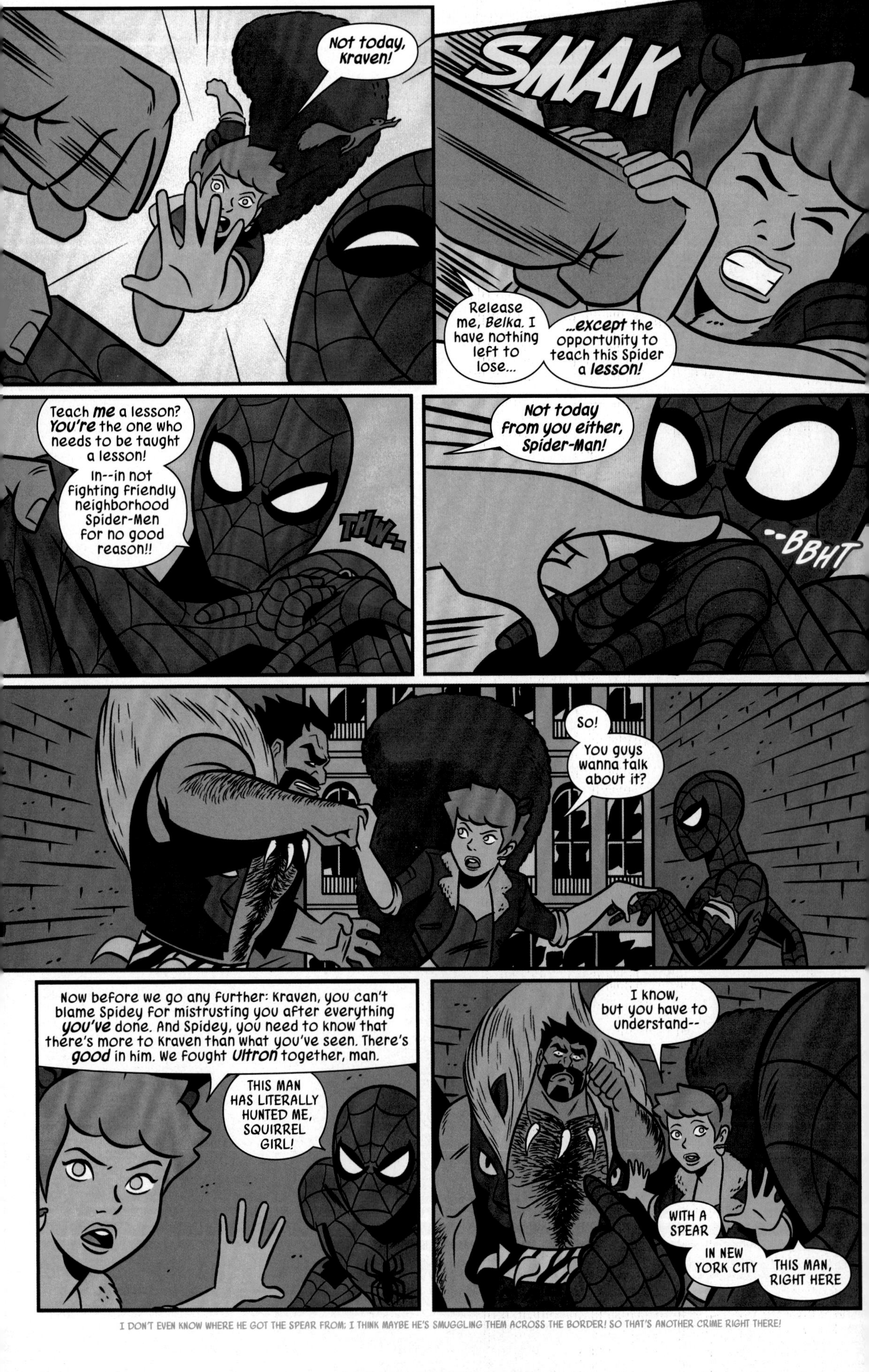
Not today, Kraven!
SMAK
Release me, Belka. I have nothing left to lose...
...except the opportunity to teach this Spider a lesson!
Teach me a lesson? You're the one who needs to be taught a lesson!
In--in not fighting friendly neighborhood Spider-Men for no good reason!!
THW--
Not today from you either, Spider-Man!
--BBHT
So!
You guys wanna talk about it?
Now before we go any further: Kraven, you can't blame Spidey for mistrusting you after everything you've done. And Spidey, you need to know that there's more to Kraven than what you've seen. There's good in him. We fought Ultron together, man.
THIS MAN HAS LITERALLY HUNTED ME, SQUIRREL GIRL!
I know, but you have to understand--
WITH A SPEAR
IN NEW YORK CITY
THIS MAN, RIGHT HERE

I DON'T EVEN KNOW WHERE HE GOT THE SPEAR FROM; I THINK MAYBE HE'S SMUGGLING THEM ACROSS THE BORDER! SO THAT'S ANOTHER CRIME RIGHT THERE!

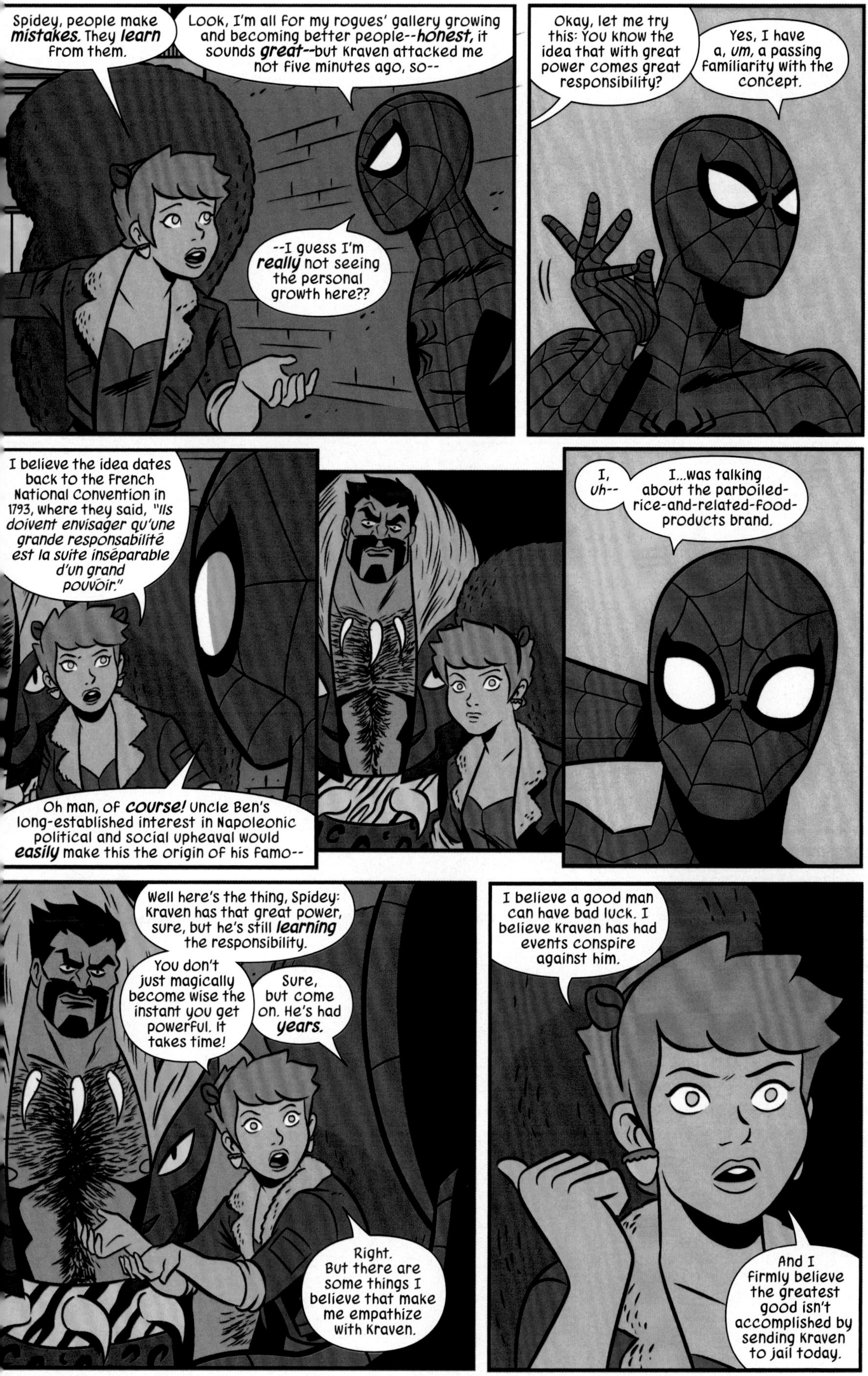
Spidey, people make mistakes. They learn from them.
Look, I'm all for my rogues' gallery growing and becoming better people--honest, it sounds great--but Kraven attacked me not five minutes ago, so--
--I guess I'm really not seeing the personal growth here??
Okay, let me try this: You know the idea that with great power comes great responsibility?
Yes, I have a, um, a passing familiarity with the concept.
I believe the idea dates back to the French National Convention in 1793, where they said, "Ils doivent envisager qu'une grande responsabilité est la suite inséparable d'un grand pouvoir."
Oh man, of course! Uncle Ben's long-established interest in Napoleonic political and social upheaval would easily make this the origin of his famo--
I, uh--
I...was talking about the parboiled-rice-and-related-food-products brand.
Well here's the thing, Spidey: Kraven has that great power, sure, but he's still learning the responsibility.
You don't just magically become wise the instant you get powerful. It takes time!
Sure, but come on. He's had years.
Right. But there are some things I believe that make me empathize with Kraven.
I believe a good man can have bad luck. I believe Kraven has had events conspire against him.
And I firmly believe the greatest good isn't accomplished by sending Kraven to jail today.

The direct translation of that French quote is, "They must consider that great responsibility follows inseparably from a great power." Uncle Ben punched it up a li'l.

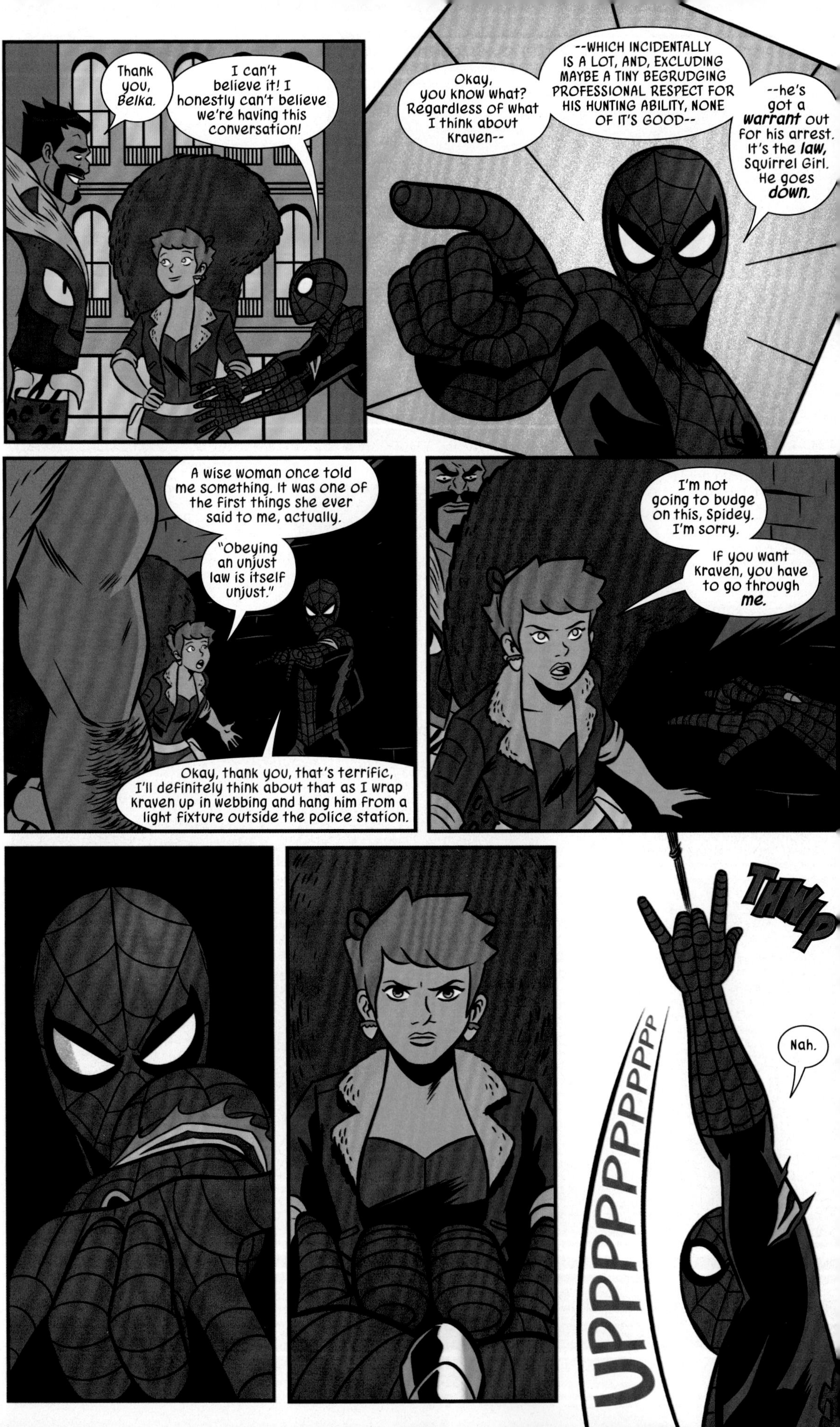
Thank you, Belka.
I can't believe it! I honestly can't believe we're having this conversation!
Okay, you know what? Regardless of what I think about Kraven--
--WHICH INCIDENTALLY IS A LOT, AND, EXCLUDING MAYBE A TINY BEGRUDGING PROFESSIONAL RESPECT FOR HIS HUNTING ABILITY, NONE OF IT'S GOOD--
--he's got a warrant out for his arrest. It's the law, Squirrel Girl. He goes down.
A wise woman once told me something. It was one of the first things she ever said to me, actually.
"Obeying an unjust law is itself unjust."
Okay, thank you, that's terrific, I'll definitely think about that as I wrap Kraven up in webbing and hang him from a light fixture outside the police station.
I'm not going to budge on this, Spidey. I'm sorry.
If you want Kraven, you have to go through me.
THWIP
UPPPPPPPPPP
Nah.

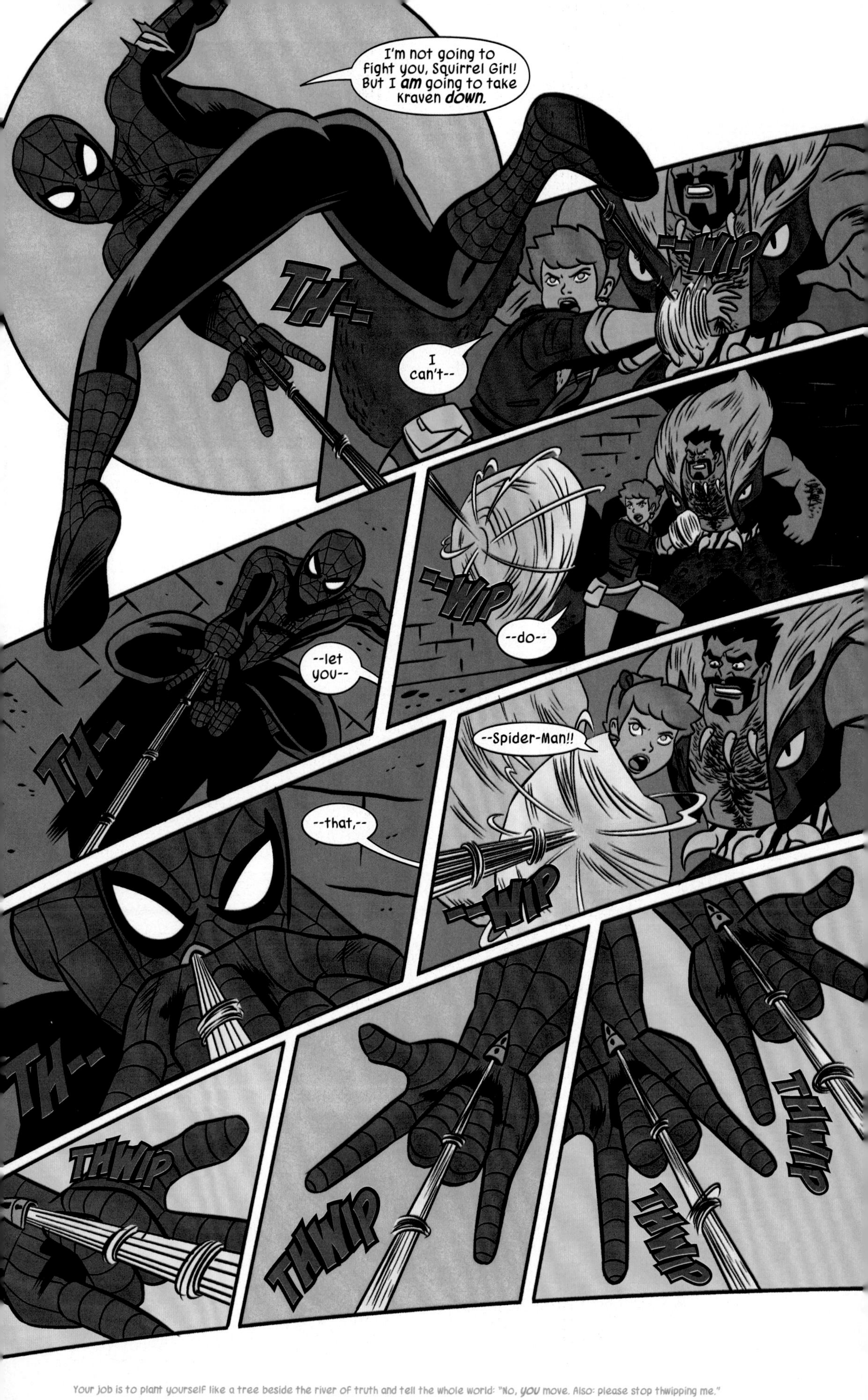
I'm not going to fight you, Squirrel Girl! But I *am* going to take Kraven *down.*
TH--
I can't--
--WIP
--WIP
--do--
--let you--
TH--
--Spider-Man!!
--that,--
--WIP
TH--
THWIP
THWIP
THWIP
THWIP

Your job is to plant yourself like a tree beside the river of truth and tell the whole world: "No, *YOU* move. Also: please stop thwipping me."

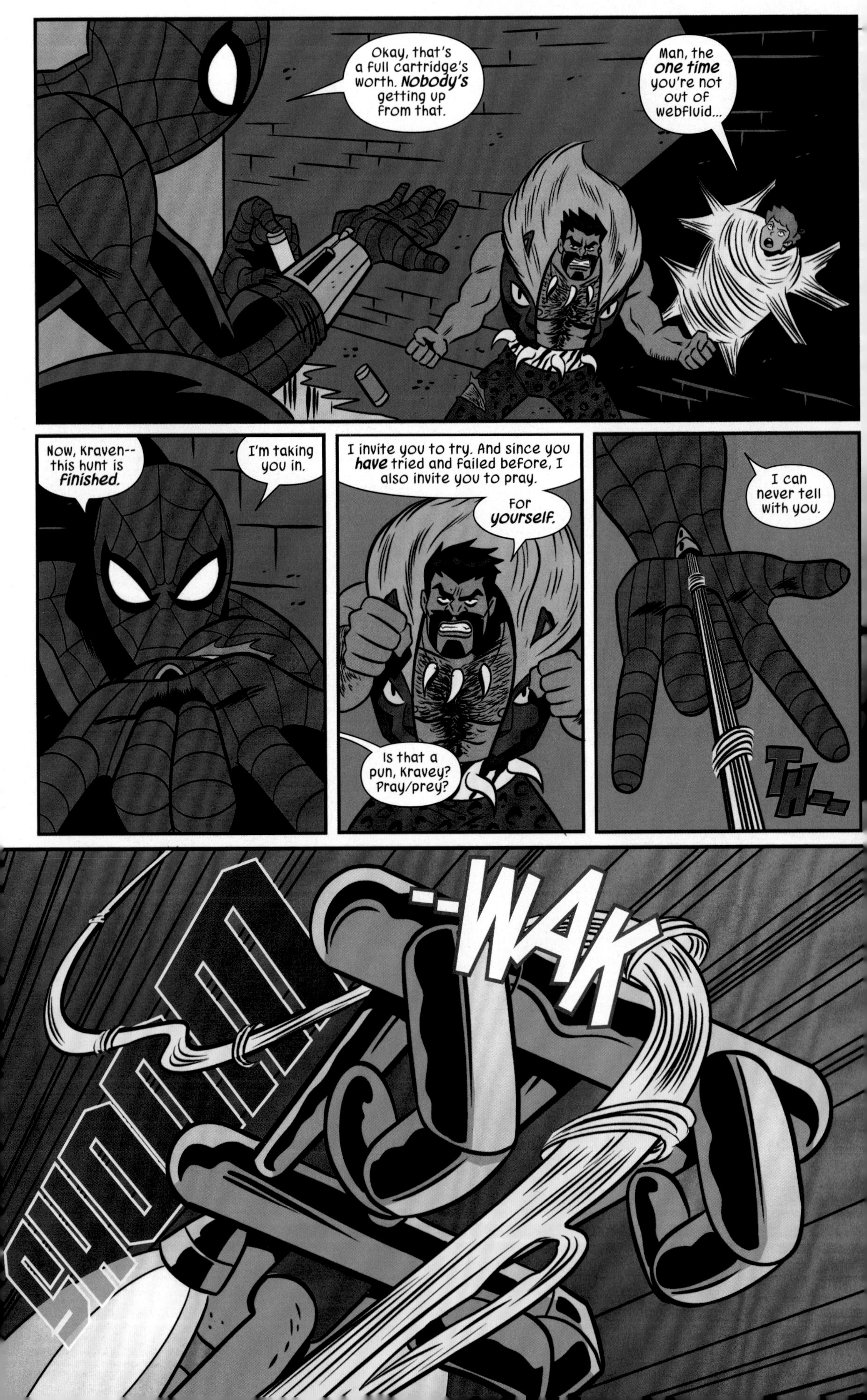

Okay, that's a full cartridge's worth. Nobody's getting up from that.
Man, the one time you're not out of webfluid...
Now, Kraven-- this hunt is finished.
I'm taking you in.
I invite you to try. And since you have tried and failed before, I also invite you to pray.
For yourself.
Is that a pun, Kravey? Pray/prey?
I can never tell with you.
TH--
--WAK

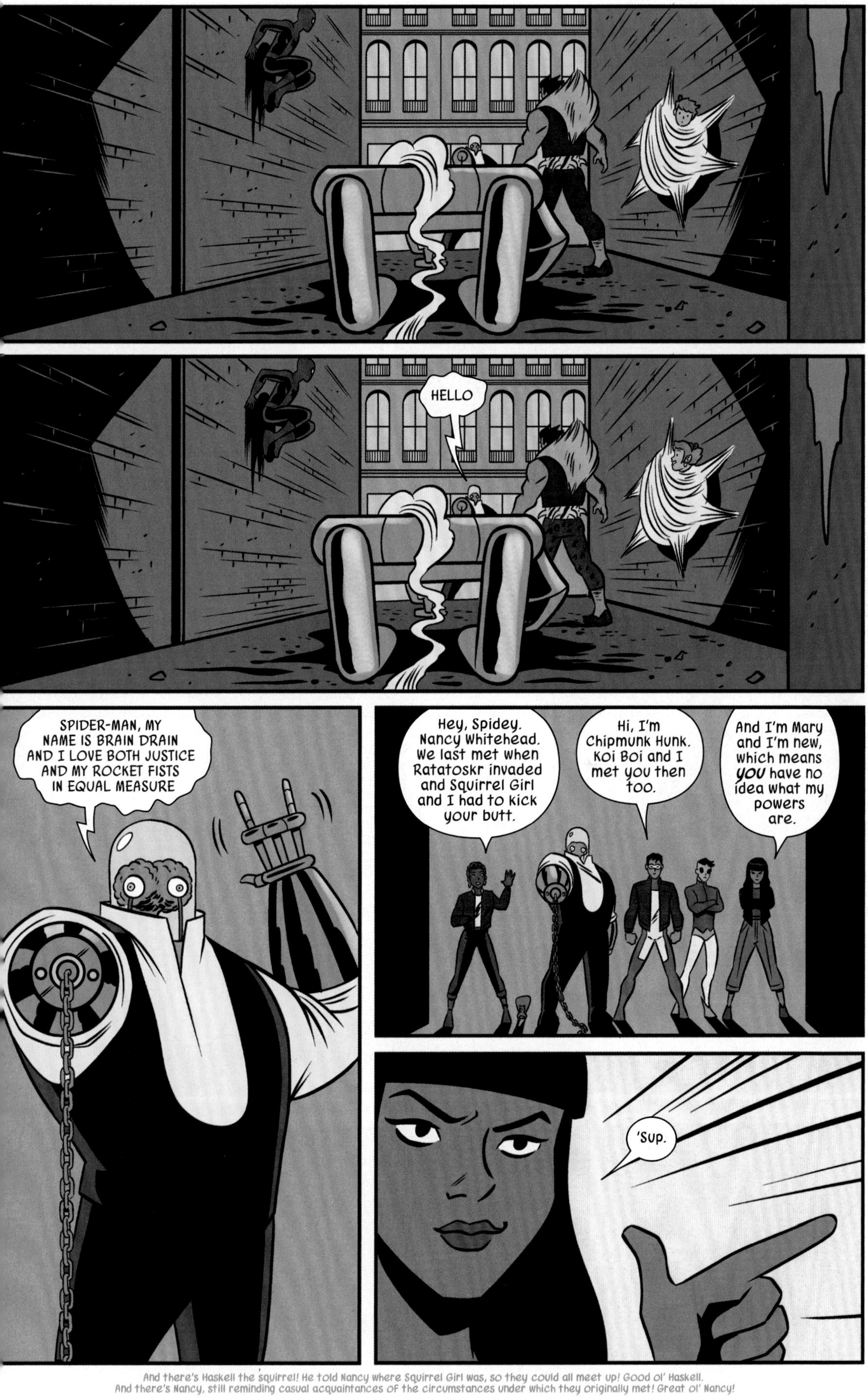
HELLO
SPIDER-MAN, MY NAME IS BRAIN DRAIN AND I LOVE BOTH JUSTICE AND MY ROCKET FISTS IN EQUAL MEASURE
Hey, Spidey. Nancy Whitehead. We last met when Ratatoskr invaded and Squirrel Girl and I had to kick your butt.
Hi, I'm Chipmunk Hunk. Koi Boi and I met you then too.
And I'm Mary and I'm new, which means *YOU* have no idea what my powers are.
'Sup.

And there's Haskell the squirrel! He told Nancy where Squirrel Girl was, so they could all meet up! Good ol' Haskell.
And there's Nancy, still reminding casual acquaintances of the circumstances under which they originally met! Great ol' Nancy!

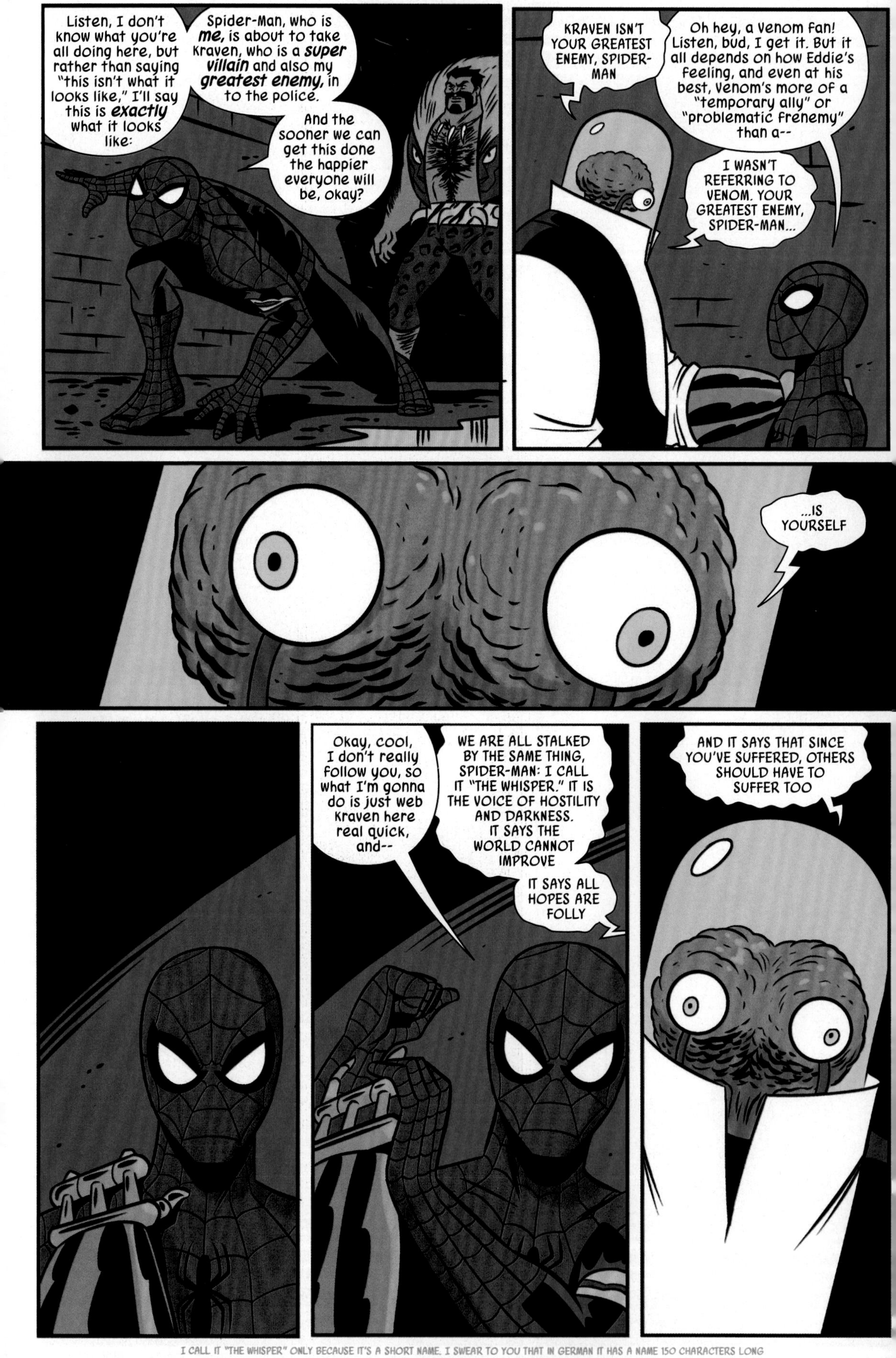
Listen, I don't know what you're all doing here, but rather than saying "this isn't what it looks like," I'll say this is exactly what it looks like:
Spider-Man, who is me, is about to take Kraven, who is a super villain and also my greatest enemy, in to the police.
And the sooner we can get this done the happier everyone will be, okay?
KRAVEN ISN'T YOUR GREATEST ENEMY, SPIDER-MAN
Oh hey, a Venom fan! Listen, bud, I get it. But it all depends on how Eddie's feeling, and even at his best, Venom's more of a "temporary ally" or "problematic frenemy" than a--
I WASN'T REFERRING TO VENOM. YOUR GREATEST ENEMY, SPIDER-MAN...
...IS YOURSELF
Okay, cool, I don't really follow you, so what I'm gonna do is just web Kraven here real quick, and--
WE ARE ALL STALKED BY THE SAME THING, SPIDER-MAN: I CALL IT "THE WHISPER." IT IS THE VOICE OF HOSTILITY AND DARKNESS. IT SAYS THE WORLD CANNOT IMPROVE
IT SAYS ALL HOPES ARE FOLLY
AND IT SAYS THAT SINCE YOU'VE SUFFERED, OTHERS SHOULD HAVE TO SUFFER TOO

I CALL IT "THE WHISPER" ONLY BECAUSE IT'S A SHORT NAME. I SWEAR TO YOU THAT IN GERMAN IT HAS A NAME 150 CHARACTERS LONG

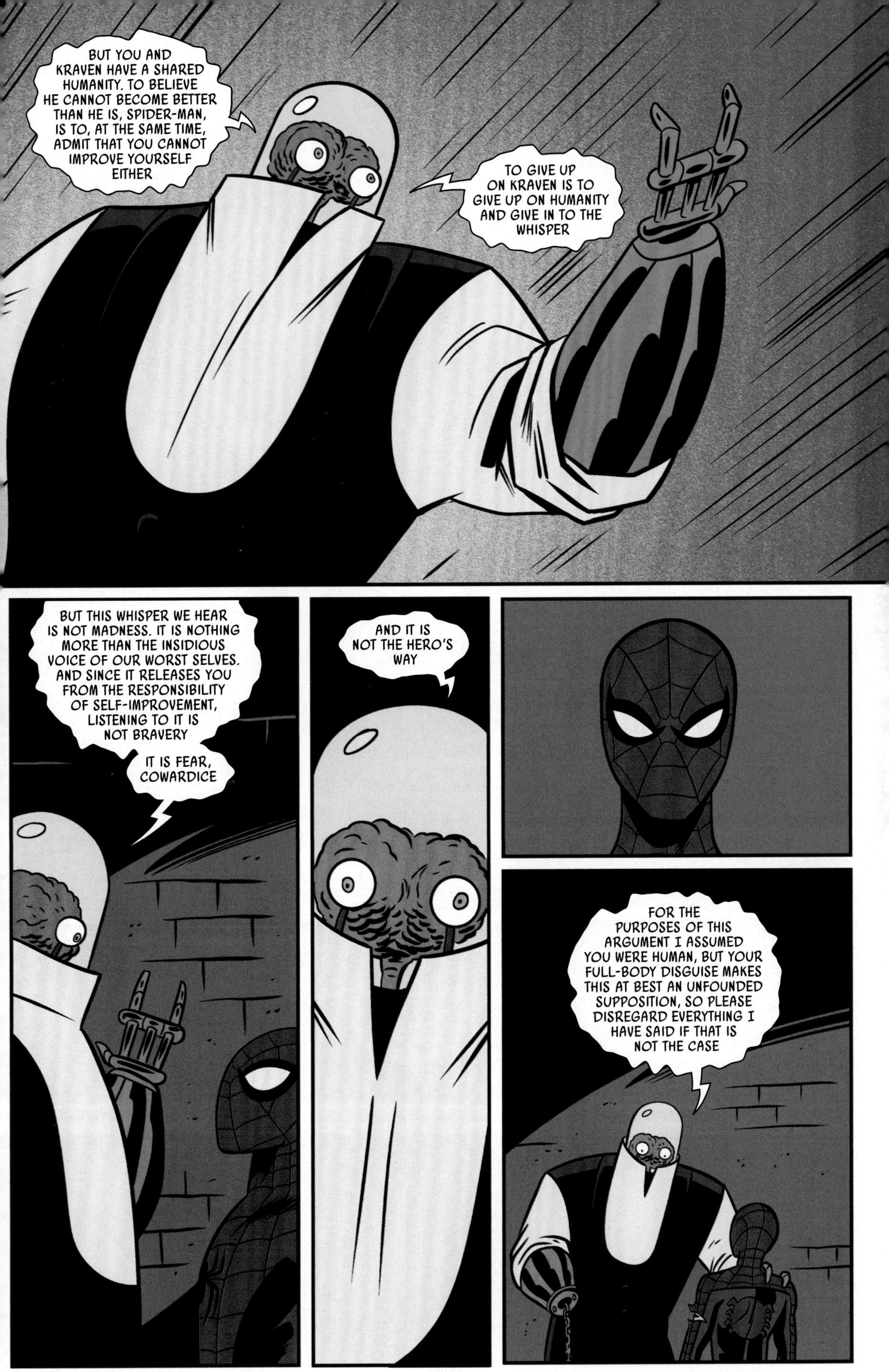
BUT YOU AND KRAVEN HAVE A SHARED HUMANITY. TO BELIEVE HE CANNOT BECOME BETTER THAN HE IS, SPIDER-MAN, IS TO, AT THE SAME TIME, ADMIT THAT YOU CANNOT IMPROVE YOURSELF EITHER
TO GIVE UP ON KRAVEN IS TO GIVE UP ON HUMANITY AND GIVE IN TO THE WHISPER
BUT THIS WHISPER WE HEAR IS NOT MADNESS. IT IS NOTHING MORE THAN THE INSIDIOUS VOICE OF OUR WORST SELVES. AND SINCE IT RELEASES YOU FROM THE RESPONSIBILITY OF SELF-IMPROVEMENT, LISTENING TO IT IS NOT BRAVERY
IT IS FEAR, COWARDICE
AND IT IS NOT THE HERO'S WAY
FOR THE PURPOSES OF THIS ARGUMENT I ASSUMED YOU WERE HUMAN, BUT YOUR FULL-BODY DISGUISE MAKES THIS AT BEST AN UNFOUNDED SUPPOSITION, SO PLEASE DISREGARD EVERYTHING I HAVE SAID IF THAT IS NOT THE CASE

ALSO IF YOU AND EVERYTHING ELSE I THINK I SEE ARE MERELY SOLIPSISTIC ILLUSIONS, PLEASE LET ME KNOW: IT WOULD ACTUALLY PUT A LOT OF LONG-STANDING QUESTIONS TO BED

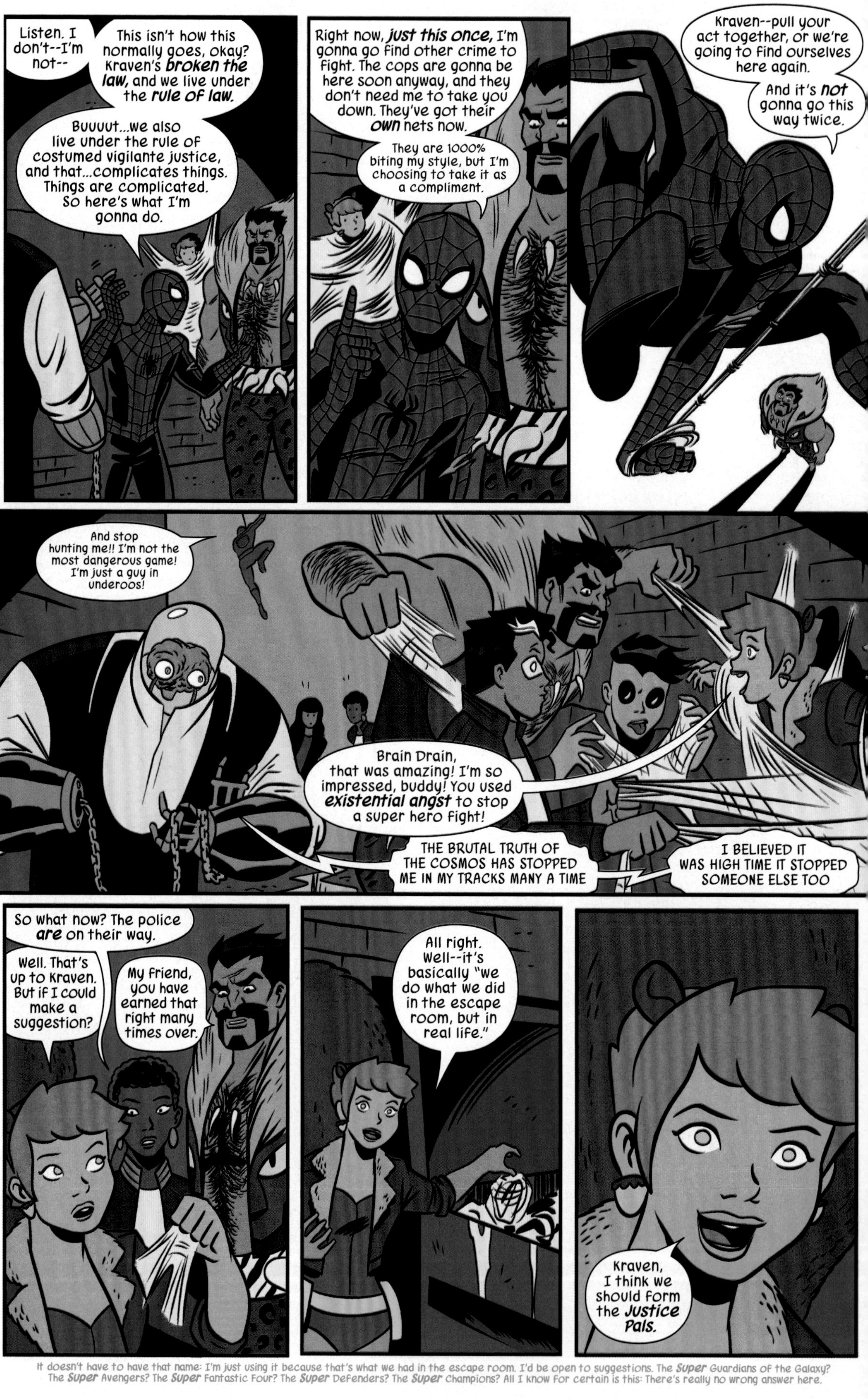
Listen. I don't--I'm not--
This isn't how this normally goes, okay? Kraven's *broken the law,* and we live under the *rule of law.*
Buuuut...we also live under the rule of costumed vigilante justice, and that...complicates things. Things are complicated. So here's what I'm gonna do.
Right now, *just this once,* I'm gonna go find other crime to fight. The cops are gonna be here soon anyway, and they don't need me to take you down. They've got their *own* nets now.
They are 1000% biting my style, but I'm choosing to take it as a compliment.
Kraven--pull your act together, or we're going to find ourselves here again.
And it's *not* gonna go this way twice.
And stop hunting me!! I'm not the most dangerous game! I'm just a guy in underoos!
Brain Drain, that was amazing! I'm so impressed, buddy! You used *existential angst* to stop a super hero fight!
THE BRUTAL TRUTH OF THE COSMOS HAS STOPPED ME IN MY TRACKS MANY A TIME
I BELIEVED IT WAS HIGH TIME IT STOPPED SOMEONE ELSE TOO
So what now? The police *are* on their way.
Well. That's up to Kraven. But if I could make a suggestion?
My friend, you have earned that right many times over.
All right. Well--it's basically "we do what we did in the escape room, but in real life."
Kraven, I think we should form the *Justice Pals.*

It doesn't have to have that name: I'm just using it because that's what we had in the escape room. I'd be open to suggestions. The *Super* Guardians of the Galaxy? The *Super* Avengers? The *Super* Fantastic Four? The *Super* Defenders? The *Super* Champions? All I know for certain is this: There's really no wrong answer here.

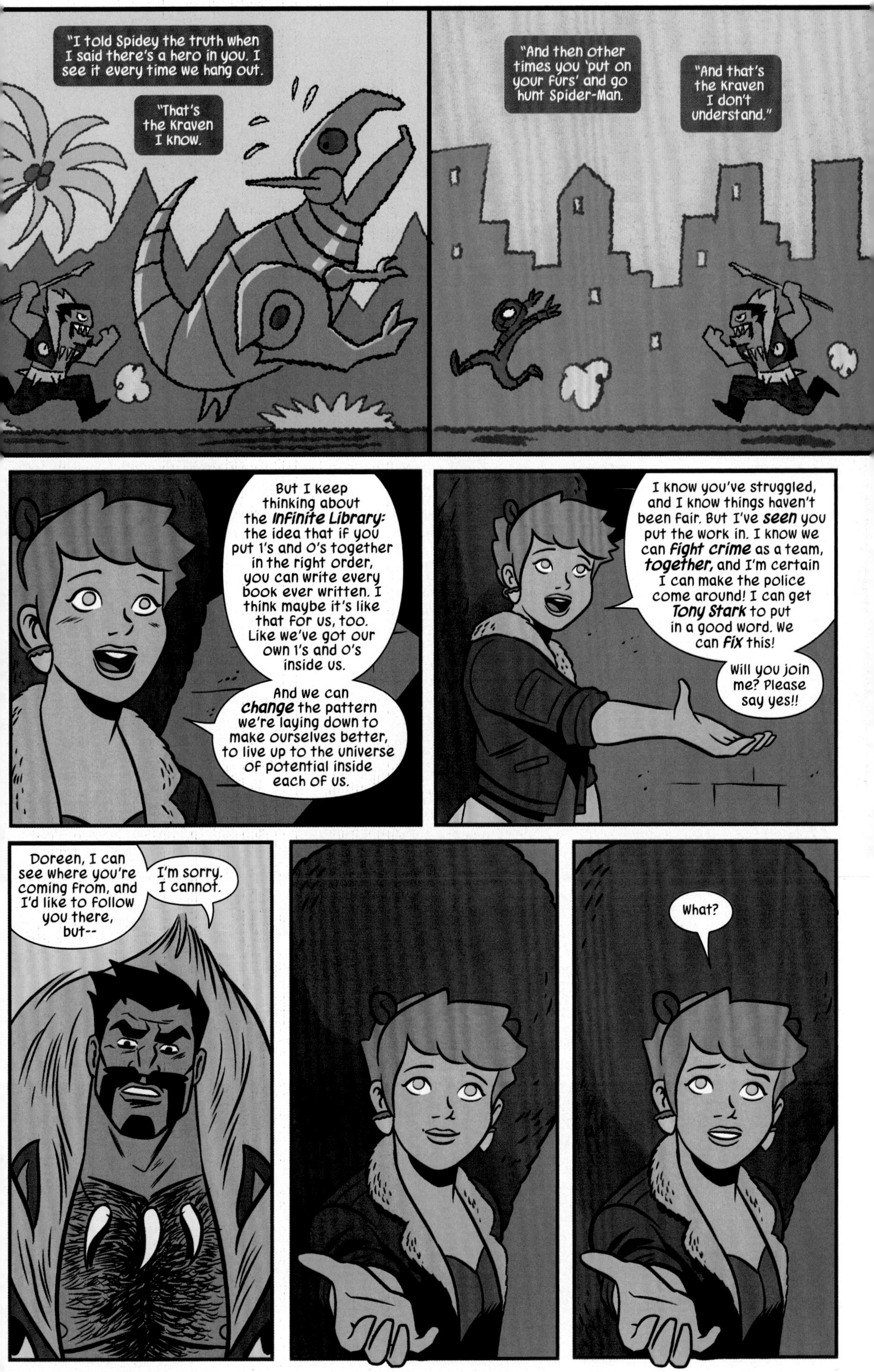
"I told Spidey the truth when I said there's a hero in you. I see it every time we hang out.
"That's the Kraven I know.
"And then other times you 'put on your furs' and go hunt Spider-Man.
"And that's the Kraven I don't understand."
But I keep thinking about the Infinite Library: the idea that if you put 1's and 0's together in the right order, you can write every book ever written. I think maybe it's like that for us, too. Like we've got our own 1's and 0's inside us.
And we can change the pattern we're laying down to make ourselves better, to live up to the universe of potential inside each of us.
I know you've struggled, and I know things haven't been fair. But I've seen you put the work in. I know we can fight crime as a team, together, and I'm certain I can make the police come around! I can get Tony Stark to put in a good word. We can fix this!
Will you join me? Please say yes!!
Doreen, I can see where you're coming from, and I'd like to follow you there, but--
I'm sorry. I cannot.
What?

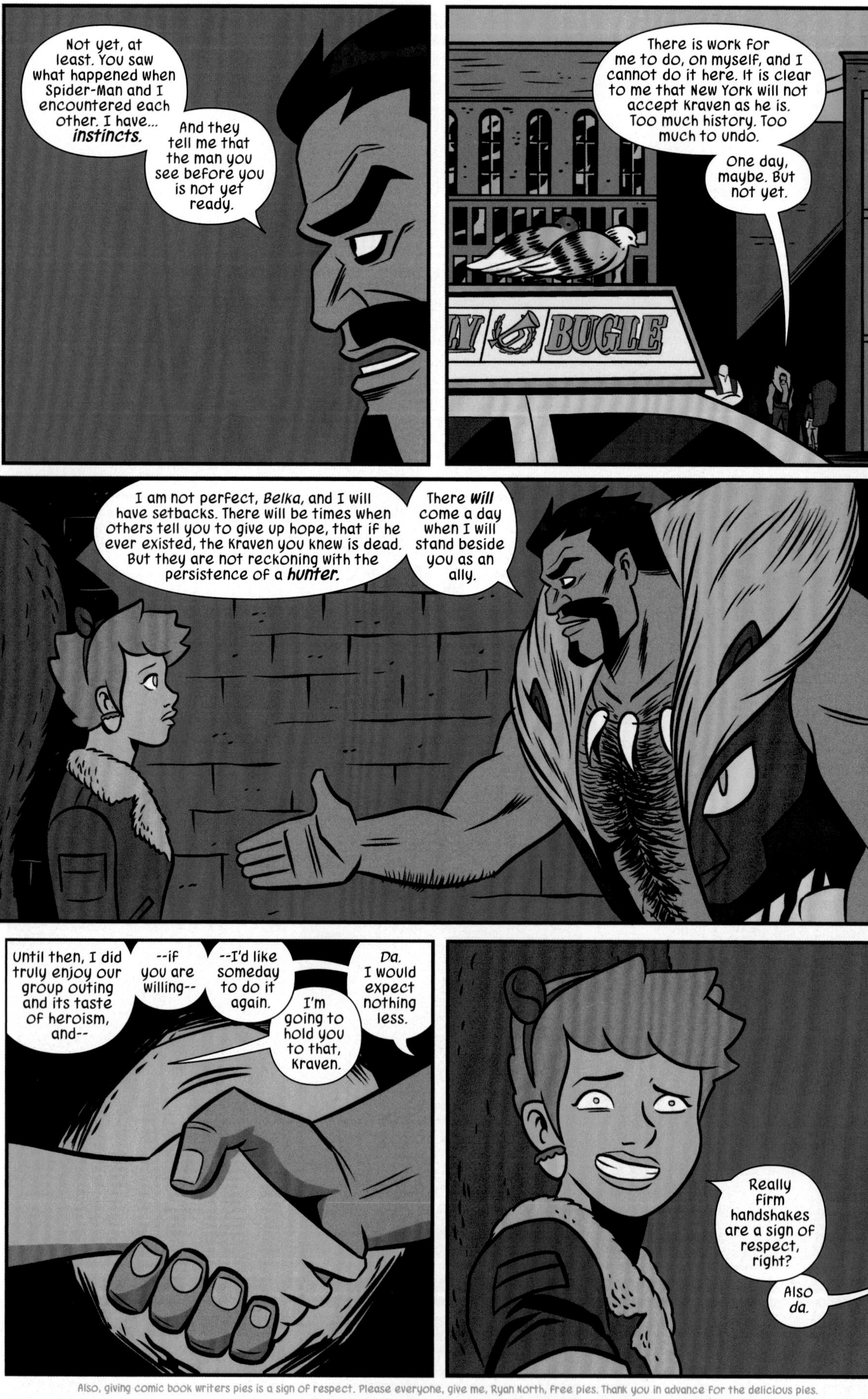

Not yet, at least. You saw what happened when Spider-Man and I encountered each other. I have... *instincts.*
And they tell me that the man you see before you is not yet ready.
There is work for me to do, on myself, and I cannot do it here. It is clear to me that New York will not accept Kraven as he is. Too much history. Too much to undo.
One day, maybe. But not yet.
BUGLE
I am not perfect, *Belka,* and I will have setbacks. There will be times when others tell you to give up hope, that if he ever existed, the Kraven you knew is dead. But they are not reckoning with the persistence of a *hunter.*
There *will* come a day when I will stand beside you as an ally.
Until then, I did truly enjoy our group outing and its taste of heroism, and--
--if you are willing--
--I'd like someday to do it again.
I'm going to hold you to that, Kraven.
Da. I would expect nothing less.
Really firm handshakes are a sign of respect, right?
Also *da.*

Also, giving comic book writers pies is a sign of respect. Please everyone, give me, Ryan North, free pies. Thank you in advance for the delicious pies.

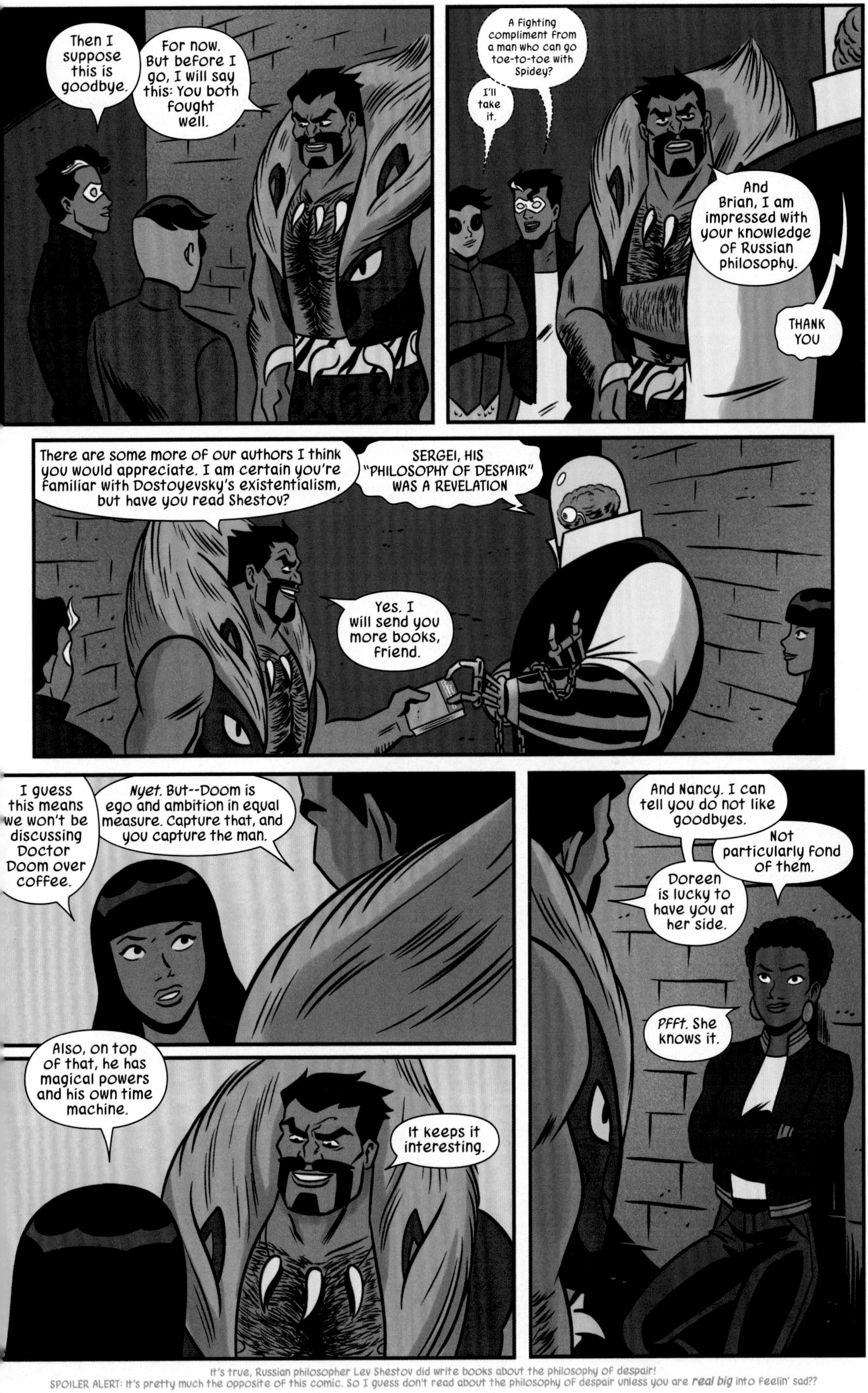
Then I suppose this is goodbye.
For now. But before I go, I will say this: You both fought well.
A fighting compliment from a man who can go toe-to-toe with Spidey?
I'll take it.
And Brian, I am impressed with your knowledge of Russian philosophy.
THANK YOU
There are some more of our authors I think you would appreciate. I am certain you're familiar with Dostoyevsky's existentialism, but have you read Shestov?
SERGEI, HIS "PHILOSOPHY OF DESPAIR" WAS A REVELATION
Yes. I will send you more books, friend.
I guess this means we won't be discussing Doctor Doom over coffee.
Nyet. But--Doom is ego and ambition in equal measure. Capture that, and you capture the man.
Also, on top of that, he has magical powers and his own time machine.
It keeps it interesting.
And Nancy. I can tell you do not like goodbyes.
Not particularly fond of them.
Doreen is lucky to have you at her side.
Pfft. She knows it.

It's true, Russian philosopher Lev Shestov did write books about the philosophy of despair!
SPOILER ALERT: It's pretty much the opposite of this comic. So I guess don't read about the philosophy of despair unless you are ***real big*** into feelin' sad??

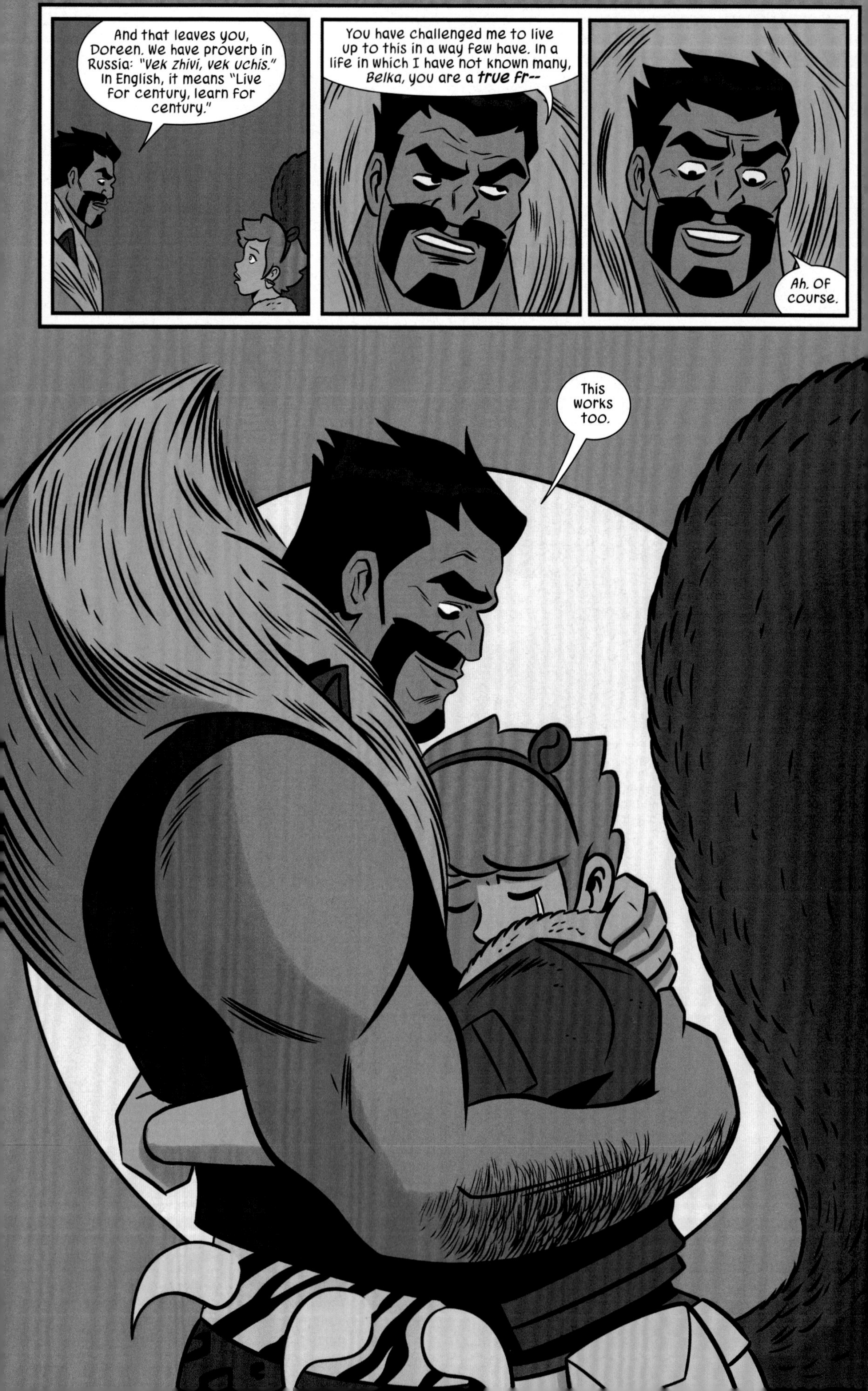
And that leaves you, Doreen. We have proverb in Russia: "Vek zhivi, vek uchis." In English, it means "Live for century, learn for century."
You have challenged me to live up to this in a way few have. In a life in which I have not known many, Belka, you are a true fr--
Ah. Of course.
This works too.

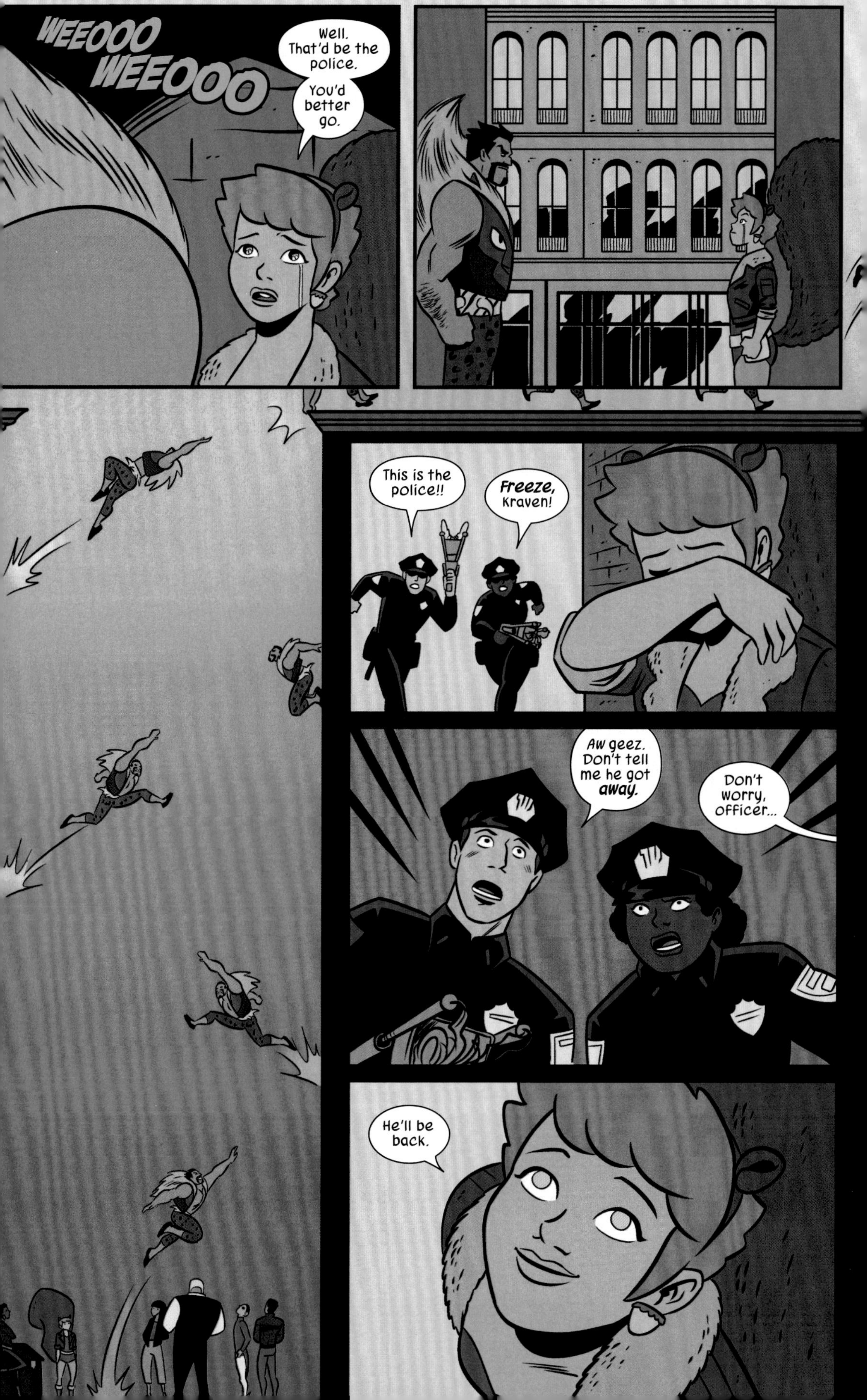
WEEOOO
WEEOOO
Well. That'd be the police.
You'd better go.
This is the police!!
Freeze, Kraven!
Aw geez. Don't tell me he got away.
Don't worry, officer...
He'll be back.

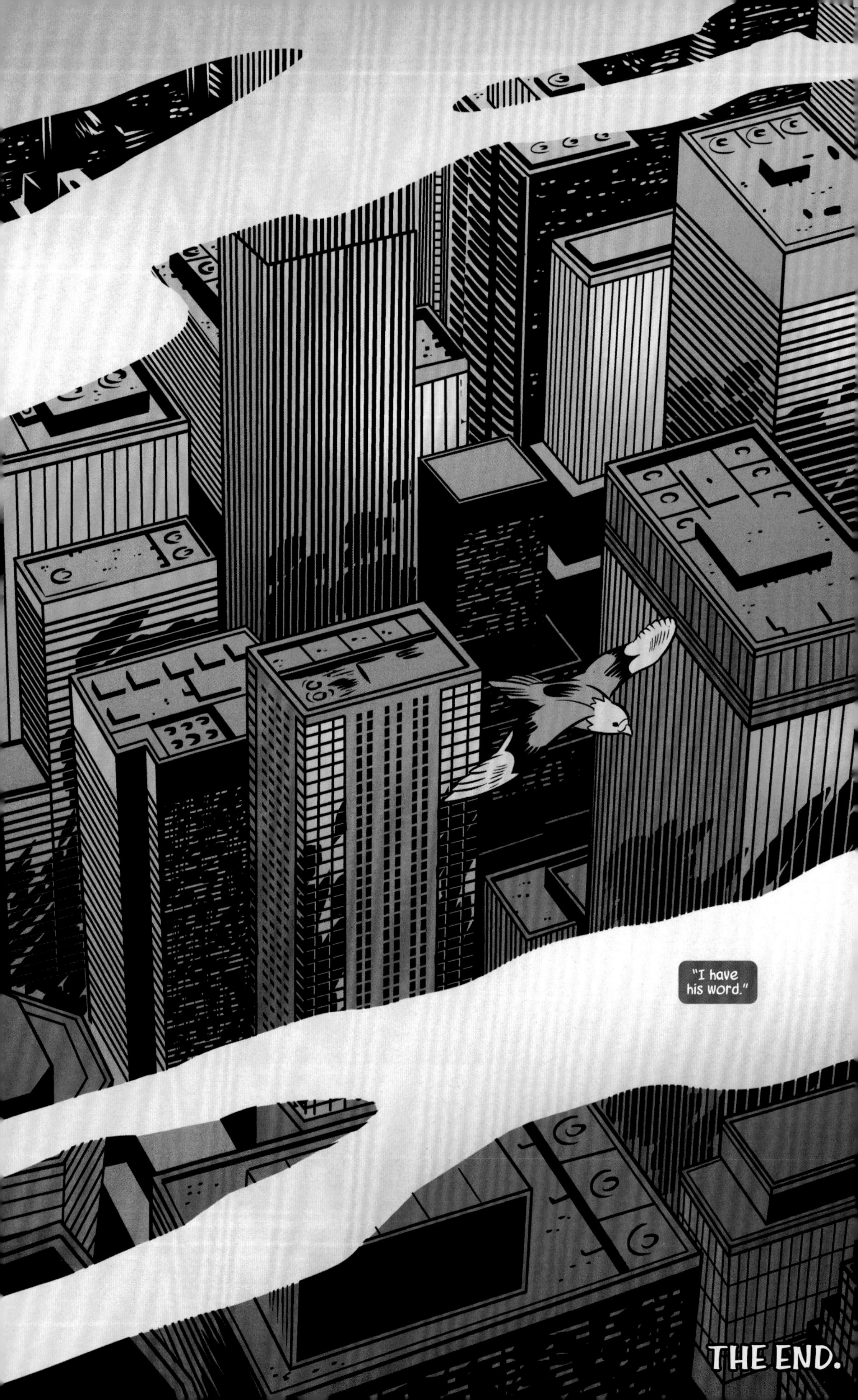
"I have his word."
THE END.

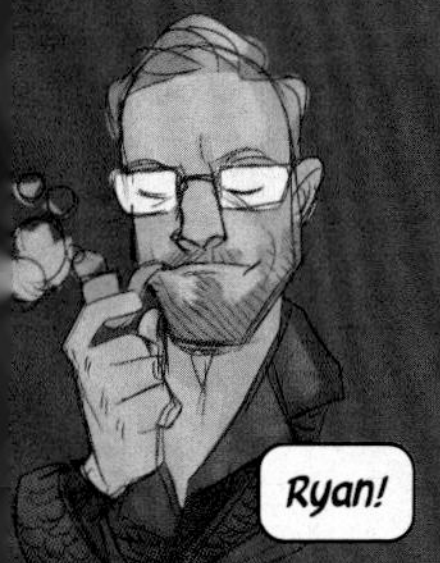
Ryan!

Letters From Nuts

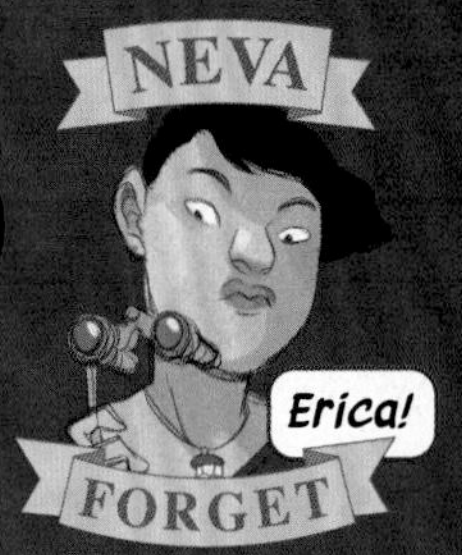
NEVA
FORGET
Erica!

Send letters to mheroes@marvel.com or 135 W 50th St, 7th Floor, New York, NY 10020 (Please mark "OKAY TO PRINT")

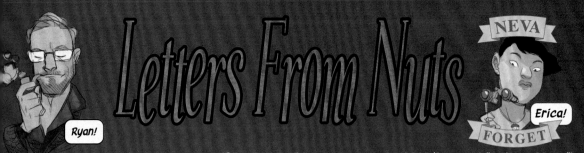

RYAN: As you may have heard, Steve Ditko passed away in July--which happened to be while this issue was being prepared for printing. In the credits of every issue, we say "Squirrel Girl created by Will Murray & Steve Ditko," but that's of course not all he created. Without him, you wouldn't have the Squirrel Girl you know and love, but you also wouldn't have Kraven, or Spider-Man, or the Doctors Strange and Octopus, along with countless other Marvel heroes and villains. Ditko brought characters to life in a way nobody else could, and he's responsible for getting many of the artists I know interested in comics!

It's a coincidence that this issue of SQUIRREL GIRL stars so many characters he co-created, but I'm glad it does, because it really shows the effect one person can have on the world: Steve Ditko was so influential that you can create a comic that works as a tribute to him entirely by accident. If you're ever in Washington, DC, you owe it to yourself to go to the Library of Congress: They have in their collection the original pages for AMAZING FANTASY #15--the issue that introduced Spider-Man!--and anyone can see them by appointment. (After the pages were thought to have been lost for decades, they were anonymously donated, and the librarian there--Sara W. Duke -- assured me that while she knew who donated them, she'd be taking that little secret to her grave.) Look at Ditko's pages carefully. In the corrections made in white-out, in the partially erased editor's notes, and most of all in Ditko's linework, you can see the beginnings of every story that followed--including the adventures of Doreen Green that you're reading right now.

The closest I ever came to meeting Ditko was there, in the Library of Congress, as Sara led my wife and I through his pages, pointing out her favorite parts and letting us study each page for as long as we wanted. His influence on my life in comics is profound, and it's just not going to be the same without him.

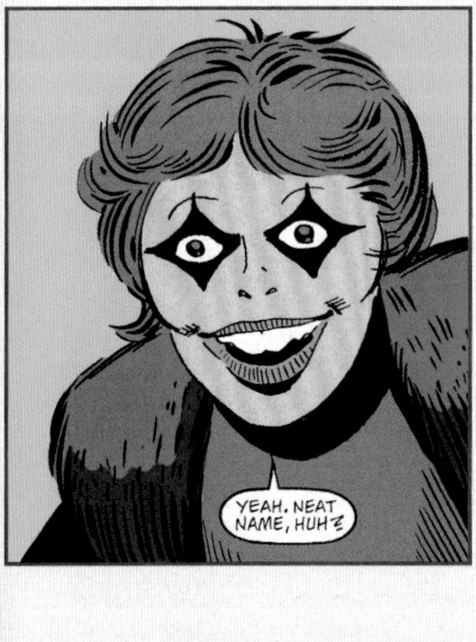
YEAH. NEAT NAME, HUH?

Hello there! There's much discussion on Squirrel Girl's love life, but Tippy-Toe is rather lovelorn. What about Hank? Or Mew?

Anne from Illinois

RYAN: Hi, Anne! That's a good question. I'll say that in MY mind Tippy doesn't really need anyone else and is fully satisfied with the platonic relationships in her life! Mew, on the other hand...

Dear Ryan, Erica and newcomer Derek!

I would like to thank you guys for the last few years of SQUIRREL GIRL. My old comic book guy recommended it to me when it was about to start. I have every issue so far, and even though I got a little off track last year, I went and found all the issues I was missing and had a binge weekend.

I love that it's not just a typical comic, but I find myself being educated throughout each read. I read the notes, and even find myself looking up some of the things you include in your comics. I loved Erica's art, and so far I find myself loving Derek's. Keep up the good work!

Kick butts and eat nuts!
Nicole
Florida

RYAN: Hey thanks, Nicole! That's the nice thing about books: they're always there waiting for you when you've got the time for them. Perhaps someone is reading these words 100 years in the future, long after I have stopped writing the comic and turned into a skeleton! Hello, future reader. I hope things are awesome for you, and I have a question: Did we ever invent time travel? If so, please send a time-traveler back to the past as I'm writing this to let me know. It's 8:54 A.M. on July 6, 2018!!!

...Dang, no such luck. :(

My name is Jahnessa (but everyone around here calls me Squirrel Girl) and I am 3 years old! Squirrel Girl is my favorite super hero ever! I dressed up as Squirrel Girl for Halloween last year;. my mommy even made my costume. I placed 4th in a costume contest at our local comic book shop!!! We live on a small island and whenever I go anywhere people say, "Hey, it's Squirrel Girl," and I reply with an ear-piercing shriek of squirrel chitter-chatter and screams. My whole family loves Squirrel Girl so much; my daddy reads her comic to me almost every day, and my mommy (who is going to school to be a kids librarian) even had a Squirrel Girl book in her class as required reading this semester. I love Tippy-Toe, she is my favorite squirrel sidekick!!! I have three squirrels (stuffed animals) that I sleep with every night and I take them to bed with me and tuck them all in with their buddy Lockjaw. I think I'm going to be Squirrel Girl every year for Halloween! My favorite thing about Squirrel Girl is her big fluffy tail and her being able to talk to all the squirrels in the world!! Thank you so much for writing about Squirrel Girl! One day when I grow up, I will read Squirrel Girl comics to my baby brother.

Jahnessa Long

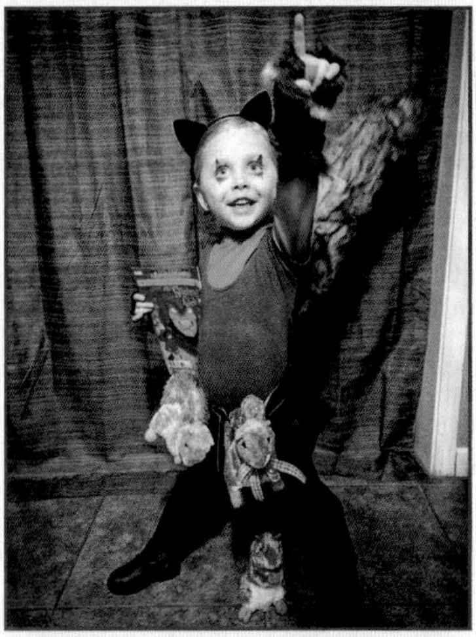

RYAN: Hi, Jahnessa--first off, your costume is AMAZING. I love that you have Tippy there and two other squirrels, too, and they're all friends with Lockjaw! And I love that you've got plans for growing up and reading to your baby brother. My nephew has a baby brother, too, and he's already helping him with that sort of thing! Here's a secret: I always wanted to live on a small island. There's an island in Toronto (named "Toronto Island," so I guess that makes sense), but the wait list to live there is literally 100 years! So I guess that's something I should've asked the time-travelers about in the last question, too. Anyway, Jahnessa, I think you're great and I'm so proud you read our comics!!

Dear Ryan and Erica,

I might be obsessed with Squirrel Girl and Ms. Marvel! My dad got me THE UNBEATABLE SQUIRREL GIRL: SQUIRREL MEETS WORLD novel and I got hooked. Then he got me the graphic novels (the ones you guys make) and I read it all in an hour. At this point, I was finished with the first book and went on to the second one. Then he got me the second graphic novel and MS. MARVEL and, again, I read both of them in two hours. Then, GUESS WHAT? My dad got me two more MS. MARVEL graphic novels and the third UNBEATABLE SQUIRREL GIRL graphic novel (THE UNBEATABLE SQUIRREL GIRL BEATS UP THE MARVEL UNIVERSE--the one I am reading at the moment of writing this letter). So, yeah...I may be obsessed. I really like all the puns and funny names of the graphic novels. So in the book, she is in middle school and she meets a girl named Ana Sofía and I was wondering if you were going to put in things like that, almost as Easter eggs. Also, she has Squirrel Scouts, which I would like to join very badly! When Squirrel Girl becomes a movie (which it has to), I wonder what timeline and/or storyline they are going to use. I really want a Ms. Marvel/Squirrel Girl crossover! But who really doesn't? I also had to throw a game for my class, since I was a V.I.P. in my class for the day. I made a Kahoot! (online live quiz) where it asked questions about me, and one of the questions was, "Who is my favorite super hero?" The answer was Squirrel Girl!

Thank you,
S.E.R. (Sadie E. Rosenblatt)
New Milford, New Jersey

P.S. I live in the same place as the Hales' Squirrel Girl, I am freaking out!

RYAN: Aren't the Hale novels great? As you saw in the recent issues of this story, we did give Ana Sofía a shout-out, but it would be great to work her into the story at some point. Also, the Ms. Marvel/Squirrel Girl crossover is happening AS WE SPEAK, in the MARVEL RISING series of comics! So basically, Sadie, if this letter you sent was a wish, it has all come true ALREADY. Well done on that! P.S. I am 100% in favor of your comics-reading lifestyle, and shout-out to your dad for enabling it!! P.P.S. If I made an online quiz, my answer would be the same as yours. NO REGRETS.

After I read SQUIRREL POWER in my after-school art class I made this and my teacher said I was really good and when I grow up I should write for SQUIRREL GIRL.

Yael Burstein
Brookline, Massachusetts

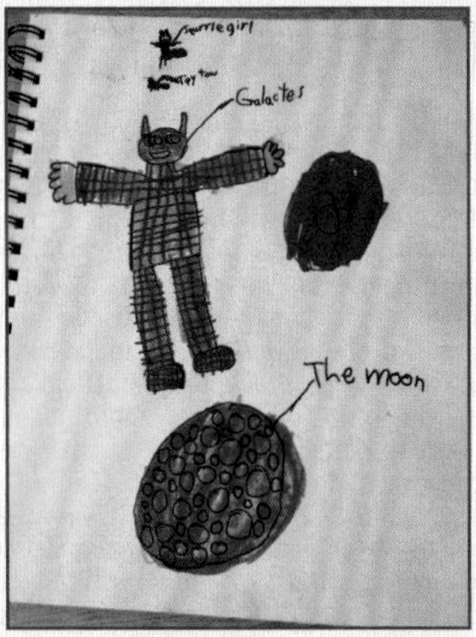
Galactes
The moon

RYAN: Yael, your teacher is not wrong, and there is literally no reason why this dream can't come true! Here's how I got to write SQUIRREL GIRL: I started making my own comics and then eventually Marvel asked me if I would be interested in writing for them, too. It's very hard to get a big company to hire you if you approach them out of the blue and say "Hey, I'm great, you should hire me," but if you make comics that they love, then they will eventually come to you and then you can say "Sure, Marvel, I guess I'll write your comic for you, no problem!" So my advice is to make your own comics, even BETTER than SQUIRREL GIRL, about whatever you want--and as you do that you'll have more and more fun, and get better and better at making comics, and eventually one day the publishers of SQUIRREL GIRL will come to you and say "Yael, do you want to write SQUIRREL GIRL?" and you can say "You will find my answer in the letters page of THE UNBEATABLE SQUIRREL GIRL #35, published back in 2018." Then they'll track down this issue in their archives, and they'll read these words just as you are, and they will find your answer at the end of this sentence: YES. Let's DO this.

Dear Ryan, Erica, Wil and everyone who helps make SQUIRREL GIRL happen:

I've been reading SQUIRREL GIRL since the first issue and have found the comic book a joy to read. I have twin daughters, Elisheva and Yael, who are 8 years old as I write this (and will be 9 years old when you publish this letter). I have shared SQUIRREL GIRL with both of them and Yael has come to love SQUIRREL GIRL as much as I do. You can see the attached picture of her with her own Tippy-Toe.

Back in December 2017, I posted on Twitter the drawing Yael did of the scene where Squirrel Girl and Tippy-Toe meet Galactus on the moon. Ryan and Erica both replied perfectly, to my daughter's delight; she loved knowing that she did the very first drawing ever of "Plaidlactus." I am sending you this email to accompany hers, and hope you will see fit to print her picture and her art in the letter column.

Thank you for making a comic that has allowed me to share my love of comics and super heroes with my children.

Best,
Michael A. Burstein
Brookline, Massachusetts

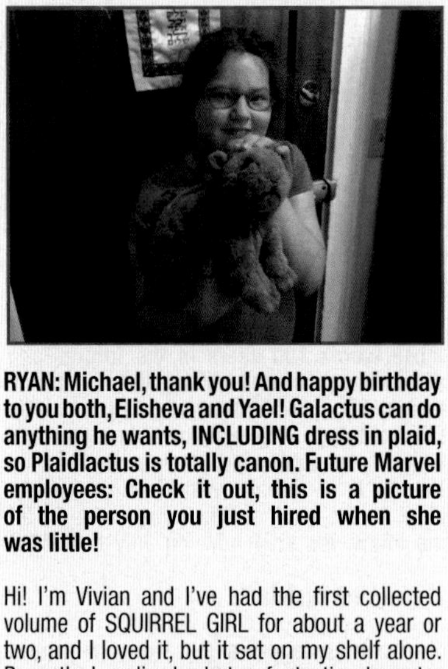

RYAN: Michael, thank you! And happy birthday to you both, Elisheva and Yael! Galactus can do anything he wants, INCLUDING dress in plaid, so Plaidlactus is totally canon. Future Marvel employees: Check it out, this is a picture of the person you just hired when she was little!

Hi! I'm Vivian and I've had the first collected volume of SQUIRREL GIRL for about a year or two, and I loved it, but it sat on my shelf alone. Recently I realized what a fantastic character she is when I rediscovered the series, so I did what any sensible 14-year-old would do and I ordered the rest of the issues. I even ordered some other comics like HELLCAT and HOWARD THE DUCK, and I plan to order even more.

I finally caught up and when the time was right and the planets aligned I finally got a print subscription! I've been waiting to send a letter so I could show my appreciation--and a sculpture I made in art class a few months ago.

I know it doesn't look much like Doreen (she isn't made of metal, to my knowledge) and Tippy has black fur suddenly, but I'm pretty proud of it!

(I made Tippy myself out of two pipe cleaners!)

(The background may or may not be a pillow.)

(P.S. Keep up the good work! I'll miss your art, Erica!)

One big SG fan <3 <3 <3

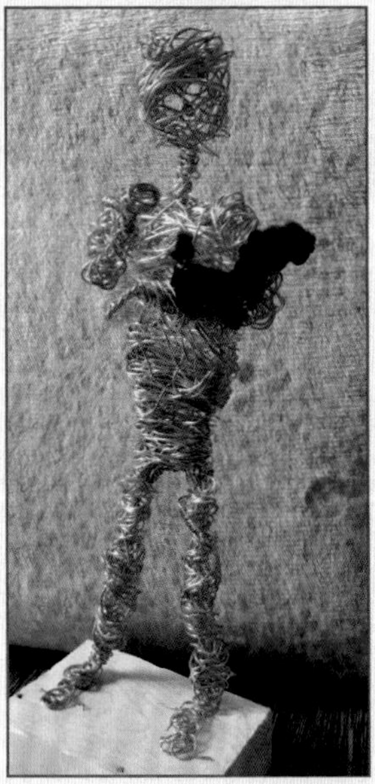

RYAN: Vivan, that's awesome. When I was in school we didn't get to work with metal or anything--it was just paints on paper. Wait, that's not true: We got to do some sculpture, too, but it was with papier-mâché. My friend Anneke pranked our art teacher by making a sculpture of a guy holding his head in his hands, but put his hands on backwards: the left hand was on the right arm and the right hand was on the left arm. The teacher never noticed what she'd done, but kept commenting on how her piece was "interesting" and that "his eyes were drawn to it," etc. As I recall, she got an A, so there is a School Hack for everyone: Swap the hands on your masterpiece and unsuspecting teachers might subconsciously notice something is wrong but not realize why and give you a good grade for such compelling art.

Next Issue:

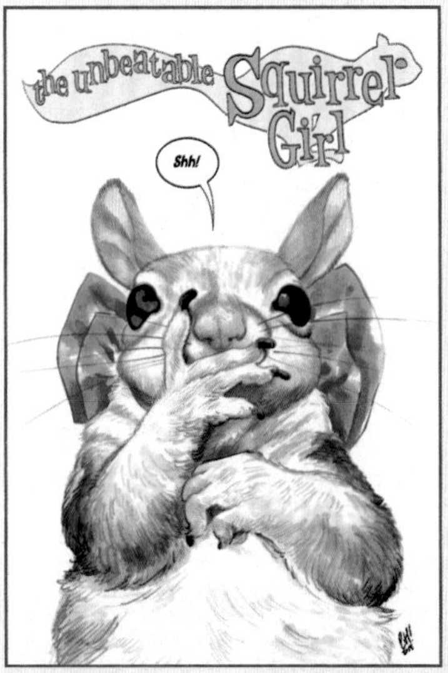
the unbeatable Squirrel Girl
Shh!

Attention, Squirrel Scouts! Make sure to check out our production blog, **unbeatablesquirrelgirl.tumblr.com**, where we post behind-the-scenes stuff on how the book gets made, along with all sorts of cool things *you* make: fanart, cosplay, whatever!

Two weeks later...

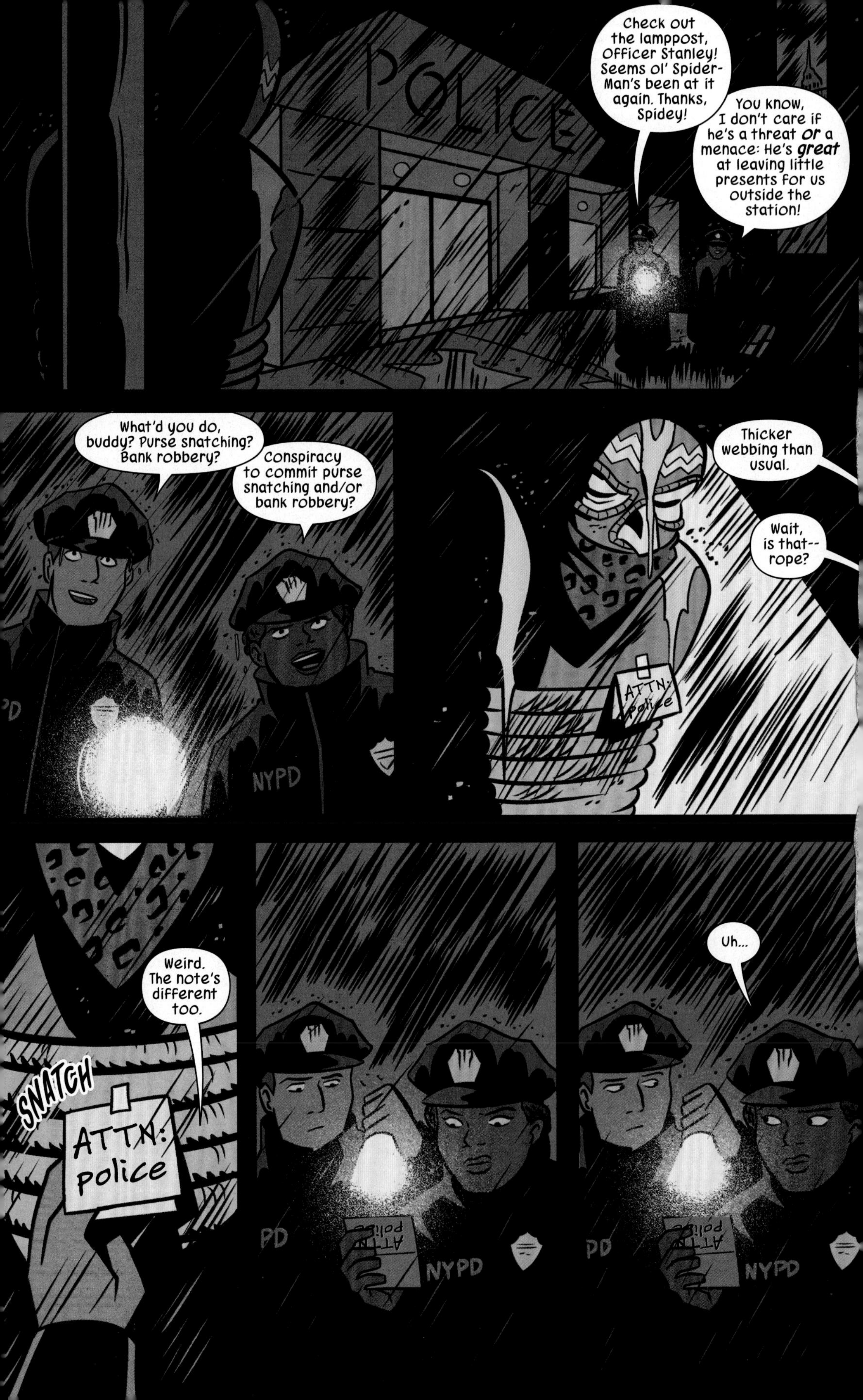
POLICE
Check out the lamppost, Officer Stanley! Seems ol' Spider-Man's been at it again. Thanks, Spidey!
You know, I don't care if he's a threat or a menace: He's great at leaving little presents for us outside the station!
What'd you do, buddy? Purse snatching? Bank robbery?
Conspiracy to commit purse snatching and/or bank robbery?
NYPD
Thicker webbing than usual.
Wait, is that--rope?
ATTN: Police
Weird. The note's different too.
SNATCH
ATTN: police
NYPD
Uh...
NYPD

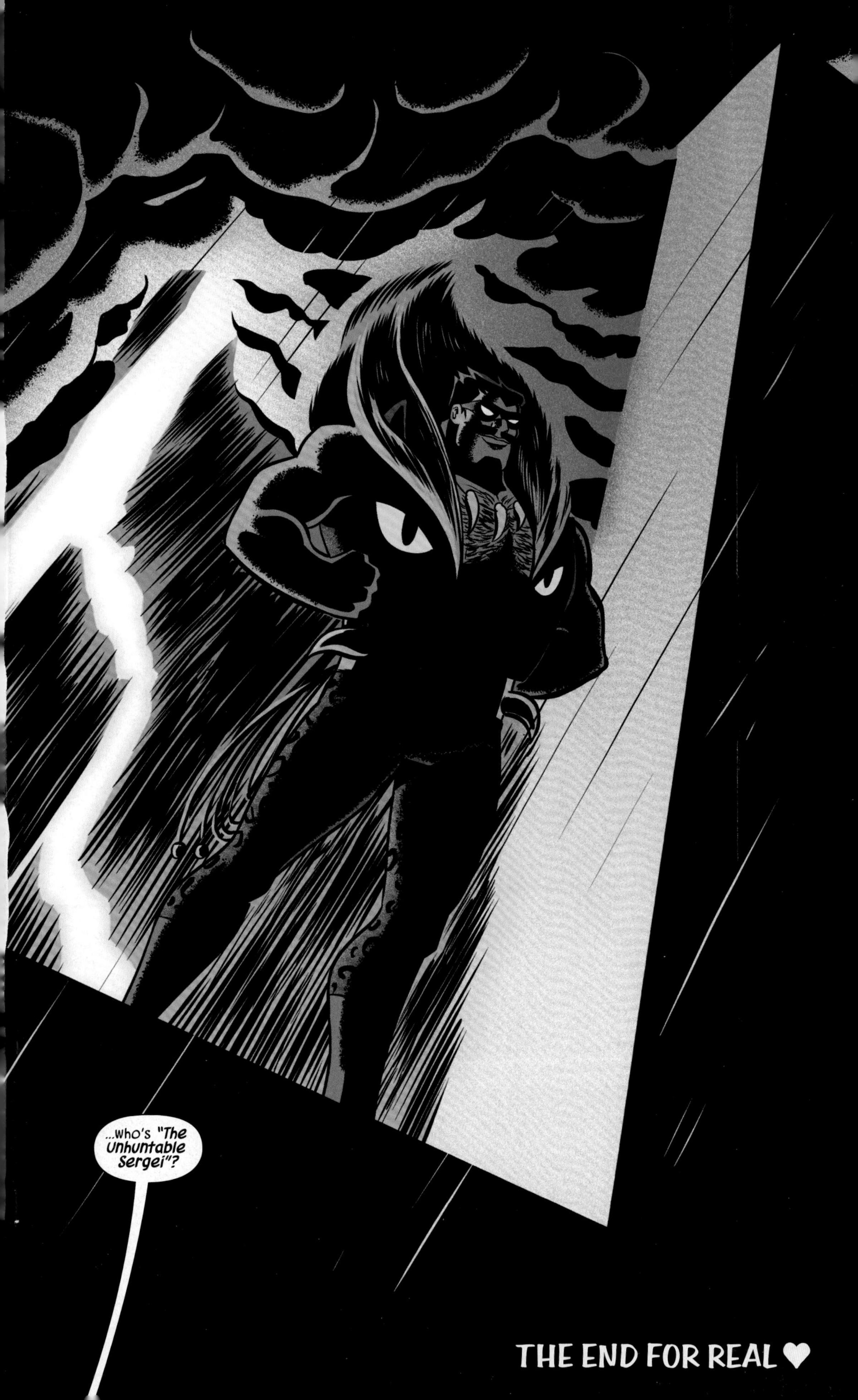
...who's "The Unhuntable Sergei"?
THE END FOR REAL ♥

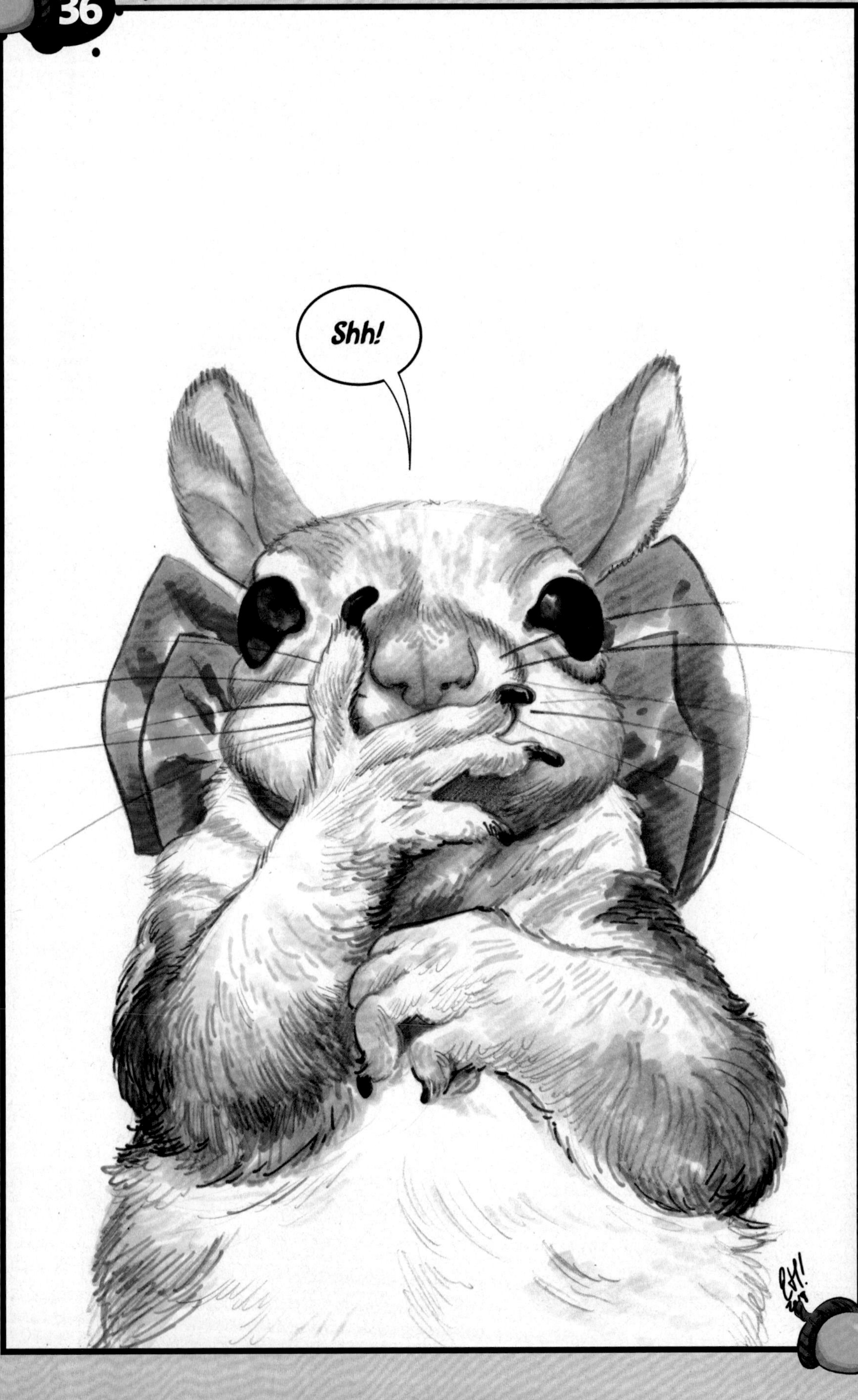
Shh!

Doreen Green isn't just a second-year computer science student: she secretly also has all the powers of both squirrel and girl! She uses her amazing abilities to fight crime **and** be as awesome as possible. You know her as...**The Unbeatable Squirrel Girl!** Find out what she's been up to, with...

Squirrel Girl *in a nutshell*

search! 🔍

#...

#...

#...

#...

#...

#...

Squirrel Girl @unbeatablesg
Hey, you know how sometimes you think you're going to have a fun day escaping a room, but then instead you get accosted by a super villain from another dimension and then you all get arrested and then one of your friends escapes court and you and him and Spider-Man get into a fight?

Squirrel Girl @unbeatablesg
MONDAYS, AM I RIGHT

Squirrel Girl @unbeatablesg
(even though that adventure took place over the course of more than one day, one of them was a Monday, GARFIELD WAS RIGHT ALL ALONG)

Nancy W. @sewwiththeflo
@unbeatablesg called it

Squirrel Girl @unbeatablesg
ANYWAY let's just say that some days are easy, and some days are unexpectedly hard, but we all get to the end of them one way or the other!!

Squirrel Girl @unbeatablesg
Plus, PLUS, Spider-Man and I worked everything out later on with a hearty handshake! I forgave him for webbing me to a wall for no reason, and he forgave ME for being so correct in all my many opinions

Squirrel Girl @unbeatablesg
✦★✦ FRIENDSHIP ✦★✦

Squirrel Girl @unbeatablesg
But here's the point of all this: I thought it'd be a nice break from the Big Important Feelings to have some fun! So me and @starkmantony are going on patrol tonight!!

Squirrel Girl @unbeatablesg
I know what you're thinking: TONY STARK? The BARON of BANTER? The REPOSITORY of REPARTEE? The QUARTERMASTER of QUIPS?

Squirrel Girl @unbeatablesg
And I am here to say: YES, that's the very same Tony Stark I'm talking about, and also, wow you know a lot of synonyms for this guy

Tony Stark @starkmantony ✔
@unbeatablesg You missed one.

Squirrel Girl @unbeatablesg
@starkmantony which one?

Tony Stark @starkmantony ✔
@unbeatablesg "The Never-Finer One-Liner Designer."

Squirrel Girl @unbeatablesg
@starkmantony Oh I wouldn't say I MISSED it, Tony

Tony Stark @starkmantony ✔
@unbeatablesg Hah! Hey, keep that up and you might reach Stark-level banter in--wow, projections say 25 years??

Squirrel Girl @unbeatablesg
CRIMINALS! AS YOU CAN SEE, DELIGHTFUL JOUSTING BOTH VERBAL AND PHYSICAL AWAITS YOU IF YOU DECIDE TO DO ANY CRIMES TONIGHT!!

Squirrel Girl @unbeatablesg
wait that makes it sound like a good and fun thing: don't do any crimes tonight just because you want to see me and @starkmantony hang out!

Squirrel Girl @unbeatablesg
in fact...don't do any crimes in general!! this has been a Squirrel Girl Crime Tip™

Tony Stark @starkmantony ✔
@unbeatablesg "Don't do any crimes in general"--gotta work on the battle cry, SG.

Squirrel Girl @unbeatablesg
@starkmantony We'll talk about it tonight dude

Tony Stark @starkmantony ✔
@unbeatablesg Looking forward to it. There's not a force on Earth that could shut THIS metal-miner never-finer one-liner designer up...

Squirrel Girl @unbeatablesg
@starkmantony omg it got worse

Squirrel Girl @unbeatablesg
@starkmantony YOU DON'T EVEN DO YOUR OWN MINING

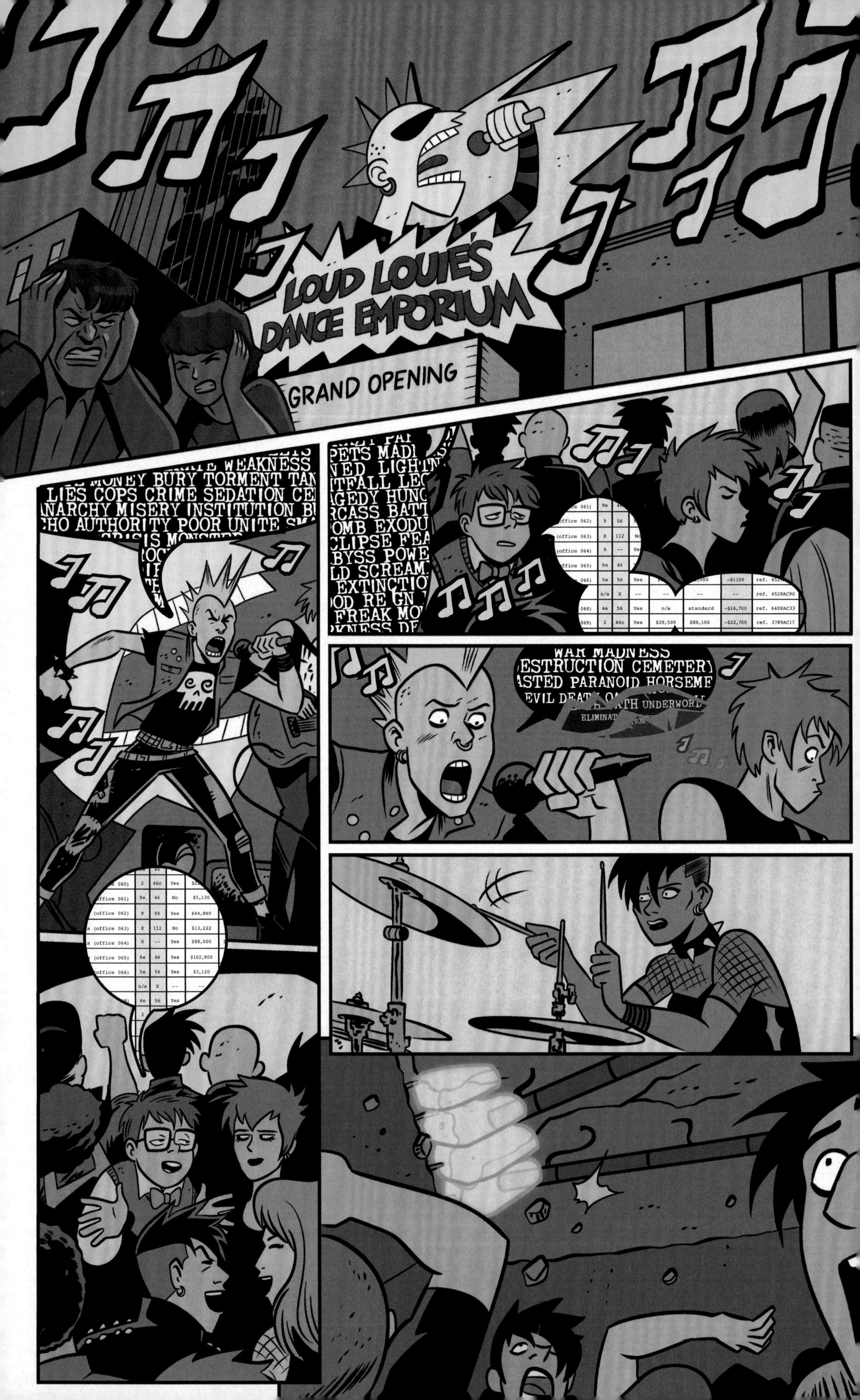
LOUD LOUIE'S DANCE EMPORIUM
GRAND OPENING
MONEY BURY TORMENT TAN
LIES COPS CRIME SEDATION CE
ANARCHY MISERY INSTITUTION B
CHO AUTHORITY POOR UNITE S
PETS MADI
NED LIGHT
AGEDY HUNG
RCASS BATT
OMB EXODU
CLIPSE FEA
BYSS POWE
LD SCREAM
EXTINCTIO
FREAK MO
n/a X -- -- -- -- ref. 4529AC90
068) 4e 56 Yes n/a standard -$16,700 ref. 6408AC33
069) 2 46c Yes $28,500 $88,100 -$22,700 ref. 3789AC17
WAR MADNESS
DESTRUCTION CEMETERY
ASTED PARANOID HORSEME
UNDERWORLD
(office 061) 9e 46 No $5,130
(office 062) 9 56 Yes $44,860
(office 063) X 112 No $13,222
(office 064) X -- Yes $88,000
(office 065) 6e 46 Yes $102,900
(office 066) 5e 56 Yes $3,120

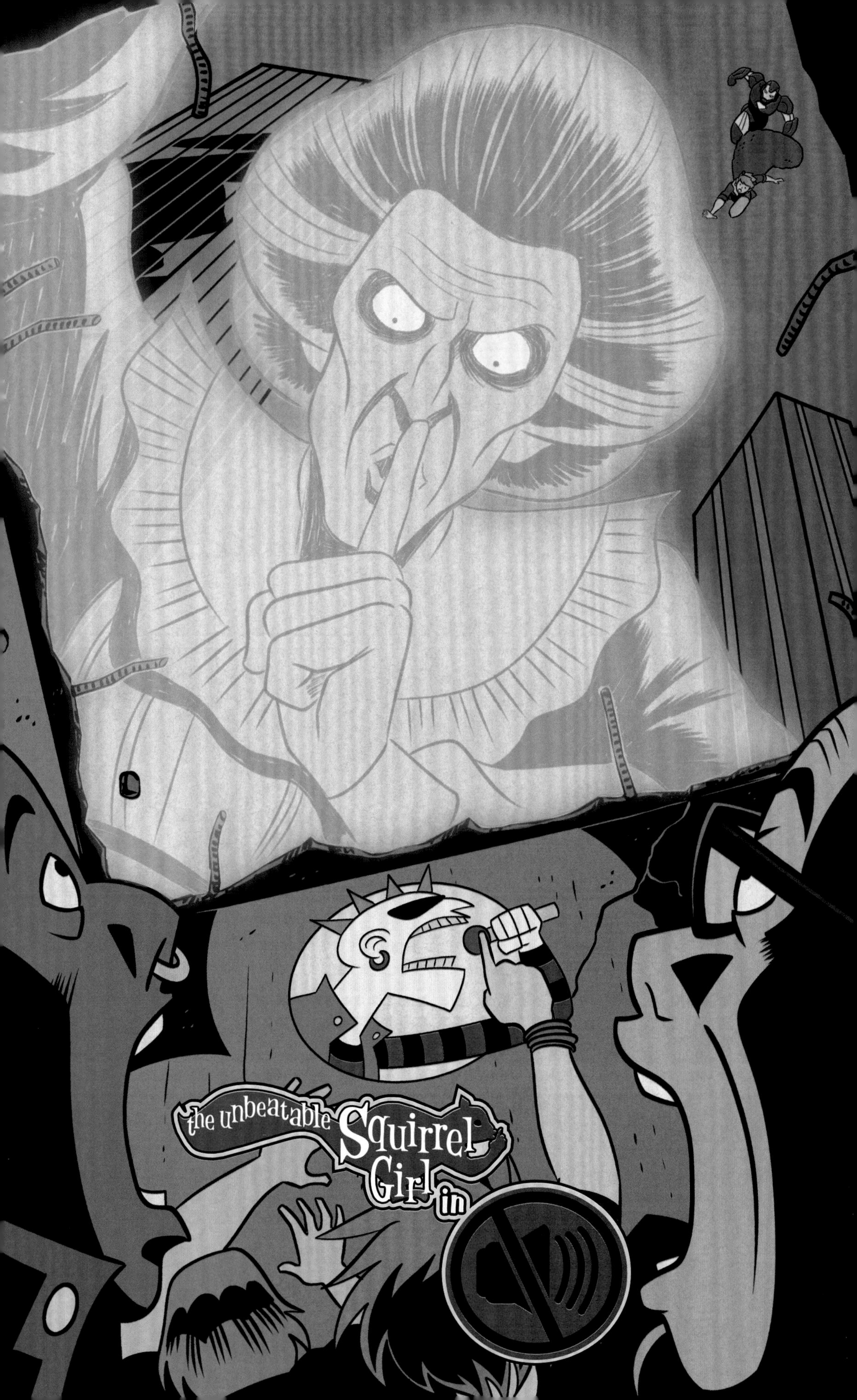
the unbeatable Squirrel Girl in

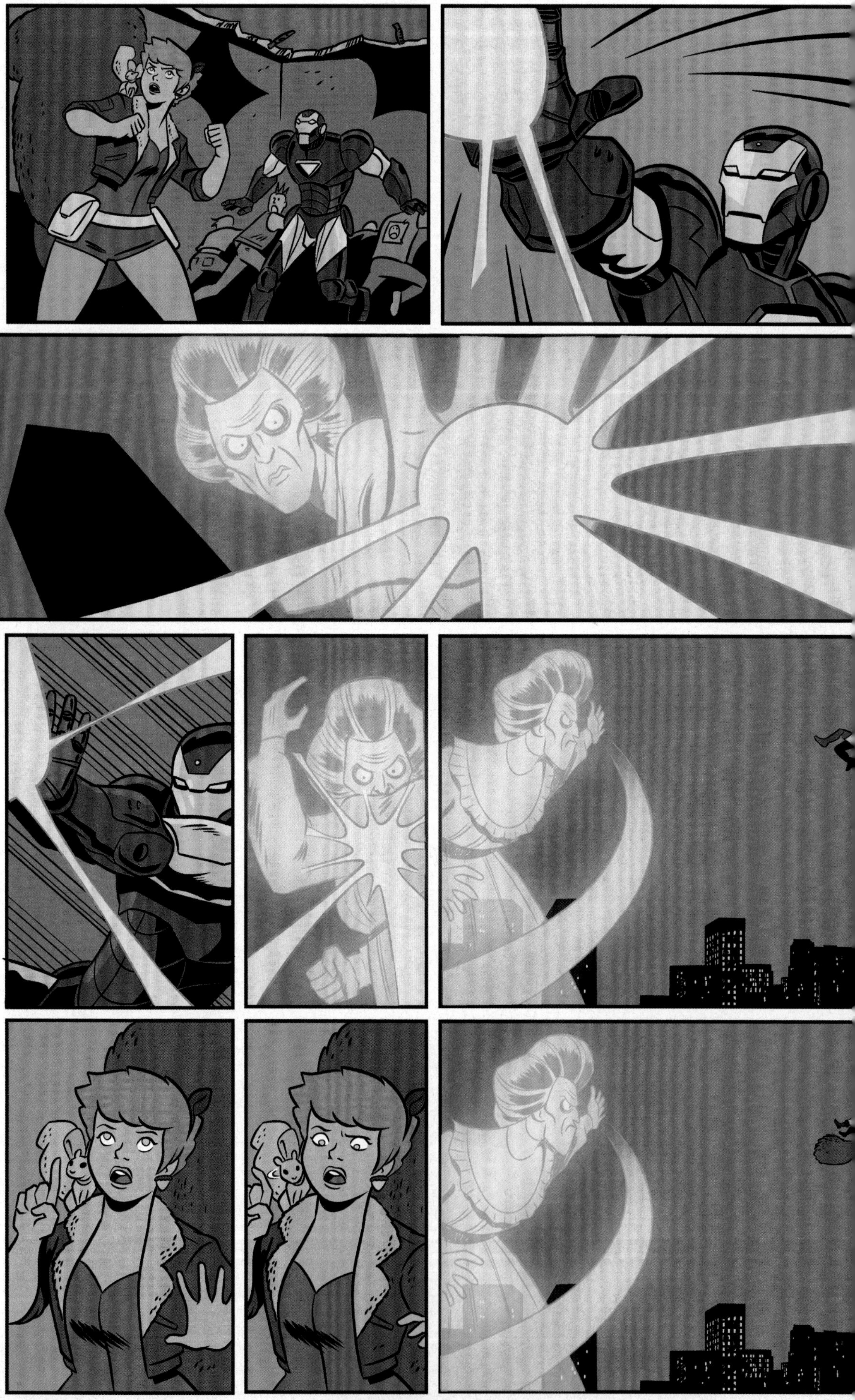

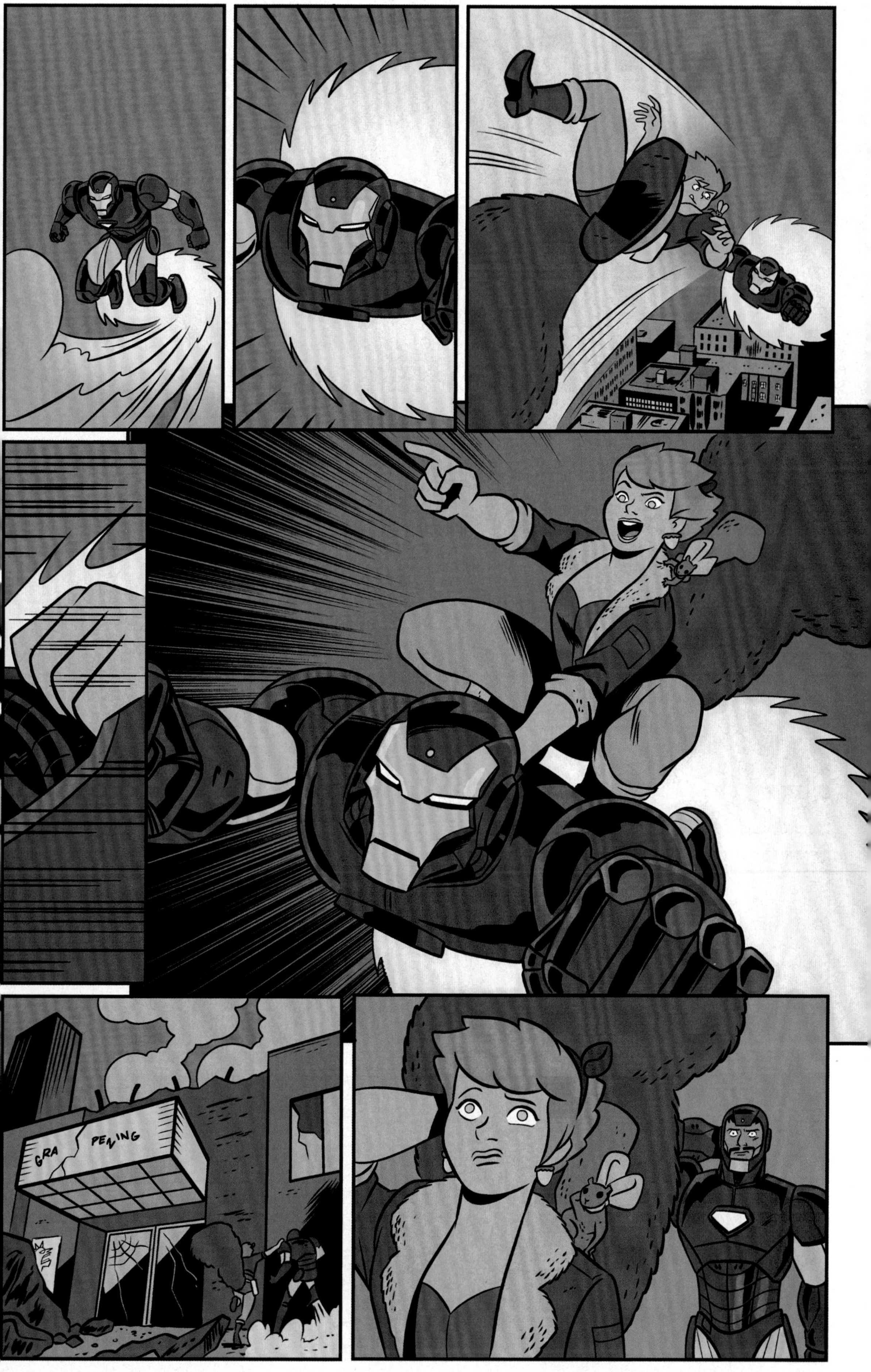
GRA
PENING

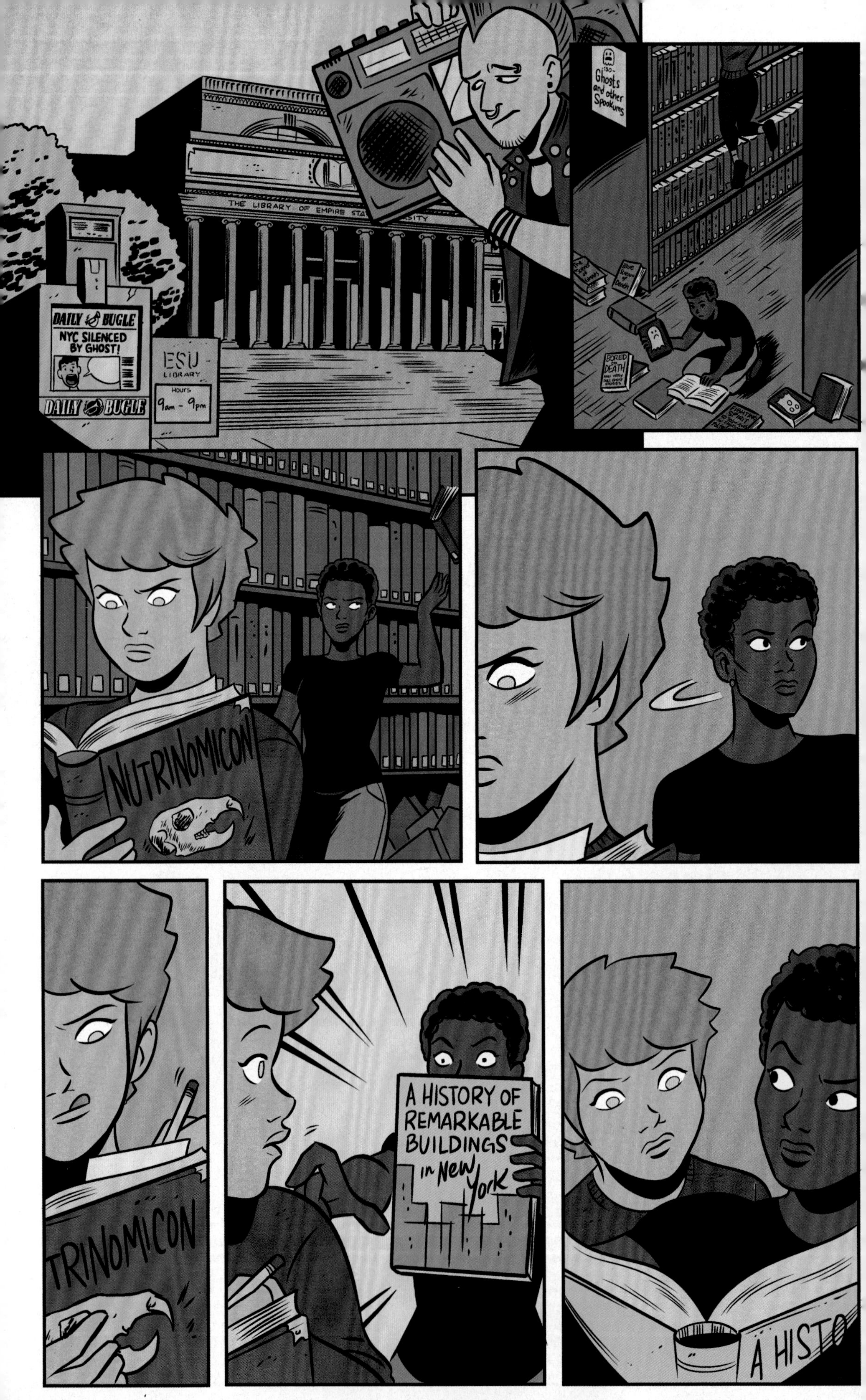
THE LIBRARY OF EMPIRE STA
SITY
DAILY BUGLE
NYC SILENCED BY GHOST!
DAILY BUGLE
ESU LIBRARY
Hours 9am - 9pm
-130-
Ghosts and other Spookums
The Science of Ghosts
Blue Scream of Death
BORED TO DEATH
FIGHTING SPIRIT
NUTRINOMICON
TRINOMICON
A HISTORY OF REMARKABLE BUILDINGS in New York
A HISTO

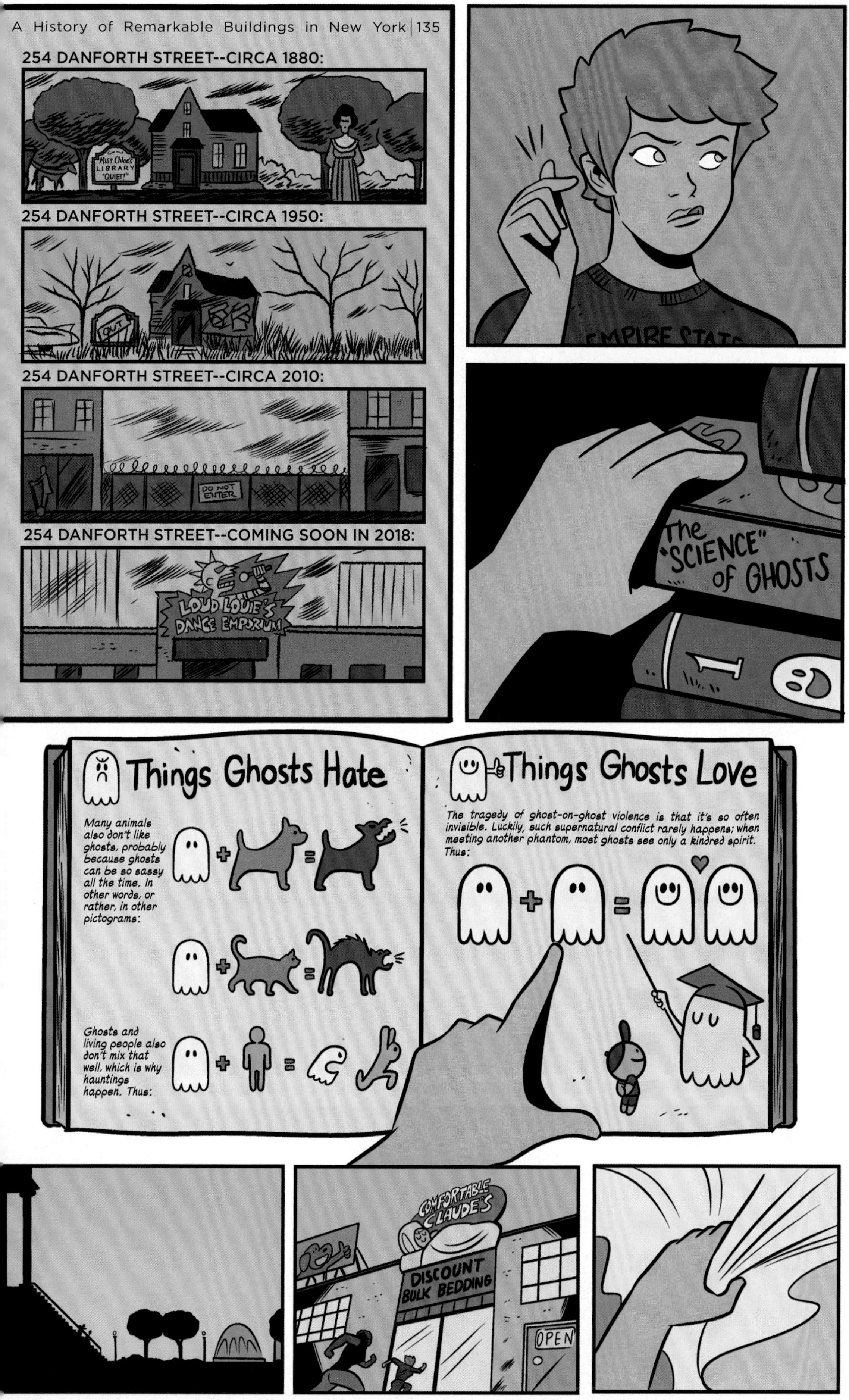

A History of Remarkable Buildings in New York | 135
254 DANFORTH STREET--CIRCA 1880:
Miss Chloe's LIBRARY "QUIET!"
254 DANFORTH STREET--CIRCA 1950:
OUT
254 DANFORTH STREET--CIRCA 2010:
DO NOT ENTER
254 DANFORTH STREET--COMING SOON IN 2018:
LOUD LOUIE'S DANCE EMPORIUM
The "SCIENCE" of GHOSTS
Things Ghosts Hate
Many animals also don't like ghosts, probably because ghosts can be so sassy all the time. In other words, or rather, in other pictograms:
Ghosts and living people also don't mix that well, which is why hauntings happen. Thus:
Things Ghosts Love
The tragedy of ghost-on-ghost violence is that it's so often invisible. Luckily, such supernatural conflict rarely happens; when meeting another phantom, most ghosts see only a kindred spirit. Thus:
COMFORTABLE CLAUDE'S
DISCOUNT BULK BEDDING
OPEN

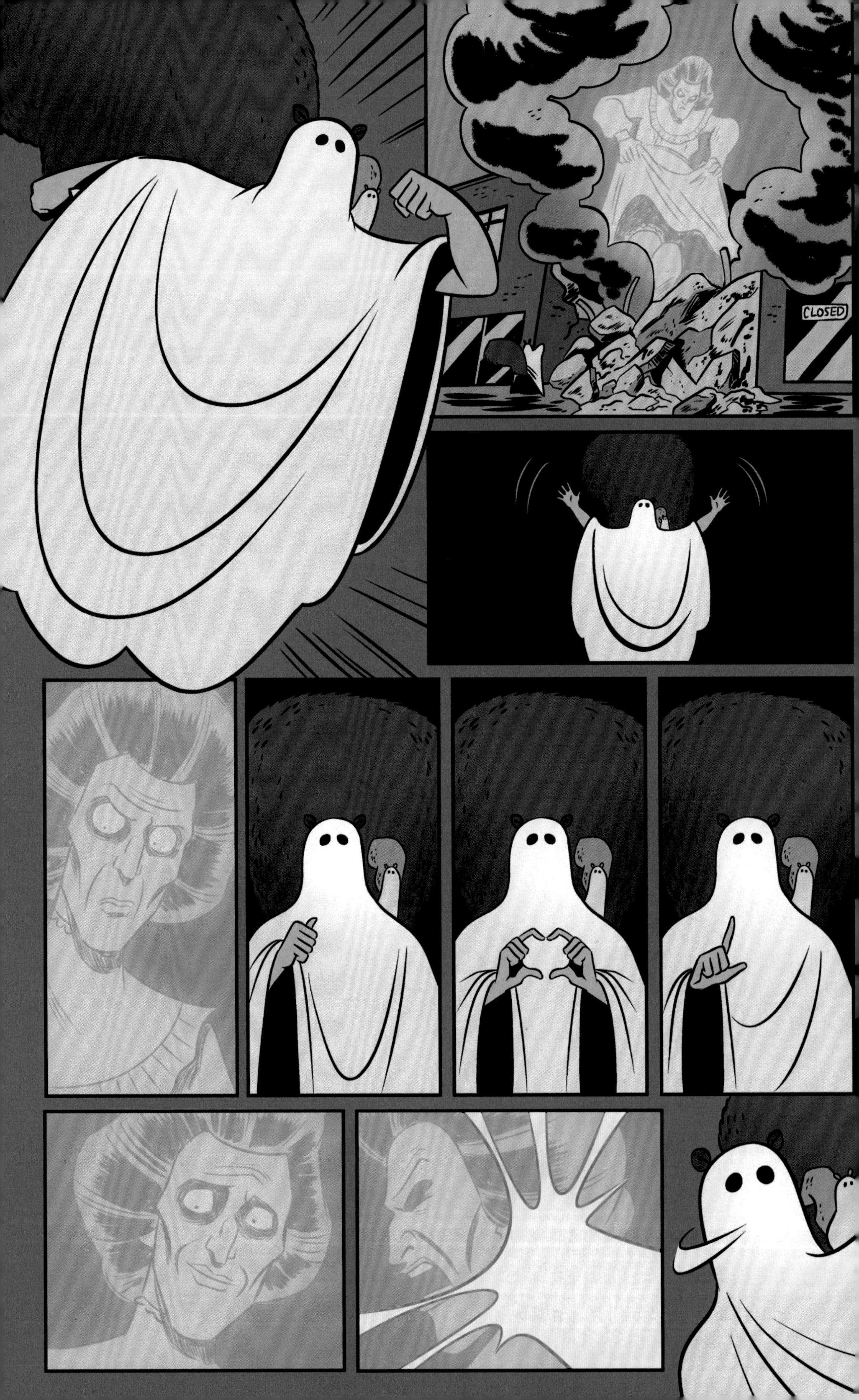
CLOSED

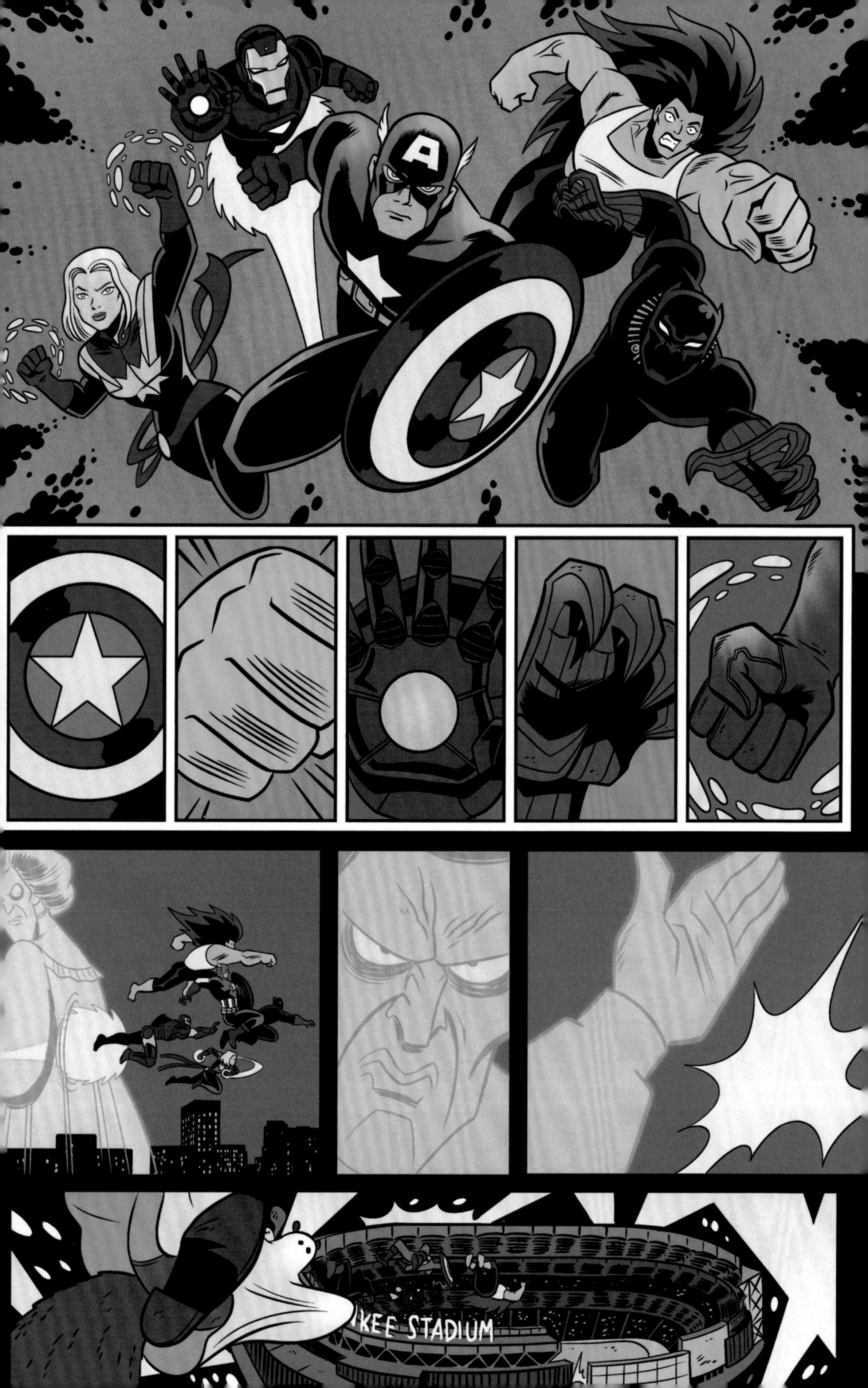
KEE STADIUM

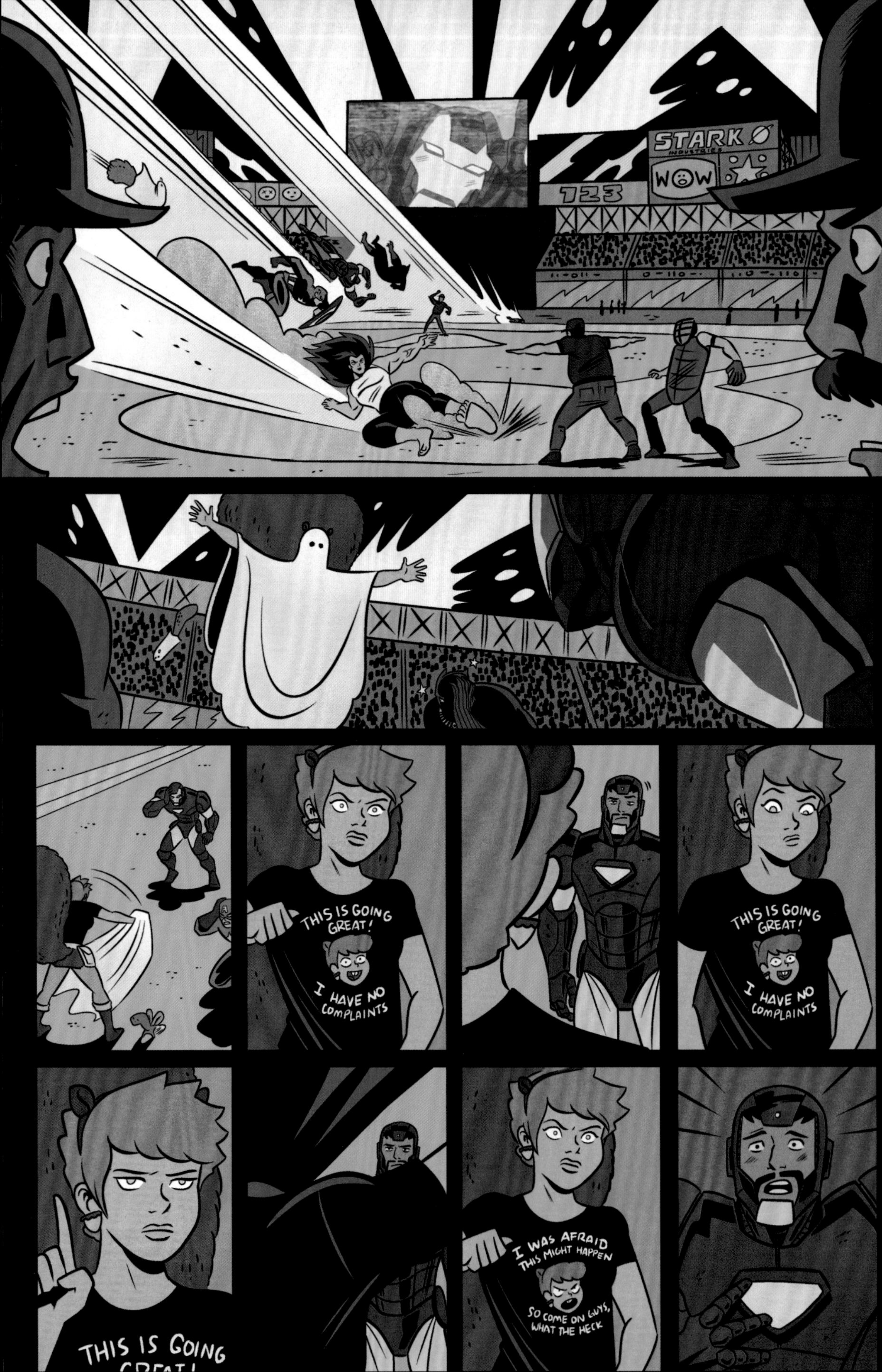
STARK
INDUSTRIES
WOW
123
THIS IS GOING GREAT!
I HAVE NO COMPLAINTS
THIS IS GOING GREAT!
I HAVE NO COMPLAINTS
THIS IS GOING
I WAS AFRAID THIS MIGHT HAPPEN
SO COME ON GUYS, WHAT THE HECK

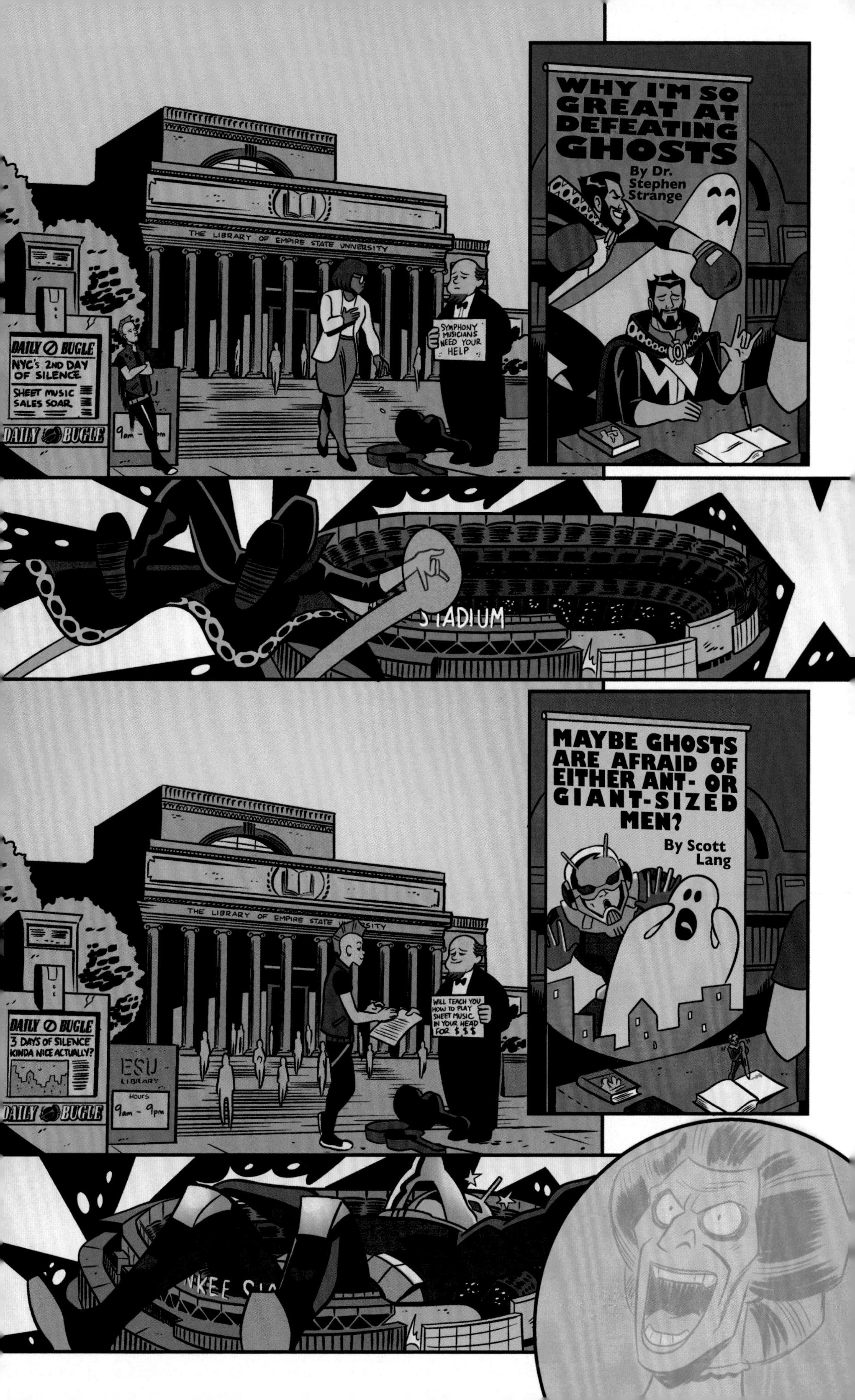

THE LIBRARY OF EMPIRE STATE UNIVERSITY
DAILY BUGLE
NYC's 2ND DAY OF SILENCE
SHEET MUSIC SALES SOAR
DAILY BUGLE
SYMPHONY MUSICIANS NEED YOUR HELP
WHY I'M SO GREAT AT DEFEATING GHOSTS
By Dr. Stephen Strange
STADIUM
MAYBE GHOSTS ARE AFRAID OF EITHER ANT- OR GIANT-SIZED MEN?
By Scott Lang
DAILY BUGLE
3 DAYS OF SILENCE KINDA NICE ACTUALLY?
DAILY BUGLE
ESU LIBRARY
Hours
9am - 9pm
WILL TEACH YOU HOW TO PLAY SHEET MUSIC IN YOUR HEAD FOR $$$

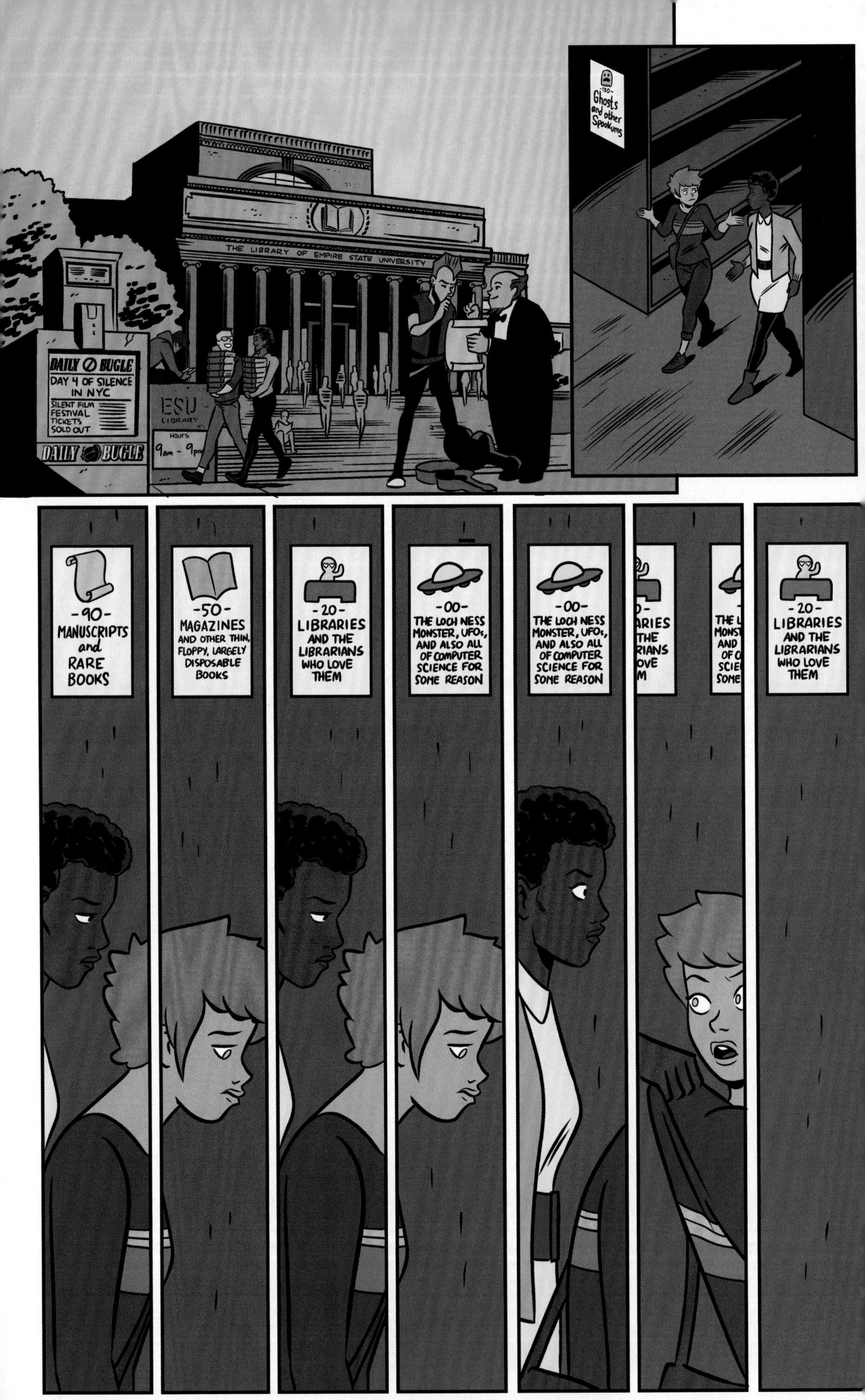
THE LIBRARY OF EMPIRE STATE UNIVERSITY
DAILY BUGLE
DAY 4 OF SILENCE IN NYC
SILENT FILM FESTIVAL TICKETS SOLD OUT
DAILY BUGLE
ESU LIBRARY
HOURS
9am - 9pm
-130- Ghosts and other Spookums
-90- MANUSCRIPTS and RARE BOOKS
-50- MAGAZINES AND OTHER THIN, FLOPPY, LARGELY DISPOSABLE BOOKS
-20- LIBRARIES AND THE LIBRARIANS WHO LOVE THEM
-00- THE LOCH NESS MONSTER, UFOs, AND ALSO ALL OF COMPUTER SCIENCE FOR SOME REASON
-00- THE LOCH NESS MONSTER, UFOs, AND ALSO ALL OF COMPUTER SCIENCE FOR SOME REASON
-20- LIBRARIES AND THE LIBRARIANS WHO LOVE THEM

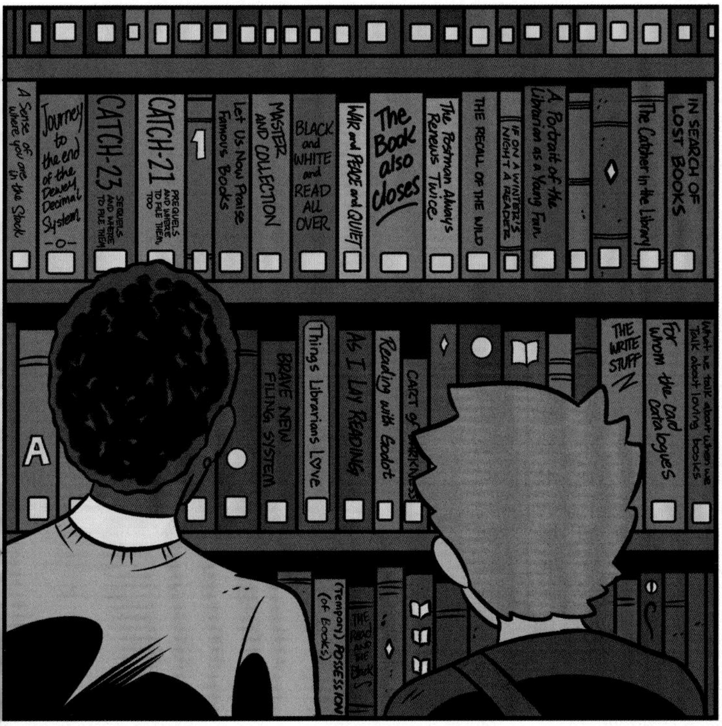
A Sense of where you are in the Stack
Journey to the end of the Dewey Decimal System
CATCH-23 SEQUELS AND WHERE TO FILE THEM
CATCH-21 PREQUELS AND WHERE TO FILE THEM, TOO
Let Us Now Praise Famous Books
MASTER AND COLLECTION
BLACK and WHITE and READ ALL OVER
WAR and PEACE and QUIET
The Book also closes
The Postman Always Renews Twice
THE RECALL OF THE WILD
A Portrait of the Librarian as a Young Fan
The Catcher in the Library
IN SEARCH OF LOST BOOKS
BRAVE NEW FILING SYSTEM
Things Librarians Love
As I Lay Reading
Reading with Godot
CART OF DARKNESS
THE WRITE STUFF
For whom the Card Catalogues
What we talk about when we talk about loving books

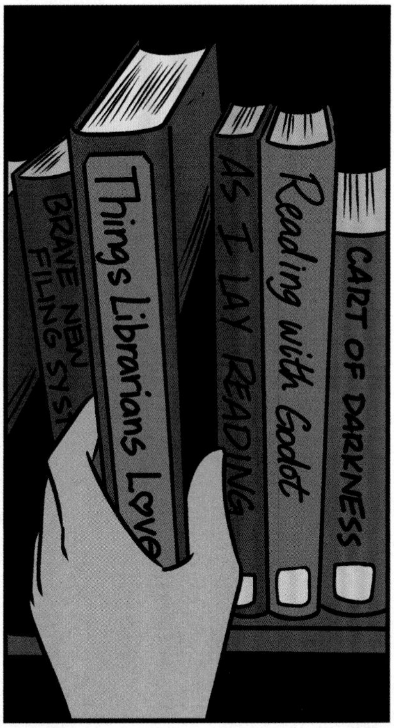
BRAVE NEW FILING SYST
Things Librarians Love
AS I LAY READING
Reading with Godot
CART OF DARKNESS

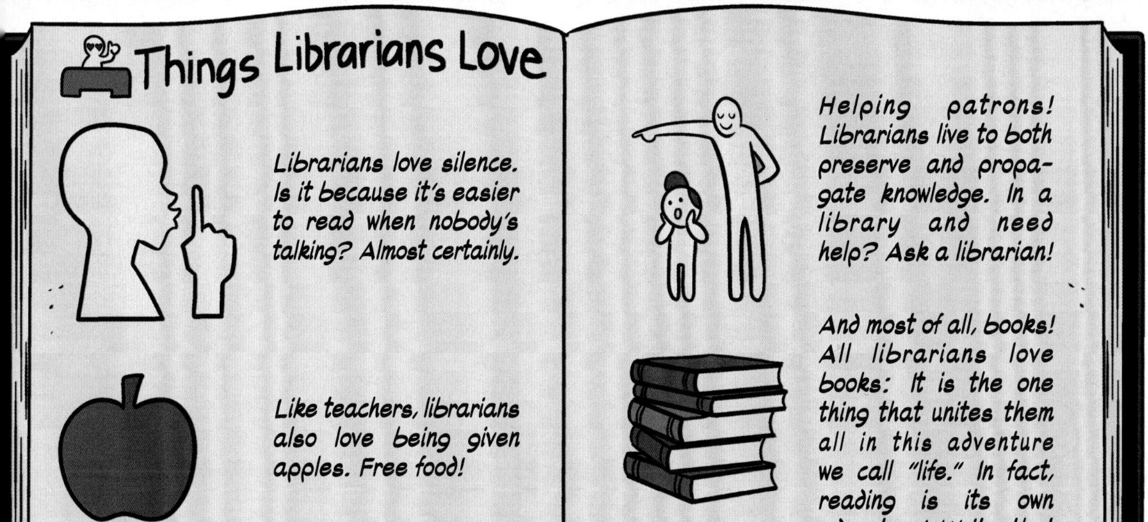
Things Librarians Love
Librarians love silence. Is it because it's easier to read when nobody's talking? Almost certainly.
Like teachers, librarians also love being given apples. Free food!
Nothing beats a free tote bag, especially if it advertises reading to people who must already know how to read in order to understand that message!
Sorry, my weekend's BOOKED
Helping patrons! Librarians live to both preserve and propagate knowledge. In a library and need help? Ask a librarian!
And most of all, books! All librarians love books: It is the one thing that unites them all in this adventure we call "life." In fact, reading is its own adventure! Write that down.
Also, most library systems are criminally underfunded and deserve way more money, so there's that too.

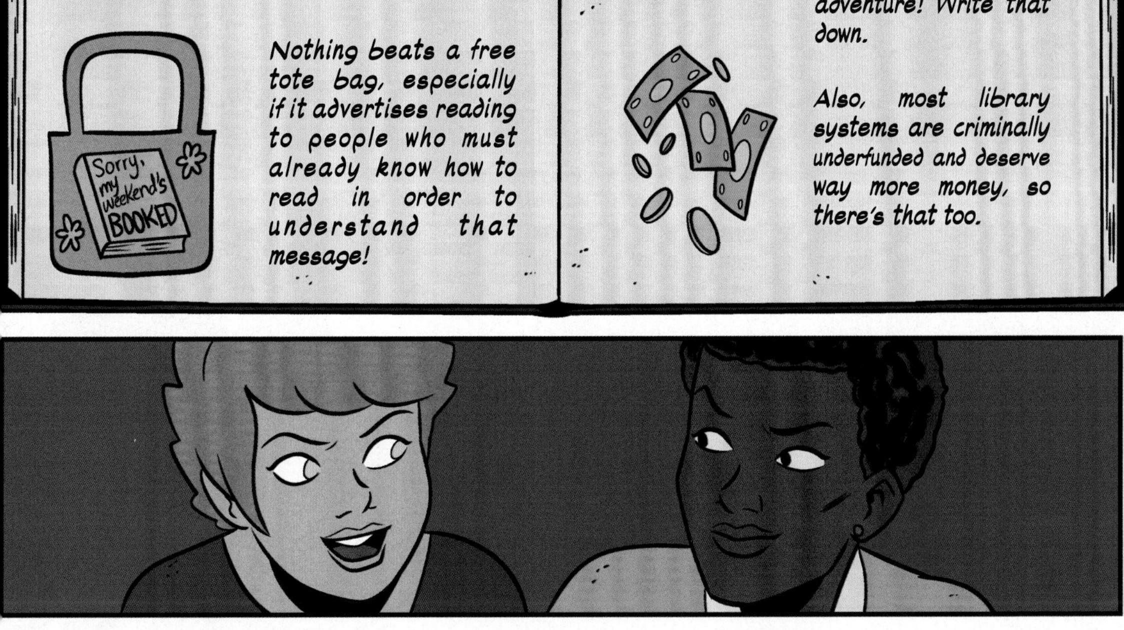

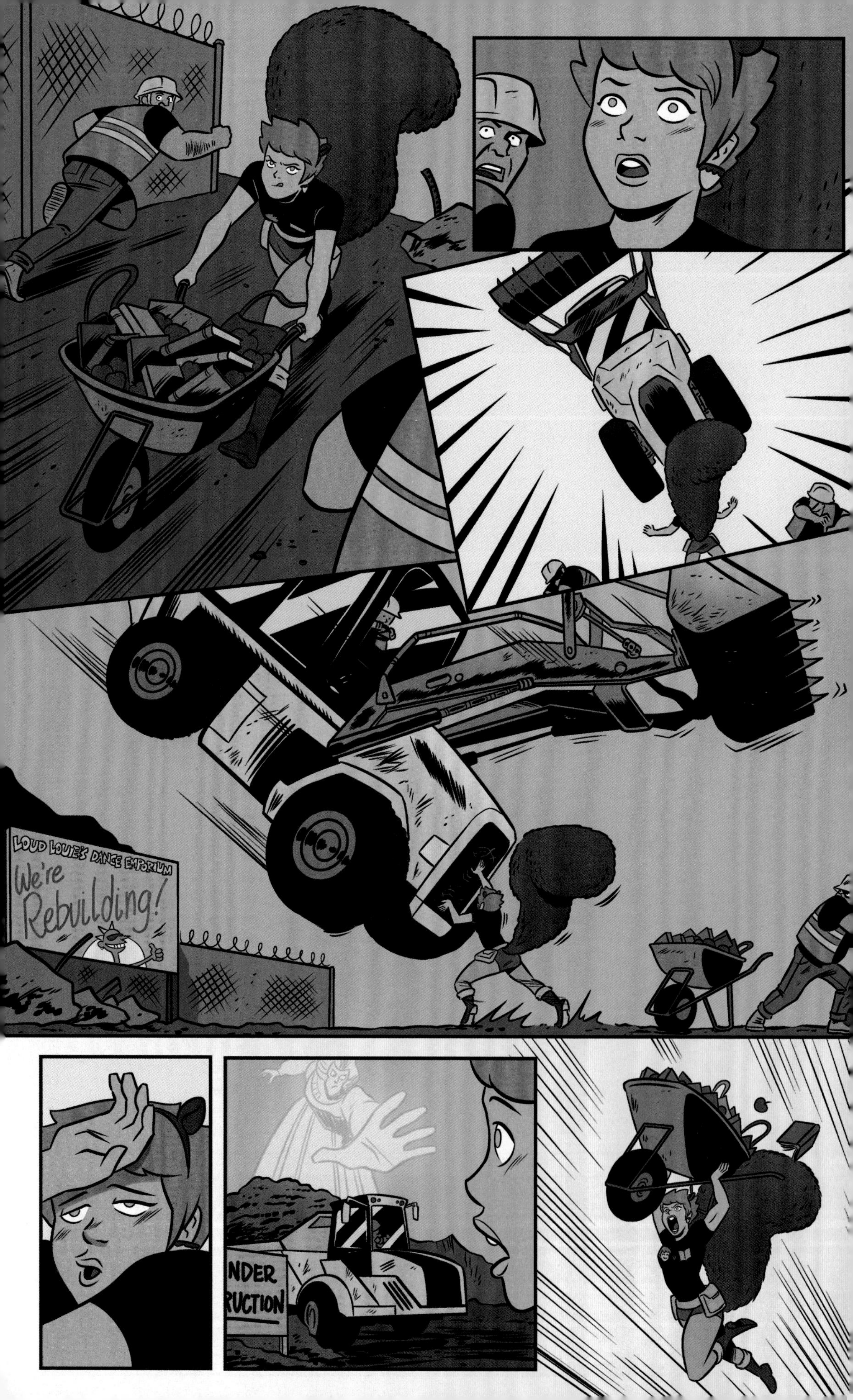

LOUD LOUIE'S DANCE EMPORIUM
We're Rebuilding!
NDER
RUCTION

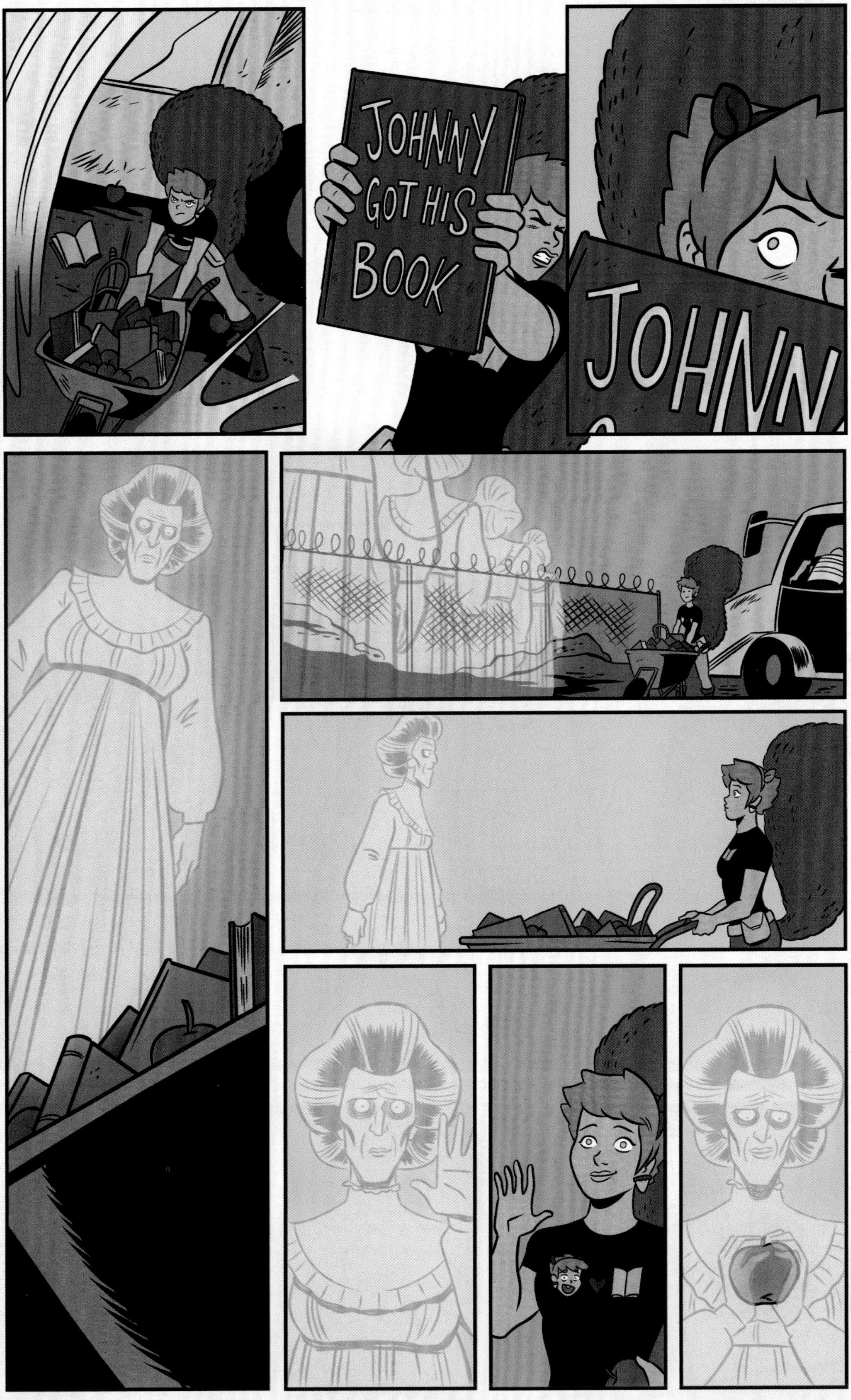
JOHNNY GOT HIS BOOK
JOHNN

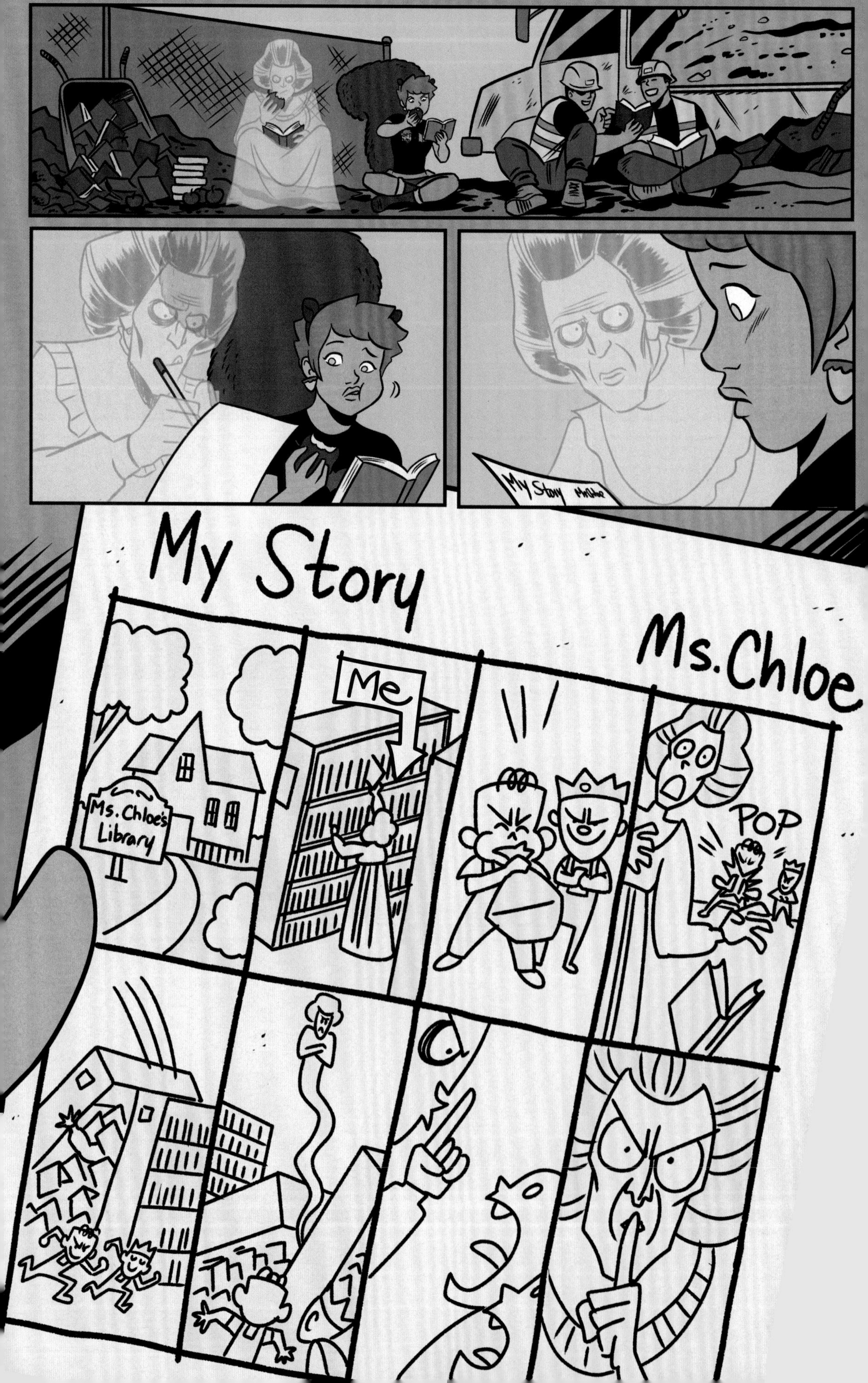
My Story
Ms.Chloe
My Story
Ms.Chloe
Ms.Chloe's Library
Me
POP

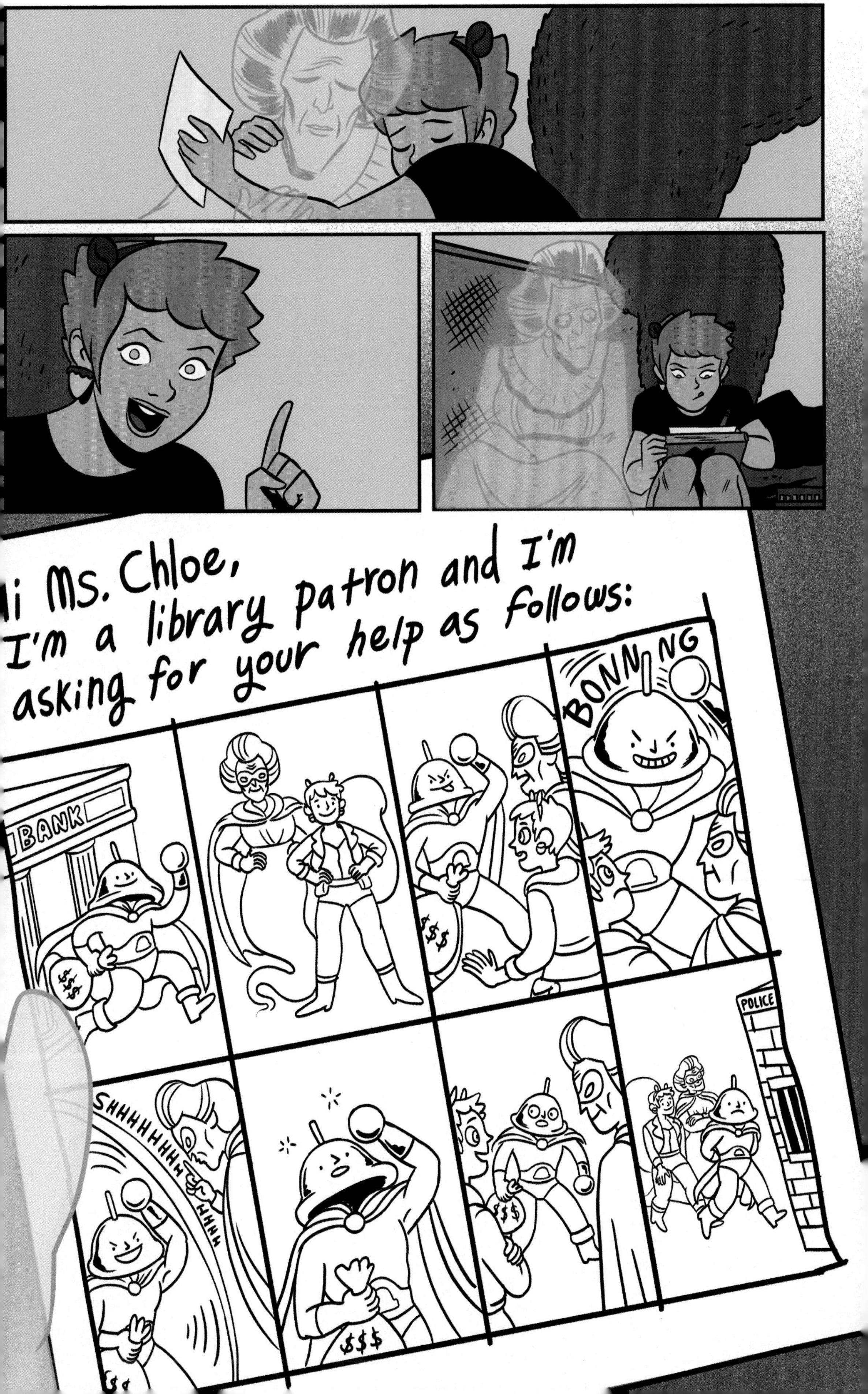

i Ms. Chloe,
I'm a library patron and I'm
asking for your help as follows:
BANK
BONNNNG
POLICE
SHHHHHHHHHHHHH
$$$

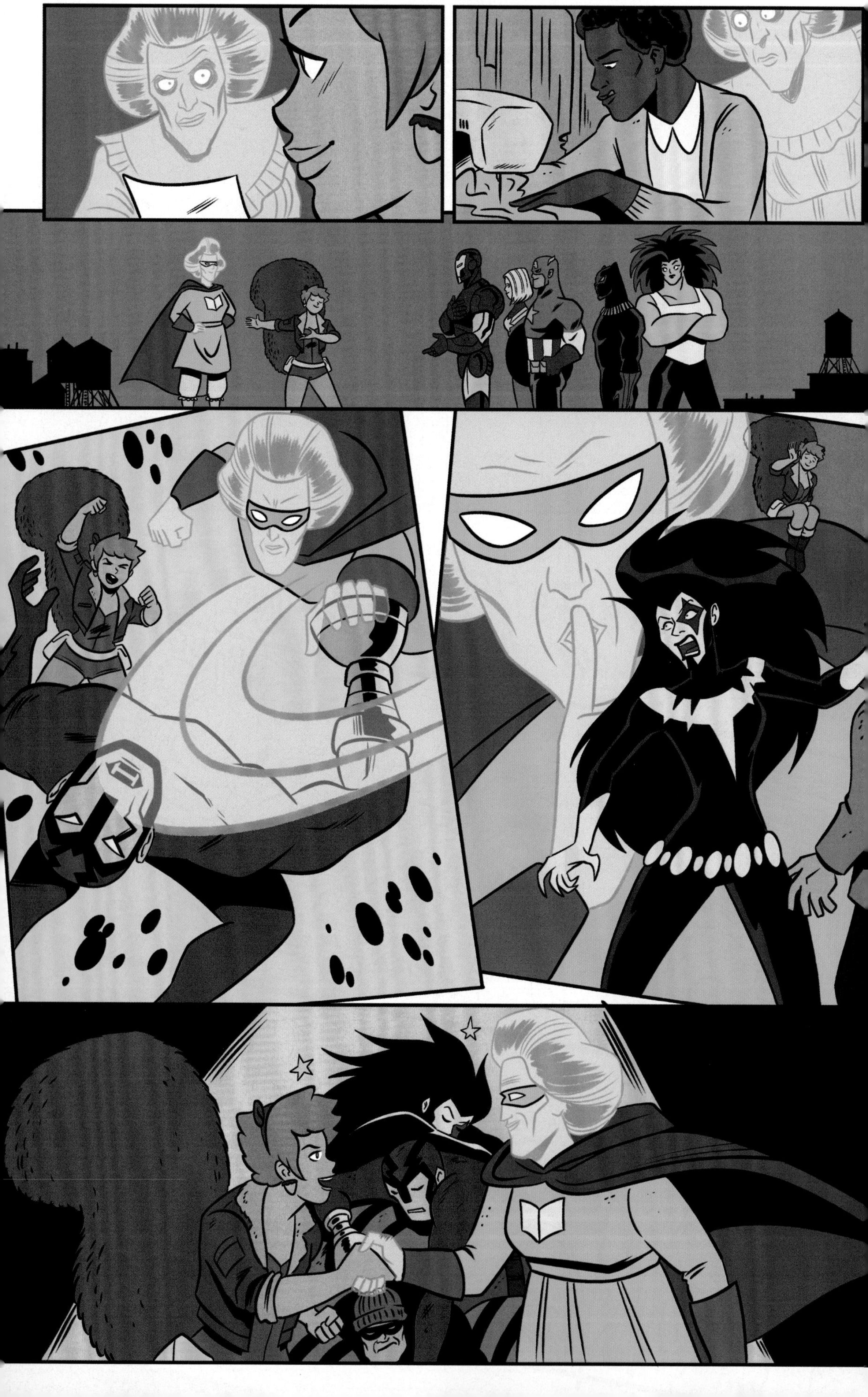

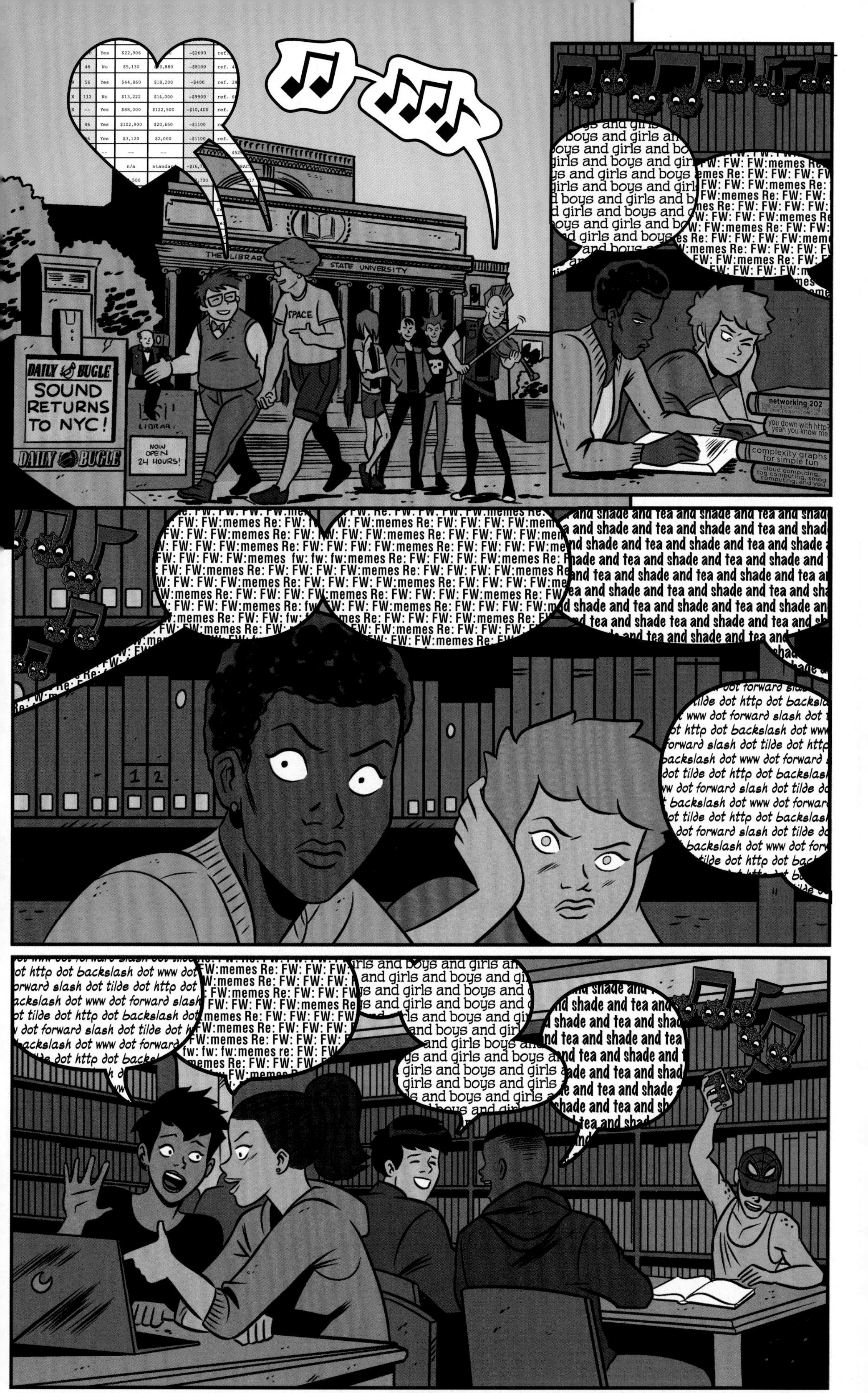
THE LIBRARY
STATE UNIVERSITY
SPACE
DAILY BUGLE
SOUND RETURNS TO NYC!
DAILY BUGLE
NOW OPEN 24 HOURS!
boys and girls and girls and boys and girls and boys and girls and boys and girls and boys and girls and boys
FW: FW: FW:memes Re: FW: FW: FW:memes Re: FW: FW: FW:memes Re: FW: FW: FW:memes
networking 202
you down with http? yeah you know me
complexity graphs for simple fun
cloud computing, fog computing, smog computing, and you
FW: FW: FW:memes Re: FW: FW: FW:memes fw: fw: fw:memes Re: FW: FW: FW:memes Re: FW: FW: FW:memes
and shade and tea and shade and tea and shade and tea and shade and tea and shade and tea and shade
dot forward slash dot tilde dot http dot backslash dot www dot forward slash dot tilde dot http dot backslash
dot http dot backslash dot www dot forward slash dot tilde dot http dot backslash dot www dot forward slash
FW:memes Re: FW: FW: FW:memes Re: FW: FW: FW:memes fw: fw: fw:memes re: FW: FW:memes
girls and boys and girls and boys and girls boys and girls and boys and girls and boys and girls
shade and tea and shade and tea and shade and tea and shade and tea and shade

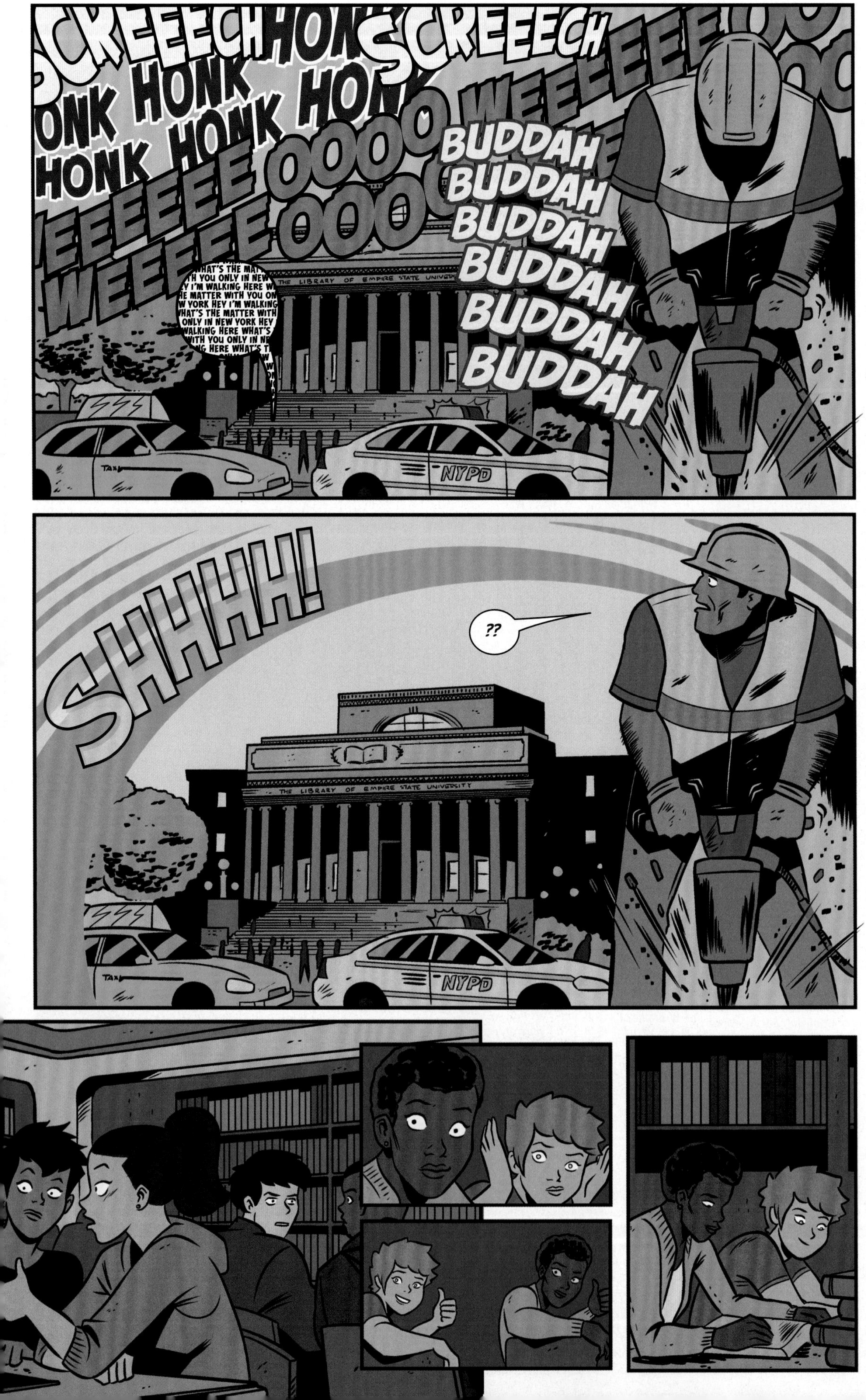
SCREEECH
HONK HONK
HONK HONK HONK
SCREEECH
WEEEEEE OOOO
WEEEEEE OOOO
WHAT'S THE MAT
TH YOU ONLY IN NEW
Y I'M WALKING HERE W
HE MATTER WITH YOU ON
W YORK HEY I'M WALKING
WHAT'S THE MATTER WITH
ONLY IN NEW YORK HEY
WALKING HERE WHAT'S
WITH YOU ONLY IN N
G HERE WHAT'S T
THE LIBRARY OF EMPIRE STATE UNIVERSITY
BUDDAH
BUDDAH
BUDDAH
BUDDAH
BUDDAH
BUDDAH
BUDDAH
NYPD
SHHHH!
??
THE LIBRARY OF EMPIRE STATE UNIVERSITY
NYPD

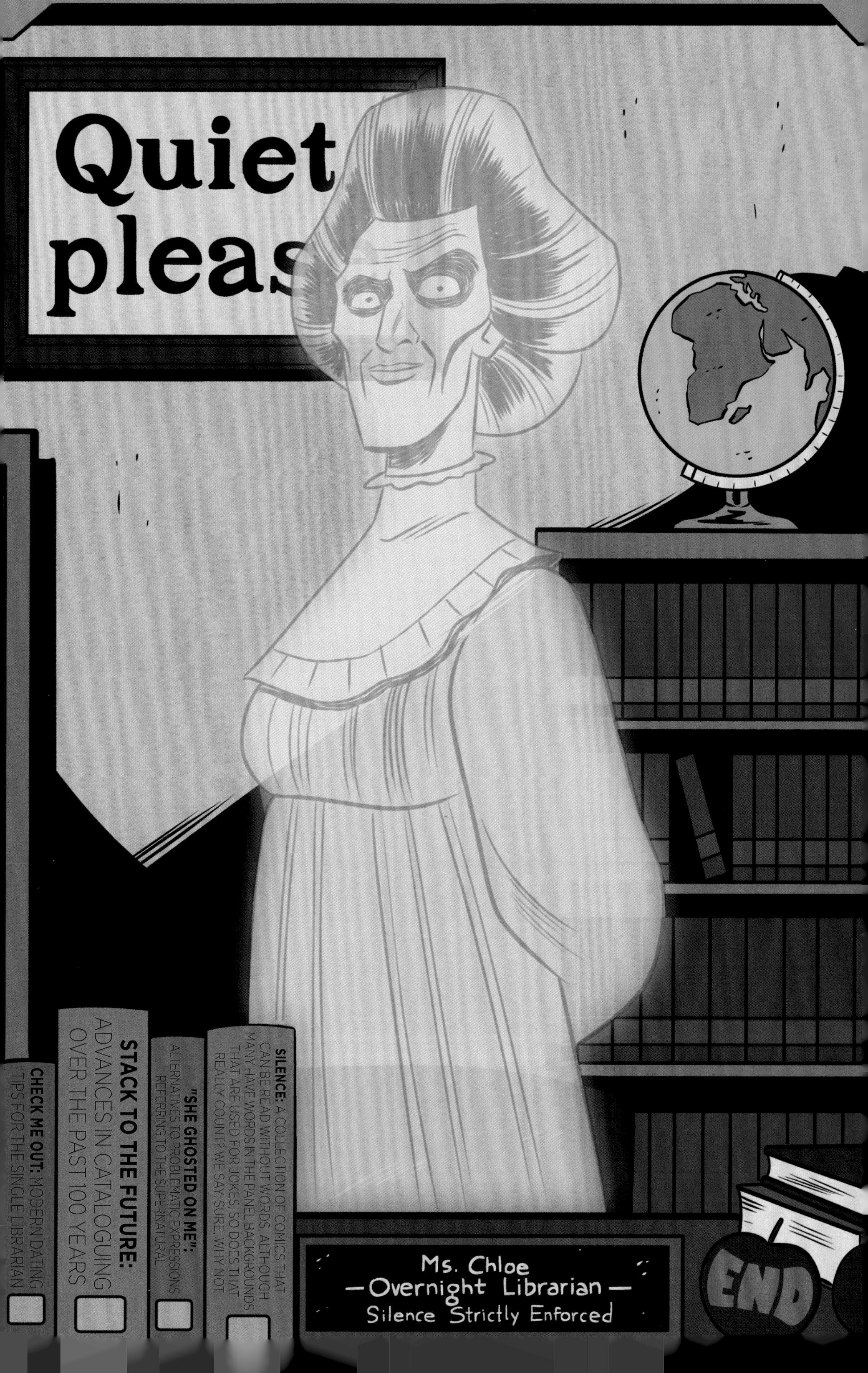

Quiet
pleas
CHECK ME OUT: MODERN DATING TIPS FOR THE SINGLE LIBRARIAN
STACK TO THE FUTURE: ADVANCES IN CATALOGUING OVER THE PAST 100 YEARS
"SHE GHOSTED ON ME": ALTERNATIVES TO PROBLEMATIC EXPRESSIONS REFERRING TO THE SUPERNATURAL
SILENCE: A COLLECTION OF COMICS THAT CAN BE READ WITHOUT WORDS. ALTHOUGH MANY HAVE WORDS IN THE PANEL BACKGROUNDS THAT ARE USED FOR JOKES. SO DOES THAT REALLY COUNT? WE SAY SURE, WHY NOT
Ms. Chloe
—Overnight Librarian—
Silence Strictly Enforced
END

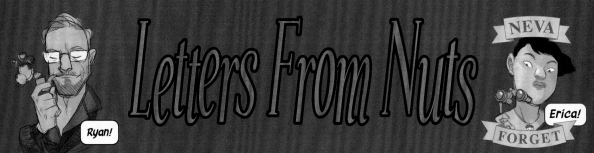

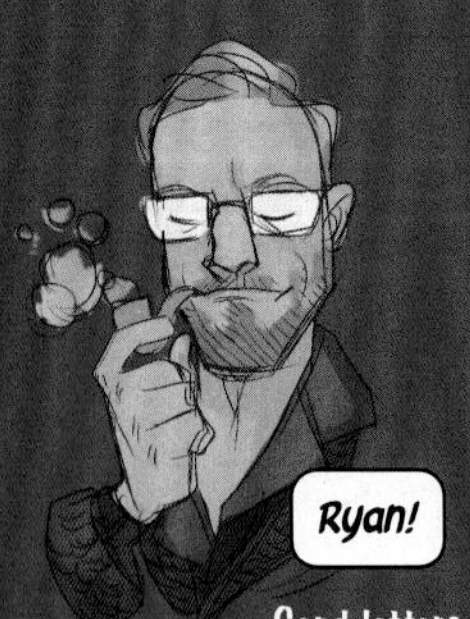
Ryan!

Letters From Nuts

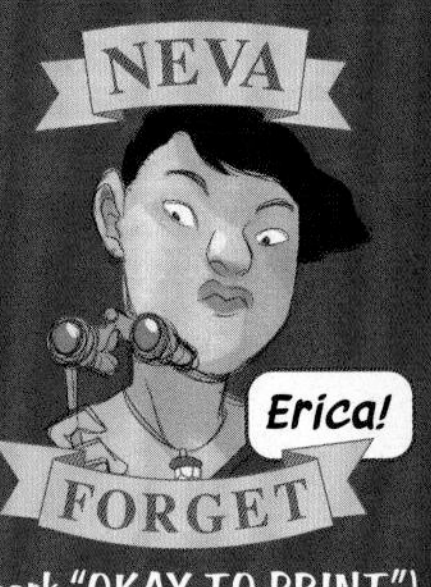
NEVA
Erica!
FORGET

Send letters to mheroes@marvel.com or 135 W 50th St, 7th Floor, New York, NY 10020 (Please mark "OKAY TO PRINT")

Hey readers! Hope you enjoyed this (mostly) silent issue! We've loved the work that Derek Charm has been doing on SQUIRREL GIRL since Erica left (haven't you??), but kudos to Derek on this issue especially since he had to do more of the storytelling than usual due to this issue being (mostly) silent! No easy thing to pull off, trust us -- but Derek sure makes it seem like it is! And we also wanted to thank Madeline McGrane for drawing the minicomic that Squirrel Girl made for Ms. Chloe. Some of you will no doubt remember that Madeline drew Squirrel Girl's contribution to our "zine" issue, #26 -- so we just HAD to bring Madeline back for Squirrel Girl's latest comic! Check out Madeline's website to see a bunch more awesome comics and drawings: www.madelinemcgrane.com. Okay, now on to your letters!

Dear UNBEATABLE Team,

I am not sure of your target demographic, but in my home a 2-year-old, a 4-year-old and a supposed adult all love reading USG! So far, Volume 7 is our favorite because…dinosaurs! And a robot dinosaur! Plus, obviously, squirrels! Thanks for giving us something to share where heroes can kick buts, eat nuts and problem solve with cooperation and CS.

Jeffrey

P.S. The picture shows a 4-year-old drawing like Erica, but she also tells stories like Ryan.

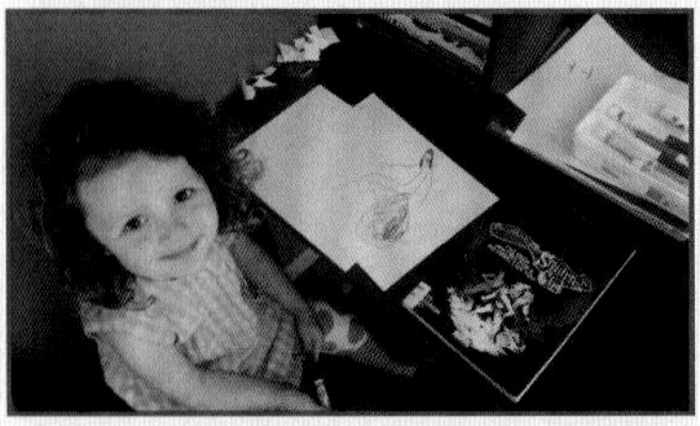

RYAN: I am in favor of ALL OF THIS. And you're ALL in the target demographic! Surprise! I want this book to be all ages, so that means everyone from 2 to 1,002 can enjoy it! I don't know if we have any 1,002-year-old readers, BUT IF WE DO: Awesome, well done, congrats on staying alive for so long and thanks for reading our comics during that period!! Vol. 7 is one of my favorites, too, because it was the story that Erica and I came up with while hanging out at that year's San Diego Comic-Con. Her rule was that if they go to the Savage Land, the first thing Doreen is doing is picking up a Savage Land torn leopard-print outfit.

Hey guys,

I love your books. I mean, I LOVE them. Mom helped make me a costume and I will describe my costume in the form of an algorithm. (I've read past issue #11 but I still have an interest in algorithms.)

I (have so much interest in the books)

I (want a costume)

}WHILE{ mom_helps_me_make_my_

costume

I(find out how to make a tail)

tell_other_people_how_to_use_a_towel_

as_a_tail_

}ELSE{ I_tell_them_myself

I included a photo. I'm a kid, so please don't call it cosplay!

Stay squirrely,
Lia Alexander, age 8

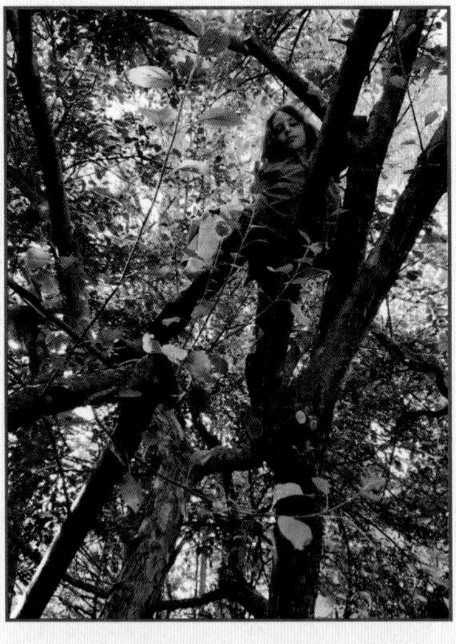

RYAN: Lia: AMAZING. And I've never seen a towel used as a tail before, but I can tell from the photo it looks great! Well done on the brilliant idea (and excellent algorithm!). Also: You look pretty high up in that tree. When I was 8 we had a tree in our front yard, and I challenged myself to climb it as quickly as possible. After a few weeks I could reach the "top"--defined as "as far up as I could go before the branches got too thin and my parents said I couldn't climb up any farther"--in 3.5 seconds. I still remember the time because I was so proud! Ha ha! And I'm just now realizing that may have been practice for writing a tree-climbing super hero. IT ALL PAYS OFF.

Hello,

So I just finished issue #34, and let me say it was one of my favorites so far. All I can think about is how I need a Courtney Alaska-centered TV show or comic made mockumentary style (a la *The Office* or *Parks and Recreation*) where Courtney's team, despite their talents and skills, is inept at putting super heroes behind bars. THE CITY MAY BE A JUNGLE, BUT THIS COURTROOM IS A TUNDRA (tagline, work in progress).

Anyway, I digress... Ryan, I had the pleasure of meeting you at SDCC in my Squirrel Girl cosplay! Your kind words were amazing! I love what you are doing with this comic and with MARVEL RISING, so much so that I made my friend rush to make a Ms. Marvel cosplay so we could rock being super hero friends. I chose to make my cosplay after my favorite Squirrel Girl costume, but I love how she switches up her crimefighting garb. Since we have an addition to the artist family with Derek, any chance that our hero will be given another addition to her costume closet?

Keep up the fantastic work,
Bridgette

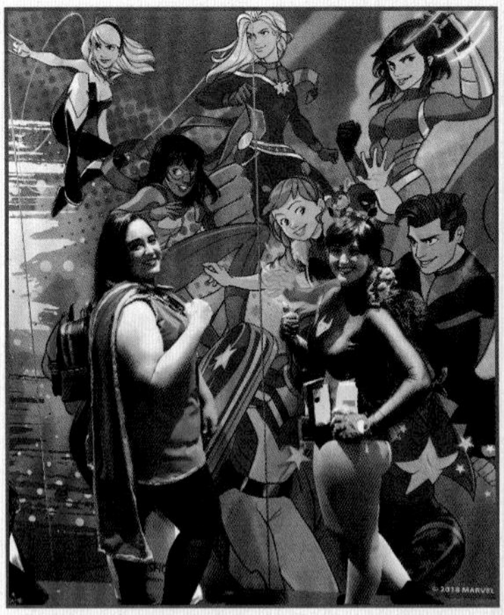

RYAN: Bridgette, I LOVE COURTNEY ALASKA TOO. She's so mean, but secretly, so awesome. It is my sincere wish--especially since there's not that many established assistant district attorneys in the Marvel Universe--that she shows up in other places because she's the best. ALSO: Your costume is amazing and I can't believe your friend's costume was last-minute! I love the "Flying Squirrel" costume in particular because it's the one where Squirrel Girl gets to have a little super hero logo on the front. I'd love to see a Derek-designed costume but I don't think we have a plot reason for Doreen to switch things up in the near

future--in the next arc (NO SPOILERS) she actually spends most of her time OUT of costume for very important plot reasons. But that DOES give us a chance to see some Derek-designed casual wear!

Hey gang,

With all of the anger, hate and general unpleasantness in the world today, can I just say what a pleasure it is to read UNBEATABLE SQUIRREL GIRL every month? Doreen and her pals kick butts (and believe me, when they kick posteriors, those posteriors stay kicked), but their true super-power is their relentless optimism. They're really, truly trying to help make the world a better, gentler place, and I say God bless 'em for it. Thank you so much--it's a balm for my weary soul. (Oh, and let me request, in the strongest possible terms, a SQUIRREL MOM comic. This would be holy and perfect and would deserve to be worshipped.)

Regards,
Terry Dickerson
Redondo Beach, California

RYAN: Thank you, Terry--I'm really glad you're liking what we're doing! And I agree: I do love Doreen's mom a lot--and given the fact that she's currently caring for Oak Tree Ultron up in Canada, there seems to be SOME story potential there...

Dear amazing SQUIRREL GIRL team,

Your comic is amazing! I had never read any Marvel or super hero comics before this one, and in my opinion this one is the best! It is so good that I don't need to bother reading any of the other Marvel comics.

Ryan: Great job on the story lines; I love all the interesting villains and alien squirrels. Please please please introduce Cat Brat! Here is a photo of me as Cat Brat and her sidekick, Eclipse!

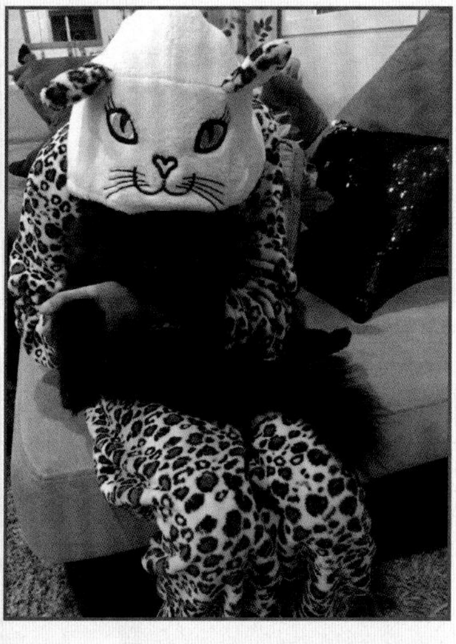

If you do introduce Cat Brat I think that her sidekick should be named Eclipse Lunar Mooney McNamee and should be a black Siberian cat with a white chest patch (I'm just describing my cat).

Erica: I am so sad to see you go. I love your art and it really brings Squirrel Girl to life. I will really miss all your creative outfits and amazing expressions. My first reaction to your "goodbye letter" was pretty much: NOOOOOOOOOOOOOOOOOOOOOOOOOOO DON'T GO ERICA!!!!!

But I now realize that even thought I will be sad and miss your art, it will be interesting to see another artist's style. Enjoy your soon-to-be wedding and good luck! Maybe another time you will come back to SQUIRREL GIRL and be the artist once again.

Thank you for this amazing comic and keep writing and drawing!

Ruby, A.K.A. Cat Brat, and her sidekick, Eclipse

P.S. Cat brat, cat brat, parts of both cat and brat, talk to her, she'll be all bratty, bark at her, she'll be all catty...

RYAN: RUBY. Your Cat Brat is amazing and SO FASHIONABLE. So great--with the theme song all ready to go too. And all evidence points toward her sidekick being a very good cat.

If you get the trade paperback collections of the comics (they're like the monthly comics, but in book form) you'll know that we usually put a quote at the top of each of them. I would LOVE for the next one to read, "It is so good that I don't need to bother reading any of the other Marvel comics." – Ruby, A.K.A. Cat Brat, but then it'd make all the other comics feel bad, so probably it's not in the cards.

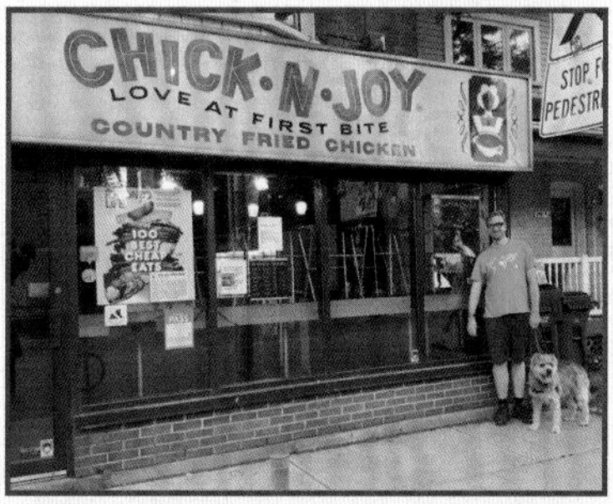
CHICK-N-JOY
LOVE AT FIRST BITE
COUNTRY FRIED CHICKEN

RYAN: Hey, here's a picture of me and my dog Noam Chompsky in front of our local fried chicken store, the Chick-N-Joy! I go there all the time on account of how much I love delicious fried chicken (NO REGRETS) and it's a family-run business, all staffed by members of the same family. I've become friends with the daughter, Dimitra, and the chef, Bill! And as one of the best parts of writing SQUIRREL GIRL is coming up with names for all the squirrels (if you send a picture of a squirrel you encounter to @unbeatablesg, she'll tell you its name and story!), a few months back I named a squirrel after Dimitra--SORRY, BILL--and put her into the comic. And then they blew up the cover of the issue--and Dimitra the Squirrel's panel!--and put it up in the window of their store! So that was an awesome surprise, and if you're ever in Toronto, go to the corner of Queen St. East and Woodfield Road, walk into the Chick-N-Joy, and tell them Dimitra the Squirrel sent you. (If you are vegetarian like Doreen, you probably won't want any chicken, but the fries are delicious too!)

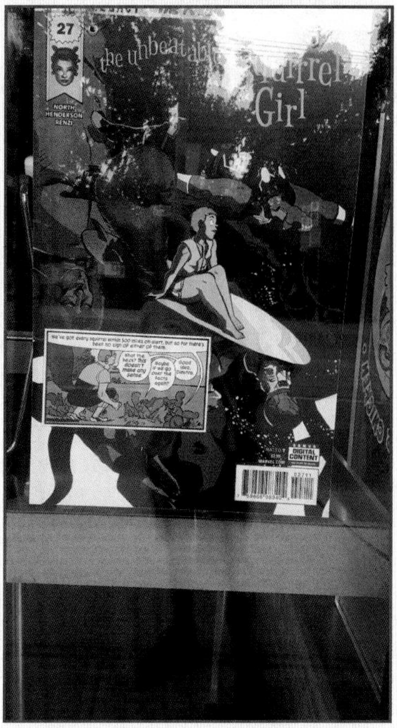
27
the unbeatable Squirrel Girl

Next Issue:

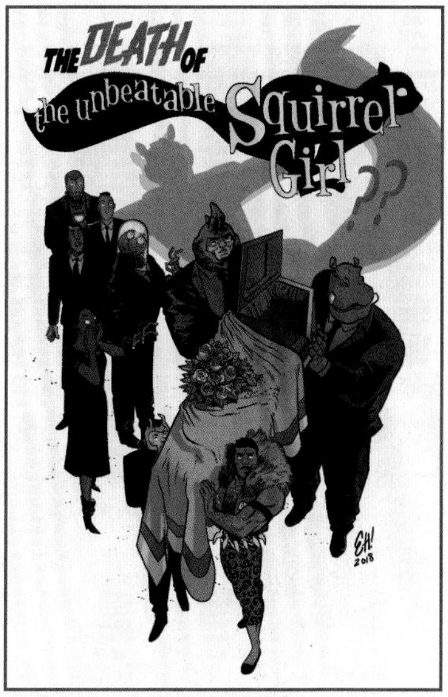
THE DEATH OF the unbeatable Squirrel Girl ??

WHAAAAT

Attention, Squirrel Scouts! Make sure to check out our production blog, **unbeatablesquirrelgirl.tumblr.com**, where we post behind-the-scenes stuff on how the book gets made, along with all sorts of cool things *you* make: fanart, cosplay, whatever!

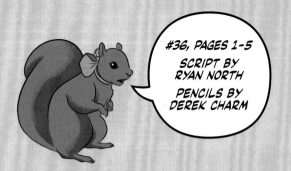

#36, PAGES 1-5
SCRIPT BY RYAN NORTH
PENCILS BY DEREK CHARM

THIS IS OUR SILENT ISSUE! My big goal here is to make a comic that can be read by kids who aren't reading yet, so all the words in the comic are there either symbolically (a word balloon full of math symbols or a spreadsheet, for example), or are optional — the idea is you can read and enjoy the story without knowing English (though there are some jokes there for people who do).

NOTE: In this "silent" issue, when we show dialogue, the words are meant more to be "seen" than read. Rather than standard balloons that encompass the text inside, these word balloons are special: They're like a window into a wall of text. It's as if the text runs out and past the balloons, and we don't see the beginning or end — the effect is one of endless words. Like so:

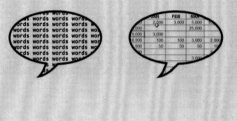

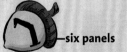

—**six panels**

1.1: Establishing shot: a dance club in NYC, a two-story building, with a big sign that reads "LOUD LOUIE'S DANCE EMPORIUM," and a "GRAND OPENING" banner hanging underneath. For those who can't read, the building has a distinctive sign on the top: a giant punk singer, shouting into a microphone. Think those giant rooftop typewriters or lighters that were always in Batman comics in the '50s: this is a giant plywood singer, so even people who can't read know this is a place that's LOUD.

It's night in NYC, and music notes are coming out of the venue. This place is loud!

A middle-age couple, walking their dogs, is walking past, covering their ears from the noise.

SFX: [harsh punk music notes]
SFX: [stars]

1.2: Now we're inside a dance club — a big sign on the wall reads "LOUD LOUIE'S DANCE EMPORIUM." There's a live punk/metal band onstage, the singer screaming into the mike. In front of them are people dancing and cheering. There's a nerdy guy talking to a bored-looking woman in the FG.

SINGER: struggle death cuss punk streets fear kicks cobwebs desperate weakness decay concrete state money bury torment tantalize garbage lies cops crime sedation cemetery poison anarchy misery institution burning psycho authority poor unite smash crisis monster rocket dirty threat mess

SFX: [harsh punk music notes]

NERDY GUY: [image of spreadsheets]

1.3: More of the singer singing, the band rocking out, everyone dancing. The nerdy guy looks sad as the bored-looking woman walks away.

SINGER: run crazy paranoid puppets madness stained lightning nightfall legacy tragedy hunger carcass battle tomb exodus eclipse fear abyss power wild screaming extinction dark fate blood reign beast sickness war freak monster darkness destroy

SFX: [harsh punk music notes]

NERDY GUY: [image of spreadsheets]

1.4: Suddenly, all sound disappears. All the word balloons are popping — physically bursting — to show their voices going away. The harsh punk music notes are cracking and breaking.

1.5: The band looks down at their instruments. Is something wrong? The singer looks confused. Why aren't any words coming out?

1.6: Suddenly, the roof is torn off the building. Everyone scrambling, running for safety.

LOUD LOUIES DANCE EMPORIUM
GRAND OPENING

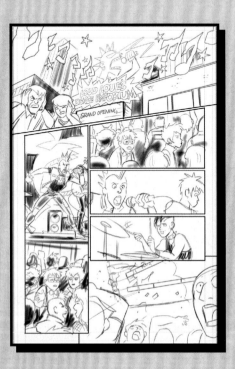